FREE COUNTRY

A penniless adventure the length of Britain

George Mahood

Acknowledgements

Firstly, I would like to thank Ben for taking part in this challenge with me. I may have painted a picture of him throughout this book as being a whinging, immature moaner – which is completely accurate – but he was also hugely entertaining, full of enthusiasm and brilliant company. His boundless energy and wit helped keep my motivation levels up throughout and I can't think of anyone else I would rather have completed the journey with.

Huge thanks to Mark and Victoria for their part in this project and I hope that all of their hard work is rewarded.

Special thanks must also go to Rachel for her love, support… and proof reading.

And finally, and most importantly, I would like to thank the hundreds of amazingly kind and generous people that helped us along the way. Whether this was with food, clothes, bikes, accommodation, directions, conversation or beer, we are incredibly grateful for their part in proving how brilliant the people of Britain are. Without these people, this adventure would simply not have been possible.

BIG LOVE to all of you.

For Mum and Dad

All of the photographs in this book are available to view in colour on Facebook
www.facebook.com/georgemahood
www.twitter.com/georgemahood
www.georgemahood.com

Day 1
The adventure begins...
Land's End to Zennor - 16 miles

We were standing in our pants on the end of Britain. The sea chewed at the land around us, and the wind and rain attacked from all angles. We had the skin of freshly plucked turkeys. Cycling 1000 miles to the top of Scotland without any money, clothes, shoes, food or bikes, suddenly felt like a really stupid idea.

Land's End is frequented by three types of people; disillusioned holidaymakers who imagine that a trip to Britain's most south-westerly point is a rewarding experience, tourists who arrive there by mistake when they run out of road, and those who are starting or finishing the popular Land's End to John O'Groats expedition. We fell awkwardly into the latter category.

The plan was simple. We had three weeks to get from the bottom of England to the top of Scotland – by foot or by bike – without spending a single penny. Setting off in just a pair of Union Jack boxer shorts, we hoped to rely on the generosity of the British public to help us with everything from accommodation to food, clothes to shoes, and bikes to beer.

I was working as a photographer at the time. At least, that's what I told people. I quit my stable, easy and fairly well paid job a few years previously to become a full-time photographer. In truth, I spent my days doing unstable, mundane and badly paid temping jobs in order to pay the bills. The photography jobs did come in very occasionally and they provided me with enough credibility to convince those around me that the decision to leave my job was a wise one. I took a picture of a friend of a friend's dog the previous month and I had a bar mitzvah booking for the following year. Business was really booming, oh yeah.

My travelling companion was Ben. Ben worked as a composer and an actor, appearing in a number of Oscar-winning blockbusters such as *Harry Potter*, *The Phantom of the Opera* and *Lord of the Rings*. He had also appeared in countless TV shows including *Eastenders*, *The Bill* and *Casualty*. When I say 'actor', I mean 'extra', and you would have to be incredibly quick-fingered with the pause button to spot him in ANY of his roles. As I mentioned, he was also a composer. Specifically, he made music for film and television. Three seconds of his music once featured in a Taiwanese computer advert - shown only on the internet - and he was still reeling in the glory of that moment. He spent his days watching *Bargain Hunt* and waiting for the advertising agency to phone back.

I asked Ben to join me on LEJOG (this is what those in the know call the Land's End to John O'Groats trip. It's an acronym, you see), because he was the only one of my friends that fitted the necessary criteria; he was a self-employed layabout like me who did not need permission to take three weeks off work at short notice.

We started early, at about 7.30am, in order to minimise the amount of people that would have to witness our scrawny bodies. The coastline around Land's End is impressive, but there is no sense whatsoever of being at the end of the country. Try standing there in your pants in the wind and rain, however, and it definitely heightens the experience.

The footpaths around the Land's End complex were not designed with the barefoot walker in mind, and the heavy gravel cut into our feet at every step. In fairness, it is unlikely that many visitors to that part of Cornwall come without shoes. Even the notorious 'Naked Rambler' wore a pair of walking boots. The cheating bastard. You can visit his boots –

if you are really bored - in the 'End to End Experience' museum, which forms part of the Land's End complex. He is mentioned alongside Ian Botham, who has famously walked the route twice, and next to the story of a man who tried to push a pea with his nose the entire way. He got about two miles before he realised that it made his nose hurt.

We met up with Jemma - the End to End co-ordinator. Jemma had possibly the most enviable job in the world. Her working day involved sitting in a little office by a log fire, looking out to sea. She occasionally had to say 'Good Luck' to people like us who were setting off to John O'Groats, or 'Well-done' to those who had finished their journey. This, it seemed, was all she did. I was incredibly jealous.

We asked her if she had any interesting stories of fellow End to Enders, and she told us about a cyclist being hit by a car and killed, and another one concerning a group being robbed at gunpoint. These were not the inspirational, feel-good stories we were hoping for.

The idea of the penniless challenge was founded on the belief, that, as a nation, we have lost sight of the basic values of humanity and kinship. We tend to be very suspicious of those that we don't know, and of anything that falls outside the realms of normality. Britain is broken, or so we are led to believe, and every unfamiliar face masks an axe murderer or terrorist. We choose to close our doors and hide from the outside world.

I wanted to prove this notion wrong. I strongly believed that there was still a lot of good to be found in society, and that there lies within everyone, the desire to help others. By travelling without money and provisions, we were putting ourselves completely at the mercy of strangers, relying on their generosity to get us through.

The Land's End to John O'Groats challenge is an iconic British journey, and it seemed to tie in perfectly with the penniless format of the trip as it encapsulated the whole of Great Britain.

Clothes were a priority.

We stood little chance of getting food, accommodation or bikes with our pasty bodies on full show. Also, it was bloody freezing and we didn't want to become the first people to die at Land's End before crossing the official start line. Although, if we had, Jemma would have had another story to tell other End to Enders before they set off.

'Well if you make it past the visitor centre,' she would say, 'you'll have done better than George and Ben. They died right here in their pants.' It would have made her day.

We wandered aimlessly around Land's End not knowing what to do or how to begin the ridiculous challenge that we had set ourselves. After a few minutes of roaming we got talking to the only other weirdoes who had decided to visit Land's End at 7.30am on that unforgiving morning. They were Australian. We explained to them why we were standing there in our pants.

'Strewth, and we thought people back in Oz were mad,' said Bruce.

'Crikey,' said Sheila. 'Bruce, go and get that old t-shirt from the car for these fellas.'

'No worries, Sheila,' said Bruce. Bruce and Sheila were not their real names. Their actual names were lost in the wind somewhere.

Bruce and Sheila were halfway through their five-week world tour and had been in England just two days. Why they had decided to come to Land's End we had no idea. They were in their early forties and were travelling with another couple, Kylie and Jason, and the four of them were dressed like a mountain rescue team, as southern-hemisphere visitors to England tend to dress. Only a few square inches of their faces were exposed to the elements, but this was enough to see their kind and genuine smiles.

Bruce returned a few minutes later with the t-shirt. It was a momentous occasion; our first freebie and we hadn't even asked for it. The t-shirt itself was an XXXL made of silky white polyester, with a cigarette burn in the back and an inescapable scent of Australian body odour. I tried it on first, as Ben seemed more comfortable than me to prance around Land's End almost naked. It was ridiculously big and made me look like I was wearing a parachute.

The t-shirt did make a huge difference, however. Not only did it repel some of the icy temperatures that were being thrown at us, but it also transformed my confidence. I was instantly changed from a shivering fool in a pair of Union Jack boxer shorts, to someone that was about to cycle 1000 miles to the top of Scotland. The fact that I was still only half clothed and didn't have a bike was purely incidental.

We thanked Bruce, Sheila, Kylie and Jason and urged them not to judge England by Land's End, or the English by us. We decided to make our way to the Land's End Hotel, as it was the only place likely to be open so early. We had high hopes of raiding the lost property for some more clothes.

On our way to the hotel, Bruce's friend Jason caught us up.

'G'day again, guys. I got this for ya, too,' he panted and handed us another t-shirt. This one was cotton, clean, white, without cigarette burns and a cosy medium fit. I regretted hastily grabbing the first one. Ben gave me a smug grin.

The Land's End Hotel is a fairly ugly building, and is therefore in keeping with the surroundings. The interior, however, is rather posh and the reception area was crammed full of elderly American tourists who had been lulled there by the notion that it was a charming hotel perched on the edge of the country. There was an air of deep disappointment in the room. The conversations stopped and they all turned to watch as we entered the reception.

'WHATTA YA DOIN?' yelled one of the Americans who looked close to a hundred and spoke at twice the necessary volume.

'WE'RE ON OUR WAY TO JOHN O'GROATS AT THE TOP OF SCOTLAND,' said Ben, replying in a volume equal to the old man's.

'YOU'LL END UP IN HOSPITAL,' shouted the old man.

We both gave a nervous laugh and shuffled our way to the reception desk. The Americans shuffled out of the door through which we had just come, ready for their day of fun.

The hotel receptionist forced a smile when she saw us. She was in her late thirties and had the look of a supply teacher who would take no shit.

'Hello... Ruth,' I said, spotting her badge and dropping her name into conversation like a sleazy salesman, 'I wonder if you can help us.' Her smile disappeared and she began to look panicked. 'We're about to attempt to cycle to John O'Groats without spending a single penny...' Her face turned to mild bemusement as though she had just been told the punch line of a joke she didn't quite understand. '...and all of our food, accommodation, clothes and hopefully bikes will have to be acquired from the generosity of the British public,' I continued, sensing she was beginning to warm up, 'and we were wondering whether the hotel had any lost property that had not been reclaimed that we could possibly have?'

There was a long pause. A sense of relief passed over Ruth. My speech was over and she realised she wasn't being robbed, she wasn't going to have to sponsor us and we weren't asking her out on a date.

'Ok,' she said, 'I'll see what I can do.' She disappeared into the back office and we were left alone.

A middle-aged man and his wife arrived at reception to check out. He was dressed head to toe in Lycra and was wearing a pair of cycling gloves. He had a cycle helmet in one hand and a drinking bottle in the other. With some careful deliberation we guessed him to be a cyclist. Our suspicions were confirmed when we noticed that he was wheeling a bicycle.

'Are you going to John O'Groats?' asked Ben.

'I sure am,' said the cyclist.

'I'm his support crew,' said his wife.

'We're cycling to John O'Groats, too,' said Ben, standing shivering in a pair of damp boxers and an ill-fitting t-shirt.

'Really?' said the cyclist, who then gave a laugh as if to say 'you nearly had me there.'

Although our goal was the same, the differences between us could not have been further apart. He had at least £2000 worth of equipment, top-of the range Lycra cycling clothing, a lightweight Gortex jacket and a devoted support crew. We were unsupported, barely clothed and without any form of bike. Oh, how we longed for a couple of carbon-fibre racing bikes, waterproof jackets and a support crew. And the Lycra was strangely alluring, too.

The cyclist's name was John and he was about to begin his second End to End trip. He had completed the trip with a friend a few years previously and wanted to do it again alone, with his wife following behind in the car. He was aiming to finish the trip in ten days. We imagined we would probably still be in Cornwall in ten days. John explained that his Dad had been a professional medal-winning cyclist and that he had always lived in his shadow. Doing the Land's End to John O'Groats trip was his way of making his dad proud.

Once he understood that we were serious about our trip, he

13

took a keen interest in how we were going to go about it.

'You'll need some shoes and socks,' he said. 'Hold on, I'll be right back.' His wife took hold of his bike and he scurried out of the door. He returned a minute later with a pair of trainers and a pair of socks.

'Take these,' he said, worryingly out of breath for someone about to cycle to Scotland. 'I brought way too many pairs of shoes and I never wear these anyway.' They were white leather trainers, slightly retro and a perfect fit for either of us. We thanked him gratefully and wished him luck for his bike ride. We had earned the respect of an End to End veteran and we had not even crossed the start line.

Ruth returned from the office holding a big box of lost property. She dropped it down on the reception desk in front of us and our eyes scoured eagerly over the contents like a couple of clothes perverts.

The first item that caught our eye was a pair of thick, woollen, pinstriped suit trousers. They were tailor-made to fit a big fat man. Ben decided I should have them, since I was the larger of the two of us. After trying them on, it was clear that there would have been room for both of us. Not only were they for a big fat man, but they were also previously owned by an extremely short fat man, or someone with a penchant for wearing their trousers at half-mast. The trousers hung halfway down my arse, and stopped halfway up my shin. I looked like the lovechild of a gangster and a sailor. It was EXACTLY the look I was going for.

Also in the box were two cardigans. Ben took the trendy, skimpy black number and I took the thick, granny blue one. We only took items that had been unclaimed for over three months, so as not to get into trouble with any angry tenants. Although, I'm pretty sure the 'finders keepers, losers weepers' defence would have held firm. We also took a baseball cap each. I'm not sure why, but it seemed like a good idea at the time. Ben had an England football cap with a St George's Cross on the front, and I had a retro Manchester United cap. We looked like a couple of chavs. Chavs in cardies.

The final item of lost property that we acquired was a child's pink umbrella. We naively thought that it would shield some of the rain for a while, and we thought it might also be a useful bartering item to swap at some stage of the trip. It proved to be neither.

We were delaying the inevitable.

At some point we were going to have to leave the relative comfort and security of Land's End and start our journey towards John O'Groats. We had scavenged as much as we could from the hotel and it was time to leave. On the way out we bumped into Jemma again. She was armed with two 'official' Land's End t-shirts, which she kindly presented to us. Normal people have to pay for these, but we had told her that payment for anything was prohibited in our world. We pulled these on over our cardigans and we were ready to go. Land's End – been there, done that, and now we had the t-shirts.

Almost fully clothed, we were about to begin our journey towards Scotland. The official start line is in the car park and not by the sign, as you would expect. Crossing it was certainly an anti-climax. Our farewell party consisted of two old ladies, but it turned out that they were just waiting for the toilets to be unlocked. Even so, they uttered a half-hearted 'good luck', raised their eyebrows and smirked at each other.

We were finally on our way.

I was dressed in my suit trousers, which I had to roll up around the waist to keep them from falling down to my ankles. I was also wearing two t-shirts, a blue cardigan, a Manchester United baseball cap (on backwards, because I'm hip), one trainer and one sock. Ben was wearing two t-shirts, a black cardigan, an England cap (on sideways, because he's rad) and no trousers. He was wearing the other sock and trainer. It was still raining, but the wind had died down once we had moved away from the exposed cliffs. It was cold but bearable.

The road climbed gradually away from the coast and the Land's End complex became a distant blemish on the landscape behind us. We had been warned that John O'Groats was just a rubbish version of Land's End, so we were in no hurry to get there.

The ground was painful underfoot. The idea of wearing one shoe each was supposed to minimise the pain for each person, but in reality, it made things worse, as we constantly had a reminder of what a luxury shoes are. We soon established that walking along the thick white line on the edge of the road minimised the discomfort.

Most travelogues such as this have a long preamble about the build up to the journey. This would include extensive details about the preparations and the arrangements involved; sourcing and buying suitable equipment, planning a route and researching the trip in meticulous detail. The training regime would also be discussed to show how a peak level of fitness was attained before undertaking such a physical challenge. You will have noticed that this book contains no such introduction. The truth was, there was no real preparation. As soon as the idea of the trip had taken shape in my mind, I suggested it to Ben who agreed straight away to join me. It then didn't prove too difficult to find three weeks that we both had free, as neither of us had much on in the way of work, or anything else for that matter. We didn't need to source or buy any equipment either, as we weren't taking anything. We didn't need to plan a route as we wanted to allow for spontaneity, and as this was the first time an End to End trip had been attempted in this manner – as far as we were aware - there was nothing productive that we could do in the way of research.

As for our training regime, that was non-existent. Be under no illusion, Ben and I were not experienced cyclists. I did ride my bike several times a week, but this was to cover the 400 metres to the local shop. Ben used his bike even less frequently. We had taken part in the London to Brighton bike ride earlier in the year, which is a distance of 54 miles, and was the furthest that either of us had ever cycled by some way. It took us most of the day and made us both realise that we were not cut out for long-distance cycling. It did however plant the seed in my mind about attempting this journey of more epic proportions.

Originally I had suggested to Ben that we try to acquire our bikes and clothes for free BEFORE heading to Cornwall and then just attempt to cycle to John O'Groats without spending any money.

'Where's the fun in that?' asked Ben. 'If we're going to do it properly then we need to start with nothing at all. No clothes, no money, no shoes and no bikes.'

'What? You want to start from Land's End completely naked? We would get arrested.'

'Maybe just a pair of boxer shorts then, if you're embarrassed about people seeing your tiny penis. But definitely no other clothes, no shoes and certainly no bikes. That would be cheating.'

'Do you really think we'll be able to get clothes and bikes for free?'

'There's only one way to find out.'

We were given a lift down to Cornwall the day before by a willing friend and we spent the night in a nearby B&B and enjoyed a 'last supper' at the local pub. Early the following morning we handed our clothes, wallets, shoes and phones to our willing friend, who then waved us goodbye and left us stranded on the cliff tops in our pants.

'Now what?' asked Ben about a mile up the road from Land's End. I wasn't sure how to respond. We had not really thought the whole thing through and it suddenly dawned on us that we didn't really know what to do next. Our aim had been to get clothes, and that had been easier than expected, but we hadn't thought past that. We continued walking and hoped for inspiration.

The first bit of civilisation we came across was a farmhouse. It was set back from the road, but we could see movement through one of the windows. We decided it was worth enquiring about another pair of shoes. We approached the door with nervous caution. Ben was still without trousers and it was highly likely that any elderly occupants of the house would have had a seizure at the sight of him cavorting down their driveway in his underwear. We knocked on the door and a man answered. He was fairly old, but fit enough to withstand the shock of seeing us on his doorstep. He thought we were after money and was relieved to hear we only wanted shoes. He invited us in and we stood awkwardly in his living room while he went off to find an old pair of wellies that he thought he had lying around in a barn. It is very difficult to stand partially clothed in a stranger's house and not feel conspicuous.

He returned a few minutes later with a pair of wellies in hand, and a look of relief on his face that we hadn't run off with his telly. We thanked him and made our way back out into the driveway. The wellies were a size 6. We were both a size 10. They were overflowing with straw and cobwebs and I gave them a good shake to remove as many spiders as possible. I offered to wear them first and with a bit of effort and manipulation of my toes I was able to squeeze into them. There was no room left for any remaining insects to breathe, let alone wriggle.

A further half-mile up the road we reached a road junction

and we were forced to make our first directional decision. We determined, with our basic understanding of British geography, that if we kept the sea on our left we would be going in the direction of Scotland. We knew that the road we were on was the A30 and would become busier the closer it got to Penzance. It didn't sound suitable for badly clothed walkers, so we turned left and hobbled along the quieter road towards St Ives and the sea.

The fog had closed in and we could only see about 20 metres in either direction. There was very little sign of life anywhere. I managed about a mile in the wellies before getting a blister. I know it sounds pathetic, but seriously, you should try walking in wellies that are four sizes too small with just one wet sock for protection. Ben offered to share the pain with me and so we wore a welly and a trainer each. This look is now quite the rage.

The morning had disappeared like smoke in the wind, but we were only three miles from Land's End. We were getting hungry and decided to seek food at the first opportunity. It was no longer as cold or wet, and we were almost beginning to enjoy the experience. Ben seemed completely at ease in his boxer shorts and displayed no shame. The occasional car passed us and either hooted their horn in a 'ha ha, look at those freaks' kind of way or just stared at us with confusion.

The smell of food wafted through the air from an unidentifiable source. Suddenly, a big white building emerged from the fog; it was about the size of a small airport. Extraordinarily, it turned out to be a small airport.

We approached the building and noticed a small handwritten notice on the door:

'Due to adverse weather conditions, all flights to the Scilly Isles have been cancelled. Please leave your luggage in the car before entering'.

19

We didn't have any luggage, or a car, so we entered.

The building was heaving with people, yet there was an eerie silence in the room. Elderly tourists, idly waiting to see if the fog would clear, occupied row upon row of seats. We had come to seek out the origin of the smell and we shambled our way clumsily through the crowds towards what looked like a café. This was to be our first request for food and we both became increasingly nervous. If we failed, we knew it would be a struggle from then on.

There were two elderly ladies at the counter ordering their cream teas, so we hung back until they had finished. If we were going to crash and burn, we didn't want an audience.

'Hi,' said Ben with a awkward smile. 'My friend George and I are on our way to John O'Groats. We started this morning at Land's End in a pair of boxer shorts and we have to get the entire way without spending a single penny.'

'Ok?' replied the man behind the counter.

'And we were wondering... ' continued Ben, 'if you had any food that you were about to throw out that we could perhaps have?' There was an uneasy pause as he looked around to see if he had any senior staff to check with. The kitchen was empty.

'How does a coffee and a bacon sandwich sound?' he asked.

It was as simple as that. We had got our first free meal. We were expecting some half-chewed bread at best, or maybe an old lettuce, but we were soon presented with a huge steaming bacon bap and a mug of freshly brewed coffee.

It transpired that John - the man behind the counter - was a pilot and had been forced to help out in the kitchen because of the flight cancellations.

Ben and I sat in silence as we ate. John's food had filled us both with a feeling of contentment and there was no need to talk. He offered to top up our coffees, and, as a way of delaying going back outside, we gladly accepted.

As we sat, satisfied, we were approached by one of the passengers from the waiting room. She had been checking out Ben's legs whilst we ate. She was about 70 and asked why we were dressed like we were.

'We're cycling to John O'Groats,' replied Ben.

'Oh, do you want some grapes?' she asked, and pulled a bunch from her bag. Remarkably, at this point, other people in the waiting room started coming towards us with offerings; chocolate bars, crisps, flapjack, apples, fruit juice and more grapes. Nobody really understood why we were dressed like we were, or where we were heading, but it was obviously clear that we were needy. Their kindness, which was completely unprovoked, gave us a renewed sense of enthusiasm for our adventure.

'You'll get there, no problem,' said one of them.

'A couple of nice guys like you. Just keep smiling and you'll be fine,' said another.

'Aww, they were smashing? I would like them as my sons,' we heard one of the ladies say as we left the building.

John, the pilot-come-dinner-lady, chased after us and gave us a bottle of water each.

'You'll need this, lads,' he puffed.

The whole trip was suddenly real. There was now every chance we could make it. To Devon, at least.

You are no doubt wondering how it was possible to take the photos in this book if we started with nothing but a pair of boxer shorts. The truth is, we also carried a camera, a notebook and pen and a wad of postcards printed with the words: 'I am OFFICIALLY a very nice person'. The notebook and pen were for me to keep a diary during the trip. I wanted to keep a record of our experiences and of the people that we met, to help compensate for my deteriorating memory.

Being a photographer, I also thought it would be a nice idea

21

to photograph the different people who helped us along the way, creating a montage of Britain's unsung heroes.

The postcards were Ben's idea. He mentioned it a couple of days before we set off and I initially dismissed the idea as corny and pointless. In my defence, he had originally suggested that the postcards be printed with the phrase: 'I am a FUCKING good person.' The thought of presenting a card like this to an old lady, who had just given us an apple, seemed slightly wrong.

'Hello, little old lady. Thank you for the apple. Here is a postcard that says what a FUCKING good person you are.'

In the end, we agreed on: 'I am OFFICIALLY a very nice person.' It was simple, inoffensive and genuine.

I should make it very clear that neither the camera, nor the postcards, were ever used to help us gain favours in any way. They were only ever introduced after a good deed had been done.

The sun had not yet emerged through the fog, and Ben's legs were beginning to feel the cold. We knocked on the door of the next house that we came across, to try and find him some trousers. A large, round-faced man answered the door. He was in his thirties and had a face that looked like it was made from mashed potato. He was stocky and over six feet tall, but his overbearing frame was counteracted by a huge smile and softly spoken voice.

We explained that we were hoping to get a pair of trousers and he invited us in while he went to have a look. He returned with a pair of grey tracksuit bottoms.

'Are these ok?' he asked.

'They look absolutely perfect,' said Ben. 'Thank you so much. What's your name?'

'Les,' said Les.

Les worked for the coastguard and had bought his house a

few years previously; it was an old chapel, which he had converted himself. The place was really striking with a low hung ceiling and clever lighting giving it a cosy feel. The kitchen units were decorated with paintings and drawings done by a small child. Either that, or Les was just really rubbish at art.

Les also offered us a rucksack after noticing our arms laden with food, water and an umbrella. We thanked him and continued walking in the fog towards the village of St Just.

The road between Land's End and St Ives is dotted with the remains of tin mines. Mining had taken place in Cornwall since stone-age times, but the discovery of cheaper ore in other parts of Europe, America and Australia practically destroyed the industry. Many mines continued to fight off international competition well into the 20th Century, but on March 6th, 1998, the pumps were finally switched off for good at South Crofty, just up the road – both Cornwall and the UK's last surviving tin mine.

We reached the town of St Just with its proud status as the most westerly town in England. The town is little more than a big village. At its centre is a pleasant little market square, which is flanked by several pubs. It had been a tough morning, and we felt like we deserved a beer so called into the first pub to try our luck. Asking for clothes and food was one thing, but asking for free beer was something completely different. Unlike food and clothes, beer was hardly a necessity, but after an exhausting morning's walking and blagging we felt like it was as essential as oxygen.

I picked the youngest and better looking of the two barmaids and decided to try the honest and direct approach.

'Hi there,' I said in a cool and slightly flirtatious manner. 'We are travelling the length of the country without spending a single penny, and we were wondering if there was any chance we could possibly have a free beer?'

'Errr, ok,' she said with a nervous giggle. 'Are two half lagers ok?'

I decided that this was not the time to ask about trying one of the local ales.

'Two half lagers would be unbelievable. Thank you very much indeed.'

Seven hours earlier we had been standing in our boxer shorts in the wind and rain. We were now fully clothed and drinking free beer in a picturesque Cornish village. Life was pretty good.

We started chatting to a guy at the bar called Steve. He was not as inebriated as some of the other locals, but his words were still slurred. We asked him if he knew anywhere or anyone that could help us out with a bike.

'If you give me an hour, I'll get someone to sort you out with a bike,' he said.

'Would it be stolen?' asked Ben suspiciously.

'Yeah, probably, but you won't get caught,' said Steve.

'Thanks, but we were hoping to get some bikes lawfully and legitimately, but we appreciate the offer,' said Ben.

Steve suggested we try another pub in St Just - the Miners Arms. It was also an excuse for another beer.

The Miners Arms was fairly grim. The walls were painted black and there was almost no light, other than the daylight that poked its way through the closed shutters. We fumbled our way to the bar, bumping from empty table to empty table and treading on the occasional sleeping dog. It was Ben's round.

'Hello,' he said, looking at all four of the guys sitting at the bar, assuming that one of them worked there.

'What can I get you?' asked the youngest and least likely looking barman of the lot of them.

'We're cycling 1000 miles to John O'Groats, but we don't have any bikes,' said Ben. The place erupted with laughter. Sniggers could be heard through the darkness from a table in the far corner. 'We were wondering…' continued Ben unfazed, 'if you knew anyone that had a couple of bikes that they were trying to get rid of.'

The laughter went up a notch. It continued for a minute or so.

'I'll take that as a no,' said Ben. 'Any chance of a free beer then?'

'Sure,' said the barman. 'You guys sound like you'll need it.'

We sat down in the darkness and drank our second beer of the day. We had only walked four miles, and at that rate, it was going to take over five months to get to John O'Groats. We had allowed ourselves three weeks.

By this point, it felt like my welly had rubbed through to the bone. I removed it in the hope of showing Ben some horrific battle wound, but was disappointed to discover a small red splodge on my heel. Still, we decided that suitable shoes were more necessary than bikes. The trip would have been over before it had properly begun if we had continued in the wellies.

I decided to speak to the guys at the bar again. Despite laughing at us before, they were very friendly and approachable.

'Do you know anywhere we could get a pair of old shoes?' I asked, 'We've got one pair of trainers and a pair of wellies that are much too small.' The laughter reached new heights and I returned to our table in the corner.

We were about to leave when one of the guys who had been at the bar approached us. He was in his late twenties, with a missing front tooth and slicked hair. He had not said a word before and had been the only person not to laugh.

'I think what you are doing is inspirational,' he said quietly, so that his friends at the bar didn't hear. 'I want you to have this.' He then glanced around to check that his friends weren't looking before removing a small crystal ear stud from his ear. He then took my arm and placed the crystal gently in the palm of my hand. 'It will bring you good luck.'

I didn't really know what to say. It was the first time I had been given jewellery from anyone, and I didn't imagine that I would lose my jewellery virginity to a young man in a pub in deepest Cornwall. There was something very poignant about it, which I liked - in a non-gay way.

'You should go with them, Eric,' one of the other men shouted. 'Go on, what's stopping you? You haven't got a job or any other commitments. You should do it.'

A look of enlightenment passed over Eric's face and we half expected him to follow us out of the door. He paused.

'Nah,' he said. 'I've still got 'alf a pint left.'

We were secretly relieved. As much as we liked Eric, we didn't want the trip to turn into a Pied Piper style affair, picking up stragglers at every village. We told him to catch us up, and I fastened the earring to my t-shirt as I had never got around to having my ears pierced.

Outside the pub we met a guy clutching a huge pair of rigger boots.

'Here you go, lads,' said the man, who we then recognised as being one of the other men at the bar. He was about 50, bald, with a big smile. 'I got these for you.'

He handed us the gigantic boots, that were caked in concrete and each weighed the same as a wet towel. They were, however, far more appealing than the wellies.

'They're from Boomer, a friend of Steve's,' he said. 'He said he had met you in The Wellington an hour ago. He doesn't wear these anymore and says you can have them if you want.'

The Wellington was the appropriately named pub we had

been to first.

'Brilliant, thank you so much,' I said. 'Please pass on our thanks to Boomer and Steve.'

'Certainly. Good luck, guys,' he said.

We had acquired our third item of footwear in less than 12 hours. The generosity and enthusiasm of the people that we had met was completely overwhelming.

I took off my welly and trainer and uncurled my toes for the first time in hours. The wellies had been a size 6; the rigger boots were about size 14. I dropped my feet into them effortlessly. Despite their size and weight, they felt luxurious. They were lined with fur and my toes were free to roam wherever they chose. If I could have only found another eight pairs of socks from somewhere, they would have almost fitted me. I agreed to do the first shift in the boots and Ben wore both trainers, which were more than adequate to get us all the way to John O'Groats

After a two hour pub break we decided to try and get a few more miles under our metaphorical belts. We originally had St Ives in mind as a destination for the night, but this was now looking completely unrealistic. St Ives was 13 miles away and it would be dark within a few hours.

There was no room in the rucksack for the wellies, so Ben hung them over his shoulder with the plan to pass them onto someone with small feet and a need for wellies. A pixie farmer, perhaps.

Cornwall was stunning. We couldn't see much of it because of the fog, but what we could see was spectacular. There was no distant hum of a motorway that disturbs the calm of many other parts of the British countryside. Even the villages had a ghostly silence. The fog caked the surrounding landscape and enclosed us in a cocoon of cloud. The fields contoured unpredictably and large clumps of rock dotted them like gravestones. The view would have changed very little in a thousand years. Apart from the road we were walking along, and the hedgerows, there was no sign of modern civilisation whatsoever. It was simply beautiful.

Just after 6pm we reached the village of Pendeen, which, by Cornish standards, was bustling. The North Star was an attractive looking pub from the outside and it didn't disappoint on the inside. England were playing a European qualifier and everyone in the bar was watching the game intently on the TV. We had to scurry across the floor so as not to block the view of those at the bar. I wanted to stay in that pub forever. There was beer, football and a big log fire. I came close to asking the landlord if we could stay, but instead reeled off the spiel about bikes.

'Sorry guys, I can't help,' he said.

Disappointed, we loitered at the bar for as long as we could. We saw Steven Gerrard score before retreating outside to the cold road.

We were warned that once we left Pendeen there was nothing in the way of civilisation until Zennor, which was eight miles away. For the first time, we had started to think about where we might spend the night. We knew that even if we miraculously managed to get bikes, it would be dark by the time we reached Zennor. Despite the possibility of not being able to find anywhere to stay, Ben and I were still full of adrenaline from the challenge that we had set ourselves, and so it was of little concern.

'What happens if we can't find anywhere to stay?' asked Ben.

'We'll just find a pub, stay there until they throw us out and then hang around outside until morning,' I replied.

'Oh,' said Ben. 'Ok.'

Just on the outskirts of the village we knocked on the door of a house with a collection of weird bits and pieces strewn across the front yard; drift wood, buoys, lobster pots and fishing nets. It was as though a high tide had spewed a shipwreck in the garden. We were several miles inland, so this was extremely unlikely.

'Come in, come in,' said the wire-haired hippy who answered the door, before even asking who we were, or what we wanted.

We had been standing in her front room for several minutes chatting about the weather and her being a psychologist and other random stuff, before she even asked why we were in her house.

'We're looking for a couple of old bikes to help us get to John O'Groats,' I said.

'Oh, I haven't got any bikes, but I have got a picnic set you can have,' she replied instantaneously, as though she had been trying for sometime to get rid of it.

'Err, ok then,' I said, 'thanks,' assuming that she would have been offended if we had declined her offer.

The lady's name was Liz and she was a psychologist, as I have already mentioned. I explained that I was trying to take a photo of all of the 'nice people' that helped us along the way, and I asked to take a picture of her.

'I'm not sure if I can trust you,' she said. 'I work with mentally ill people all day long and it makes me suspicious.'

Now, I'm no psychologist, but maybe she should have thought of that before she let two complete strangers into her house. Perhaps that's what they teach on day one of Psychology School; invite any number of random people into your home, but do not, under any circumstances, let them take a photograph of you.

She fetched the picnic set for us, which came in a handy rucksack. I had visions of trying to carry a large wicker hamper all the way to Scotland, and so was relieved to see it was a manageable size. I had been carrying the rucksack that Les had given us, so Ben took the picnic set. We thanked Liz and she thanked us for brightening up her day. She told us that we were 'wacky and zany,' which we had never been described as before, and will probably never again. She also suggested, not for the first time, that we were mentally ill.

We continued onwards towards Zennor. Cornwall became more and more hilly. The land around us undulated at random like a motocross track. It must be a real bastard for farmers. The fog closed in even further and it became dangerous for us to walk on the road, so we walked on the grass verge as much as possible and kept our ears alert for approaching cars.

After another hour's walking we reached the village of Morvah. Morvah is a tiny hamlet with an alleged population of 79. When we passed through, they were all in hiding. The few houses that we could see all had their lights off and there were no cars in the driveway. We started to wonder whether cars and electricity had been discovered in Cornwall yet.

The last house that we came across did show signs of life. There were lights on and a car in the driveway. We knocked on the door and a lady answered. She was in her mid-forties with a warm, welcoming face, frizzy hair and a baggy t-shirt.

'I'm really sorry,' she said before even asking what we wanted, 'I have just finished milking the cows and I wasn't expecting visitors.'

'We're really sorry to bother you,' I said, 'but we were wondering if you had any old bikes lying around that you were trying to get rid of.'

'I don't think we have,' she said, completely unfazed by our question. 'We got rid of ours last month. We might have an old scooter in the garden.'

'Seriously?'   we   both   responded,   perhaps

overenthusiastically as it appeared to startle her. 'A scooter would be amazing.'

'Ok, what do you need it for?'

'We're cycling to John O'Groats,' said Ben, who then described our challenge to her.

'What an adventure!' said the lady, whose name was Sue. 'Just give me a sec, and I'll see if our neighbours have anything they can give you.'

'Helen, it's Sue,' she said on the phone. 'I have got two boys with me who are heading to John O'Groats and they're after a couple of bikes. Do you have anything at your place?' There was a long pause. 'It doesn't have to be a bike,' she added, 'anything with wheels.' There was another pause. 'Yes, they both look barking,' she said laughing and looking at us both. Another long pause followed, but Sue's expression changed to suggest she was having some success. 'Brilliant,' she then said, 'any chance Ross could run it over the field with the quad? Thanks, Helen. Talk to you later.'

Our mouths had both dropped open as we stood there expectantly on Sue's doorstep, waiting to hear what Helen had said.

'Ross is our neighbour's son who lives across the field. He's going to bring over his old bike for you,' she said. 'It's very small and rusty and he doesn't know if the tyres have punctures, but it might be of use to you.'

We both grinned like lottery winners.

'He'll be over in a few minutes,' said Sue. 'I'll just go and see if I can find that scooter.'

Sue reappeared a few minutes later wheeling a scooter and a tricycle. The tricycle was pink with a little basket on the front and was clearly intended for a two-year-old.

'I don't think you'll get to John O'Groats on either of these, but this one will get you as far as Zennor or St Ives,' she said, lifting up a black WWF scooter. The former *World Wrestling Federation*, that is, rather than the World Wildlife Fund. I don't think the latter make scooters.

'Woweeeee,' I said. Yes, I know people don't say 'Woweeeee' anymore, but I did. It just slipped out in the moment. I'm not proud of it.

Ben was already testing out the tricycle and it was clear that under the weight of an adult, it would be crushed within minutes. The other one, however, was a beast of a scooter. It had a wide skateboard-sized platform, Harley Davidson sized handlebars, big foam wheels and was emblazoned with pictures of greased-up wrestlers. It would have been the Rolls Royce of scooters 'back in the day'. It also had functioning brakes and a drinking bottle holder.

We could hear the distant rumble of an engine.

'That sounds like Ross,' said Sue as she made her way through the yard towards the field.

The noise grew louder, but we still couldn't see past the thick blanket of mist. After a while, a shape emerged from the haze and we could make out a quad bike coming towards us. Ross weaved his way through the field, avoiding cow troughs and ditches. He pulled up in front of us and turned off the engine. He was about 13 and was dressed in a boiler suit

'Ross, you are an absolute legend, thank you so much,' said Ben, shaking him firmly by the hand.

'That's ok,' said Ross with the voice of a 60 year-old farmer.

He lifted the bike out of the trailer and wheeled it to Ben. It was a miniature BMX, completely rusted over and it squealed as Ross pushed it. There was an ominous looking brake cable hanging from the handlebars and there was something very wrong with one of the wheels; it wasn't round. The seat wasn't attached properly, and the handlebars were at a very odd angle. We didn't care. At that moment, it was the greatest thing we had ever seen in our lives.

'The back wheel isn't screwed on properly and it's buckled but I have put some air in the tyres for you. They should hopefully stay up,' he said as Ben climbed on.

Despite its obvious crapness, it was a wonderful piece of machinery. The basic mechanics of a bicycle – which we had always taken for granted – were now vividly apparent. It really is a magnificent invention. The fact that moving your feet around in circles could propel a crappy piece of rust along at a decent speed was quite astonishing.

'Oh, and the brakes don't work,' shouted Ross, just as Ben crashed into a huge metal barn door.

'Brakes are overrated anyway,' I said. 'Stopping is not going to get us anywhere.'

We asked Sue and Ross if they had any ideas of places that we could spend the night.

'There's nothing between here and Zennor,' said Sue, 'but I'm sure you'll find somewhere to stay there. It even has a youth hostel.'

'But there's a wedding on tonight,' said Ross, 'so it might be completely full. You should speak to a farmer called Harry Mann. He'll let you stay somewhere. Tell him I sent you. He lives in a farm at the top of the hill, just outside of Zennor.'

We thanked Sue and Ross for their incredible generosity and gave Ross the wellies that Ben had been carrying. Ross was as close to a pixie farmer as we were ever likely to meet.

It was almost dark, and we were still four miles from Zennor.

I did the first shift on the scooter and Ben pedalled the BMX. The difference they made was unbelievable. The countryside wasn't whizzing by like it would on a racing bike, or in a car, but we could feel the progress that we were making with every revolution of our bikes' tiny wheels.

bout half a mile of steady uphill we were faced with downhill. Safety was not a concern on the scooter. The tyres were made of foam and it was so slow that we had to push when going downhill. In the event that it did reach an out of control speed – which it didn't – it had a functioning back brake to bring it to a gradual stop. To make it more exhilarating on the scooter, you could stand sideways to make it feel like you were snowboarding, albeit very slowly, and on tarmac.

The BMX, however, had no such luxury. Descending a Cornish hill on that bike was like a skier attempting an icy black run on the first morning of ski school. The only way to maintain control was to dig each foot into the tarmac to try and preserve balance and keep the speed under control. We felt a rush of adrenaline after every corner that passed without a nasty accident. It continued like this all the way to Zennor; a long, slow, uphill slog, followed by a thrilling downhill. We swapped bikes regularly to even things out.

It became so dark that we could no longer see the contours of the road but we knew we were getting closer to Zennor, as we could hear the distant purr of a cheesy wedding disco.

We reached the village of Zennor at about 9.30pm. I had been to Zennor once previously, but it was so dark on this visit that I didn't recognise it. All that I remembered was a story about a mermaid, and a pub with good beer. We cared nothing about the mermaid, at this point, so headed towards the pub.

On the way, we enquired at the youth hostel, but it was fully booked with wedding guests, as Ross had predicted.

The wedding was in full swing in a marquee adjacent to the pub. There were people everywhere, and *You Can't Hurry Love* by Phil Collins wailed out from the tent.

The pub - The Tinners Arms - was rammed. A combination of wedding guests and villagers spilled out onto the street. There was a small service window by the door, which opened through to the area behind the bar. Ben poked his head through and asked if he could speak to the manager. The manager, a Brian Blessed lookalike, appeared a few minutes later.

'What do you want, guys? I'm very busy here,' he asked whilst loading the glass washer.

'We're here to offer to help you collect glasses, clear plates, pour pints, whatever needs doing,' said Ben, trying a new approach.

'What's the catch?' asked Brian Blessed.

'We need somewhere to stay tonight,' conceded Ben. 'Anywhere, just some floor space or a cupboard. Anything.'

'Sorry lads, I can't help I'm afraid. I'm fully booked with guests and I haven't got any space at all. Plus, I'm fully staffed so you couldn't help anyway.'

We noticed a man in a chef jacket leaning against the pub wall and smoking.

'How come you guys need somewhere to stay?' he said in that weird Godfather type voice that smokers use when they still have a lung full of smoke. He dropped his cigarette butt into the gravel and crushed it with his foot whilst tilting his head back and blowing out a cloud of smoke as he listened to our reply.

'We're cycling to John O'Groats without spending any money,' said Ben.

'Cool, man. Suppose you could do with some food then. Go and wait over there,' he said, pointing into the darkness. 'I'll get sacked if my boss catches me.' He swaggered off like a Cornish John Wayne towards the catering tent. We scurried off into the darkness like a pair of dirty scavengers.

'Here you go, lads,' he said a few minutes later, handing us a large ice-cream container full of unknown food. 'Better get back to work. If anyone asks, I didn't give you that, right?'

We only just got a chance to utter a brief 'thank you' as he disappeared back into the night. We decided to keep the food until after we had found somewhere to sleep.

We remembered the farmer that Ross had mentioned, so, as our luck was out at the pub, decided to give him a try. We wheeled our trusty steeds back up the hill that we had just descended, until the light of the village had faded behind us. We found what we presumed to be Harry Mann's house and knocked on the door.

'Hi there, are you Harry Mann?' I asked.

'I am,' said Harry Mann. He looked just how we had imagined he would look.

'We're looking for somewhere to stay tonight, and young farmer Ross from Morvah said you might be able to help us out. All we need is some floor space or an outhouse.'

'Yes, Ross did phone and warn me that you might call past. You can sleep in the barn round the back. There's plenty of hay to use as bedding, but you'll be sharing with a bull.'

'Cool,' I said.

'Sounds… fun,' said Ben hesitantly.

We followed Harry through the dark, around to the back of the house, through a barn full of calves and into a stable.

'Here you go. You can move that hay around to make yourself a bed and you should be pretty comfortable. Don't worry about Surprise,' he said, pointing to the gigantic bull in the neighbouring pen. 'He won't bother you. He's a prize-winner and is the sixth best bull in the country.'

Surprise was the size of a small caravan and was thankfully separated from us by some metal bars. He poked his head through and gave a huge snort to welcome us.

'So, what do you think? Is this place alright for you?' asked Harry.

Ben looked panicked.

36

'It's fantastic,' I said, 'We'll take it.'

'You should be warm enough, but I'll go and see if I can find a blanket or two just in case. There's a light just here, and you can use the toilet in our utility room,' he said, and disappeared out of the barn.

'This wasn't quite what I was expecting,' Ben uttered, after Harry had left. 'I thought we'd be able to blag hotel rooms or B&Bs. I didn't think we would have to sleep in a barn with a bull. I mean, look at the size of that beast.'

'Chill out! It's not often that you get a chance to sleep on hay next to a prize-winning bull. There's plenty of time for hotels, and B&Bs,' I said, trying to reassure him.

Harry soon returned with his wife Caroline, who was clutching two sleeping bags.

'You can keep this one,' said Caroline, holding up one of the sleeping bags, 'but we'll need the other one back in the morning. We start milking at 6am, so you'll probably hear us. Breakfast is at 8am, so come and have something to eat before you head off.'

They spoke to us as though we were the most recent of many to pass through Zennor and sleep in their barn. Not once had either Harry or Caroline questioned what we were doing or why we had nowhere to stay, but they had been extremely welcoming, in their own special way.

Ben had perked up since getting the sleeping bag, and was already moving the bales of hay around to make a bed on the floor. We both sank back into the hay and let out a simultaneous 'ahhhh'. It was possibly the most comfortable I have ever felt. After a long, hard day of walking, cycling, scootering, begging and blagging, the nest of hay was just what we needed.

It was 10.30pm and we had not eaten since the airport. It

was time to delve into the ice-cream container. Ben ripped the top off the container and we were presented with a huge pile of cold roast pork, a heap of stuffing, an enormous lump of cheese, several pieces of crackling and a stack of thick brown bread with some sachets of butter. We could not think of a single sight in the entire world that would have looked more alluring.

'The picnic set!' exclaimed Ben.

'Perfect, we can use it to eat our dinner with.'

It was as though our adventure was turning into some sort of role-playing computer game; collecting items along the way to use later.

Knock on door of house.

Collect picnic set.

Give wellies to young farmer.

Get food from wedding.

Use picnic set to eat food.

We had almost completed level one, and if we survived the night with Surprise we would have conquered the evil end-of-level boss, and moved straight onto level two.

Ben unzipped the picnic set so that we could have a proper look at it for the first time. It contained, well, as you would expect from a picnic set, everything that you need for a picnic: plates, bowls, cups, knives, forks, spoons and a corkscrew. They were all still in their individual wrappers and we decided to try and dirty as little of it as possible so that we could pass it on to someone else. Carrying an entire picnic set all the way to John O'Groats seemed rather unpractical. Ben unwrapped one plate and one knife and we began to tuck in to the feast. Half an hour previously we had been hungry and homeless, and now we were living like kings; albeit those three wise men that visited the stable.

Surprise bashed at the bars with his head. Not in an aggressive way, but he seemed keen to come and join us for dinner.

'At least we're not eating roast beef,' joked Ben.

We were just drifting off to sleep when a huge series of bangs startled us. It was the sound of fireworks from the wedding down the road. Surprise was not a fan of fireworks and bolted around his pen like he was at a rodeo. We got out of our sleeping bags and rushed to try and catch the fireworks before they finished. I mean 'catch' as in watch. Catching fireworks is very dangerous – don't try this at home, kids. The calves in the next-door barn were on a full stampede and they pounded around the yard in distress. We got outside just in time to see the extremely under-whelming grand finale, which consisted of three fireworks exploding at almost the same time. We could hear the token applause and cheers that greet the end of every firework display.

'Wooo... ahhh... yeeaaah.' Indeed. Back to bed.

On our way back into the barn we noticed a small cat-sized animal in the darkness. Ben knelt down to get a closer look and discovered it was a very old dog that was sniffing around in the corner. We had been told by Harry to keep the barn door closed, so we assumed that the dog should be shut outside, rather than in. Ben picked up the dog and kindly pushed it out of the door, but the little thing scurried straight back in before we had a chance to shut the door. He tried again, this time gently tossing it out of the door. Again, the pesky thing bounced back through the door. Ben tried again, slightly more forcefully than before and again the dog was back in the barn at lightning speed before we knew it. It was at this point that I heard the chink of metal. I bent down and discovered that the poor feeble dog was actually chained up on the inside of the barn, and the reason that it kept coming back so quickly was that it was restricted by the length of its chain. Ben instantly realised what he had done and cuddled the poor dog as best as he could. I had lost the power of speech because I was laughing so much.

I had only ever laughed this much once before in my life. When I was in the sixth-form, a friend of mine was showing a group of us a music video he had made. When his recording had finished it switched to what had previously been on the video tape. It was footage of his mum and dad filming each other naked in their bedroom. I have never seen anyone or anything move as quickly as he did when he dived across the room for the eject button. That was, until I saw the speed that this dog came back each time Ben threw it out.

We closed the barn door, with the dog inside where it belonged and we prayed that it would still be alive in the morning. The calves had just about settled down after the fireworks and Surprise was sitting on the floor and snorting quietly to himself. We drifted off to sleep without further incident.

Land's End car park

Bruce and Sheila, Land's End

Ruth, Land's End Hotel

Jemma - End to End Co-ordinator

Ross, Morvah

Somewhere near Zennor

Surprise the bull

Harry Mann's farm

Day 2
As I was going to St Ives...
Zennor to Camborne - 30 miles

We were covered in mould when we awoke. Our clothes, faces and hair were covered in black spots, which we decided must be mould spores, although for a while we were worried they were fly eggs and were going to hatch into our skin and infest our bodies like some '50s B-movie. I had thought I was being sensible by removing my boxer shorts before I went to sleep, and leaving them to air on a hay bale. They were now completely speckled with mould, whilst Ben's, which he had decided to wear all night, were spotless, albeit a little more smelly than mine.

Surprise had been a fairly quiet roommate. He had decided at about 6am to let us know he was awake by crashing into the bars and knocking over a large wooden board that had been propped against it. This in turn toppled onto our BMX and scooter that were leant against the wall, and these fell over onto my face.

There were flies swarming all around us. I pulled my whole body into the sleeping bag and scrunched it up above my head. Surprise was awake, the calves next door were awake, the sun was shining through the window bars, Harry and Caroline could be heard milking the cows and I was bursting with excitement. There was no use trying to get back to sleep.

We eventually got up and put on our spotty clothes. On the way through to the house we were relieved to see that the dog was still alive. In the daylight it looked even feebler. It whimpered in fear as Ben picked it up and gave it a cuddle.

Harry and Caroline were both in the kitchen. Caroline was at the AGA with a sizzling pan of bacon, and Harry was at the table reading the paper. It was a good-sized farmhouse kitchen with one of the walls covered in postcards and rosettes from their various prize-winning cattle. The rosettes were from the cattle, not the postcards, I should clarify. Although, if the cattle had written the postcards it would have clarified their prize-winning credentials.

It wasn't until breakfast that we got a chance to tell Harry and Caroline about our challenge. Until then, they had thought we were just a couple of travellers looking for somewhere to stay. After hearing our plans they opened up completely and we even caught them smiling a couple of times.

Harry had lived on the farm all of his life. His father had looked after the farm before him, and his grandfather before that. Caroline had been a nurse previously, but now worked on the farm full-time.

Harry gave me some bailer twine so that I could construct a belt for my enormous pin-striped suit trousers. Caroline insisted on giving us two gigantic Cornish pasties and a couple of bananas to take with us for lunch. After several attempts, Ben managed to squash the sleeping bag into the picnic set, leaving no room for anything else. We packed up our things and said goodbye to Harry, Caroline and Surprise. By the time we got going it was 10.30am and our aim to be in St Ives by 10am was already looking rather unrealistic.

Before we left, Caroline retold us the story of the mermaid of Zennor. The story goes that a lady in a long dress – to hide her fishy bits, presumably - used to attend services at the church of St Senara, in Zennor. She was enchanted by the singing voice of the chorister, Mathew Trewhella. One day their eyes met and they fell in love. He followed her down to the village stream, and then to the beach at Pendour Cove, and Mathew was never seen again. It is suggested that they disappeared beneath the waves together. Some people still

43

claim that if you sit at Pendour Cove at sunset in the summer, you can still hear Mathew's voice in the breeze.

This sounds like a load of old bollocks to me.

What really happened was that some 'out of town' hussy passed through Zennor and tempted Mathew – a suggestible and naïve village idiot - back to her flat in Penzance. Mathew then realised that eloping with some girl in the city was a better existence than being a choirboy, and so never returned to the village. As for hearing his dulcet tones floating across the waves on a summers evening - that's just Phil Collins being played at the wedding disco.

By daylight, Zennor was a picture postcard village. The road from Harry Mann's farm dipped down to the pub where the wedding had been, and the rest of the village sat on the slope beyond. Unlike the other villages that we had passed since Land's End, the main road does not pass directly through the Zennor. It had somehow secured its own bypass. The parish of Zennor also has the honour of being the last, alphabetically, in the whole of Britain. FACT!

The weather had brightened up, but there was still a thick barrage of mist in the air stopping the sun from breaking through. Our clothes were already sticky with dampness, so the extra moisture made little difference. Caroline had warned us that the terrain between Zennor and St Ives would be as tough as what we had experienced on the previous day.

'Although...' she had said, 'the last two miles are all downhill.' It was this phrase that kept repeating in our heads as we pushed our bikes up the first of many unreasonable hills.

However exhausting and painful it may be, there is no better way to see the countryside than on a scooter and a crappy BMX. You travel so slowly that you see absolutely everything; appreciating every inch of downhill freewheeling, and savouring every incline slowly and considerately on foot.

After a while, we spotted a turning to a camping and caravan park, and decided to go and check out their lost property. The caravan park turned out to be a tiresome mile-long detour from the main road. It was a completely unsuccessful trip as they had no bikes and no shoes. The receptionist, however, was one of Cornwall's finest sights and made the excursion entirely worthwhile.

On the steep downward descent into St Ives, I spotted a squash club set back from the road. I managed to swerve into the drive, but it was too late to warn Ben who shot past on the BMX completely out of control. The scraping of his boots on the road echoed up the quaint street as he tried to slow the bike down. In a moment of lunacy, he reached out and grabbed onto a lamp post as he passed, and was swung around in a circle, bumping up and over the curb, and finishing on the pavement facing back up the hill towards me. It was a move that any gymnast would have been proud of. He then wheeled his bike up the hill to where I stood in astonishment.

We had been taking it in turns to wear the rigger boots, but they were beginning to cause problems for both of us. We were now 'athletes', and clay covered rigger boots are not considered suitable athletic footwear. I had pulled over at the squash club thinking that they might have a lost property that we could scavenge through.

The squash club seemed to be a part of the bar next door, because the barman sprinted round as soon as he saw us.

'Can I help you, guys?' he said as he bounced towards us. I mean bounced as in a sort of jolly run, rather than actual bouncing. That would be weird.

'Hello,' I said, 'We were just wondering whether you had an old pair of trainers that had been left behind?'

'Did you lose a pair here?' he asked

'Not exactly,' said Ben, and then he explained the whole

situation, after which Dave – the extremely excitable barman – began bouncing up and down on the spot. This time, I mean bouncing in the literal sense.

'I love it, I love it,' he said, clapping his hands together like a small child. 'I don't think we've got any trainers at the moment, but you can come and have a look.'

We followed him through the corridors to a small broom cupboard under the stairs. He opened the Alice-in-Wonderland sized door, and removed a box containing a few random bits and pieces. There was one pink sock, a pair of tights, a baseball cap, a sweaty sweatband, a necklace and a set of car keys. Ben held up the sweaty sweatband and the tights and looked at me with a look as if to say 'How about these? Do you think these might be useful?' I raised an eyebrow at him, which made my feelings known. He got the message and put them back in the box.

'Sorry, guys. No luck, I'm afraid,' said Dave, sounding almost as disappointed as we were as he put the shoebox back. 'Hang on a minute, what are these?' He retrieved a pair of white Adidas trainers that had been hiding behind the vacuum cleaner. 'I'm not sure whose these are or where they have come from, but I would just take them if I were you.'

They were a perfect fit, and, as Ben pointed out, they were almost trendy.

'I'm sure nobody will miss them,' he said. 'They've probably been here for years. Or maybe that's where the manager keeps his trainers.'

'I thought you were the manager?' I asked.

'Noooo,' said Dave. 'I just work at the bar next door and I'm covering while he's popped out. I would disappear if I were you before he gets back.'

We tried to leave the rigger boots with him, but he thought it was a bad idea for us to leave any evidence that we had been there. We jumped back onto our bike and scooter, with proper footwear on our feet, the rigger boots on our handlebars, and freewheeled down the last few hundred metres to the sea.

St Ives was once a thriving fishing village, but following a decline it rebuilt itself as a holiday destination and art centre. Thanks largely to former artist residents such as Barbara Hepworth and Russian sculptor Naum Gabo (No? Me neither), the town is now considered an important centre for art. With the exception of Liverpool, it is the only place outside of London to have a branch of The Tate.

St Ives is a pretty little town. We were there on a sunny Sunday and the place was crawling with tourists. It has its fair share of tat, but it has still managed to maintain its charm. For a small seaside town however, the sea was very difficult to find. We spent a while trapped in the maze of tiny back streets before eventually finding it. It was the big wet bit by the harbour.

We stopped by a patch of sand by the water. I say 'patch of sand', rather than 'beach', as it was a patch of sand, rather than a beach. The fog had completely cleared and it was a beautiful day. We sat back against the harbour wall and bit into our Cornish pasties. They were immense. The seagulls swooped and dive-bombed us from above, trying to sample our lunch, but we skilfully defended our provisions with deadly backhands.

Ben propped the rigger boots against one of the large bins along the waterfront. They were in prime position for a passer-by to see, and failing that, the bin man might have been tempted by a change of footwear.

There was a 'SPEEDBOAT HIRE' sign by the harbour. Up to this point, we had only asked for things we NEEDED for our journey; clothes, food, bikes… beer. But there we were, basking in the sun, without a care in the world. We had been fed, watered and were fairly well clothed. It was time for some fun.

'Hi there,' said Ben to the guy manning the speedboat stand. 'We're cycling to John O'Groats without spending any money, and along the way we're hoping to experience some of the excitements that Britain has to offer.'

Nice. I liked Ben's approach. He was basically telling this guy that by lending us a speedboat, he would be doing his bit for good ol' Blighty.

'Sounds fun,' said the man, a little bemused and still unsure of what Ben wanted.

'Would it be possible,' continued Ben, 'for us to rent a speedboat, for free, so that we can fully experience St Ives?'

'Errr, ok,' said the man, not really knowing what else to say.

'I can't find the accelerator,' I said to St Ives' version of CJ from *Baywatch* who had helped us into the boat. Unfortunately, though, *she* was a *he* and he had considerably more chest hair, though with similar sized boobs.

'There is no accelerator,' he said. 'It has a fixed speed and you pull this cord to stop it.'

'Shit,' whispered Ben, 'this thing might get out of control.' In reality, he need not have worried. I could have swum faster than that boat. Its slowness was excruciating. Still, we were cruising around the bay in a 'speedboat' we had borrowed for free. We couldn't complain.

It was in these very waters that a great white shark was supposedly spotted in August 2007. Experts were quick to point out that it was more likely to be a harmless porbeagle shark or a basking shark. At around the same time, there were similar sightings of a great white shark in Newquay. 52-year-old security guard Kevin Keeble came forward with a picture depicting a great white with bloodied teeth, fresh from a kill.

He claimed to have taken the picture in the waters off Newquay and the local paper ran the photo on its front page. The story was soon featured in *The Sun* and various other national media. Kevin Keeble later admitted that the photo had been taken during a fishing trip in South Africa and he had only meant it as a joke.

The most exciting thing we saw on our boat trip was a dead seagull. Well, we assumed it was dead. Either that or it was swimming on its back, with its head underwater, and a hole in its body.

We spoke to CJ for a while after returning the boat, and asked him if he had any suggestions of where we might find some bikes.

'There's a farm a few miles out of St Ives where a guy does up old bikes to sell,' he said. 'His name is Badcock. Roger Badcock.' Ben sniggered at the name. 'Be warned, though, he's quite a strange bloke and if he invites you in for a cup of tea, I would definitely refuse.'

'How come?' asked Ben, still grinning at the name Roger Badcock.

'Put it this way. It's the kind of house where you have to wipe your feet on the way out.'

We had clothes and shoes, but there were a few other supplies that we thought we would need along the way. First up was an ice cream. Yes, I know an ice cream is hardly a necessity, but we were at the seaside and everyone was eating them. As the old adage goes: 'When in St Ives, do as the St Ivans do'. With a bit of sweet-talking we got two delicious Cornish ice creams from a very puzzled lady in the ice cream shop.

We prepared ourselves a mental shopping list.

2 x toothbrushes
1 x toothpaste
Towel
Soap
Plasters for our blisters

It seemed like a fairly modest selection of provisions. Acquiring such supplies in a busy seaside town was going to prove difficult, so we decided to ask at different shops for each item.

First up was Boots, the *'popular high street chemist'*. We spoke to the manager - a young, pretty, smiley lady, which is always a bonus. She seemed mildly amused when we told her what we were up to and explained why we were dressed so ridiculously. We asked first of all for a couple of their cheapest toothbrushes, and without hesitation she walked off and returned with a pack of Boots value toothbrushes and a tube of toothpaste.

'I assume you'll need this toothpaste, too. Anything else?' she asked. We were shocked. We had expected a cold response from the recognised high street chains. We imagined that a strict policy structure would be in place that would prevent people like us walking in off the street and getting things for free.

'That's brilliant. Thanks,' I said. 'Could you spare a small packet of plasters?'

'Sure,' she said and asked one of the other members of staff to pass her a packet of plasters from behind the counter. She probably would have given us everything on our list, but we decided to leave it at that and try elsewhere for the rest of our things.

There was another local chemist just up the road and we went in and asked for some soap. The man behind the counter disappeared down into the basement and emerged a few moments later holding a bottle of rather expensive looking shower gel, two gigantic beach towels and two t-shirts.

'Here you go, lads,' he said. 'Do you have towels already? If not then I'm sure these will be useful.'

'We don't have towels, but they were on our list. Thank you so much,' said Ben, open-mouthed. I mean open-mouthed as in 'surprised'. He obviously talks with his mouth open. If he had been a ventriloquist I would have mentioned that earlier.

'You're welcome. We get them free from companies when they're trying to promote a new product. You can have the t-shirts, too.' The t-shirts were huge white ones with a sun cream logo on the front and the words 'Surf's up' on the back. We had only been on the road for a day and a half, but the sight of a clean white t-shirt that didn't have any traces of mould was unbelievably appealing.

We decided to go and have a swim in the sea, give ourselves a bit of a wash and then change into our 'Sunday best'. It was Sunday after all, and it was only right that we dressed for the occasion. We wheeled our bikes and an armload of new belongings back down to the harbour.

There were already a few kids swimming in the sea and we sat on the harbour wall to try and repack our bags. Two young boys, aged about seven and nine, were taking it in turns to ride their scooter down the long boat ramp and into the water. It was a pink Barbie scooter and they soon noticed our superior WWF scooter leaning against the wall, and they eyed it with envy. They realised that their scooter was totally uncool, and that ours was the daddy.

'How about we show these mini Evil Knievels a thing or two about scootering,' suggested Ben.

'I'm not even sure that 'scootering' is a word, but yeah, I reckon we could definitely teach them how to do it properly,' I said.

Ben took the scooter and I took the BMX and we readied ourselves at the top of the ramp. The boys stood back and looked on in awe. Ben and I looked at the boys, nodded at each other, and then set off down the ramp.

We crashed into the water in spectacular fashion. The water was absolutely freezing, but we pretended it wasn't. We swam around for a few minutes and did our best to clean ourselves as much as possible. Ben swam out a little further and I started to follow him.

'Don't come any closer,' he said. 'I'm doing a piss.'

We fished our bikes out of the sea, and then dried off with our matching towels, hung our matching boxer shorts out in the sun to dry and put on our crispy clean matching t-shirts. We made a lovely couple.

Realistically, we should have cut one of the gigantic towels in half there and then and taken half each, but they were so nice and lavish that we decided to try and keep them both.

The two boys, who must have been brothers, approached us and started pointing erratically at our bike and scooter.

'You want to borrow ours?' I asked.

They nodded eagerly and started pointing frantically at the sea.

'You want to ride our bikes into the sea?' asked Ben.

They nodded even more excitedly.

'I think they're deaf,' said Ben.

They started signing to each other and it became apparent that they were not only deaf, but also mute. They picked up our bike and scooter and spent the next ten minutes riding down the ramp into the sea. At one point, one of the boys wheeled the BMX over to me and started stamping his feet, pointing at the bike's chain and then waving his finger at me. The chain had fallen off and it was clearly my fault. I reattached the chain and they carried on. They may have been a little rude, but Ben and I felt a sense of well-being that we had been generous to two disadvantaged children. This proved to be a huge mistake.

'Where have our bikes gone?' I asked Ben after a while.

'They're around somewhere. One of the boys is still there.'

'But the other boy isn't there and neither are our bikes.'

'I'll go and speak to him,' said Ben, who got up and walked over to the younger of the two boys.

'Where did you put our bike and scooter?' he asked, using gestures to ensure that he would understand.

The boy shrugged his shoulders and started to walk off.

'Then where is your brother?'

The boy shrugged again and continued walking. His brother soon appeared and gave the same expressions when we asked him what had happened to our scooter and BMX.

'We're not leaving them, Ben,' I said, getting up off the harbour wall to join him. 'Let's follow them until they show us where the bikes are.'

The older brother began to make gestures to show that they were going home and then they started to run.

We ran after them.

I noticed that the younger of the two brothers had to collect his shoes from the wall on the way past, and I got there before him and grabbed them. Now, this may seem cruel to steal a poor little deaf-mute boy's shoes, but you have to trust me, those boys were evil.

I held his shoes in the air and he jumped to try and retrieve them.

'You'll get them back when we get our bikes back,' I said like a primary school teacher.

We followed the boys for a few minutes along the waterfront and we soon saw the BMX propped against a wall on a nearby street.

'I thought you didn't know where the bikes were, you little shits?' Ben shouted angrily.

The boys smirked.

'Tell us where the other one is,' I demanded.

The older boy started pointing in the direction of Land's End, back down the coast.

'OK, then show us where,' I said.

He shook his head and started pointing the other way, as if to say they lived in the other direction.

'Well we're going wherever you go,' I said.

He stamped his feet again.

They lead us out of the harbour and round into the next bay. Sure enough, after about five minutes he pointed out the scooter, which was propped up behind a dustbin. The older boy held up his hands as if to say: 'I have no idea how that got there.'

It was absolutely astonishing. We had nearly been robbed by two little kids. There we were, on a 'niceness tour' of Great Britain, and the two most innocent and vulnerable people we had met had taken full advantage of our generosity and tried to steal our BMX and scooter. They needed to face the consequences.

We reported them to the police and after a lengthy and expensive court case they were ordered to serve eight years in a juvenile correctional facility.

'Now clear off, both of you,' is what I actually said, before handing the younger brother his shoes back. They gave us both a sarcastic smirk then turned and walked off to find their next victims.

'You really showed them,' Ben said with a chuckle.

It was strange how attached to the bike and scooter we had become in less than a day. They were possibly the most rubbish form of transport that ever existed, but to us they were priceless. They were more than just bikes, they were our method of getting from A to B quicker than on foot, and without them we would have been back where we started. I mean that metaphorically, of course. We weren't playing some role-playing game that would have meant going back to Land's End if our bikes were stolen.

Another group of older boys had been hanging around the harbour and had witnessed our pursuit of the boys. One of them approached us and asked what we were up to.

'I know where there's a bike you can have,' he said excitedly. 'There's one up by Co-op. It's been there for weeks and we just use it for messing around on. I'll go and get it for you.'

Before we even had a chance to ask whose it was, or where it had come from, he had turned and ran up one of the narrow streets into town, still wearing his dripping wetsuit. He had restored our faith in humanity. One minute 'the youth of today' were robbing us of our beloved bikes, and the next they were sprinting barefoot across town to help us out.

He returned about five minutes later wheeling what looked from a distance to be a decent looking mountain bike. On closer inspection, it was an unbelievable pile of shit.

'It'll need a bit of work,' he said, 'but you're welcome to take it if you want it. I don't think it belongs to anyone.'

There were no pedals, no chain, no brake cables or brake pads. The back wheel was severely buckled, neither tyre had an inner tube and the saddle was missing. It did have a functioning bell, though. We felt really bad turning down a bike, but the amount of work that this one required to make it useable meant that we would have taken a huge step backwards.

'That's very kind of you,' I said, 'but it looks like it needs too much work. We can't spend any money and it would take too much time and effort for someone to fix this up for us.'

'Yeah, thanks mate,' said Ben. 'We really appreciate the offer, but I think we'll stick with what we've got, for now, and hold up for something better. Apparently there's a bloke who lives just out of St Ives who has a lot of bikes at his farm.'

'Yeah, his name's Roger Badcock,' said the boy. Ben sniggered again at the mention of his name. 'And no worries about the bike. I don't think it's worth you guys keeping it. I just thought I'd show it to you. Good luck with the rest of your trip.'

We gathered our stuff together and tied our boxer shorts to our rucksacks so they could finish drying. Yes, we were both going commando. In a pair of thick woollen suit trousers, it felt incredibly liberating.

The road out of St Ives climbed steeply away from the sea. We walked for about a mile as there was simply no point trying to ride the scooter up hills. It was slower, and far more exhausting than walking.

The road then reached a plateau before descending gradually into the village of Lelant. We found Roger Badcock's house fairly easily after piecing together a variety of directions from different people.

His house was a sort of permanent mobile home, if such a paradox is possible. It was on the edge of a patch of wasteland and the door was protected with a mesh fly screen. The whole place was straight out of a 1970s horror film.

We knocked on the door. There was no answer.

I had held out great hope for Mr Badcock, and despite Ben suggesting we try a few places in the built up metropolis that was St Ives, I was adamant that Roger was our man.

We turned to leave and hung our heads in defeat. It was already 5pm and it was unlikely we would find bikes anywhere else that day.

'I guess we'll just have to head into the next village and look for...' I started, before being interrupted with a voice behind us.

'Can I help you?'

Roger Badcock was standing in his doorway. He was over six feet tall and his bulk filled every inch of the doorframe. He was wearing a green polo shirt that was covered in various stains. His hair receded almost to the back of his scalp; he had a huge shock of black hair spraying out from behind in all directions and a wonderful handlebar moustache.

'Hi there, we're really sorry to disturb you,' I said. 'Are you Mr Badcock?'

Ben sniggered to himself.

'Aye,' said Mr Badcock. 'That's me.'

'We've been told by several people that you might be able to help us out,' said Ben. 'We're cycling to John O'Groats without spending any money and we were wondering if there was any chance that we could swap these bikes for something a bit more suitable for long distance cycling.'

There was a pause while his tried to clean his smeared glasses on his t-shirt which only made them worse.

'Well I don't know if I have got anything suitable at the moment,' he said, 'but we can have a look.' Roger stepped down from his house with a mammoth struggle. He swaggered across the driveway and unlocked the door to the adjacent barn.

The building was packed full of bike parts. There were whole bikes, half bikes, bike wheels, chains, inner tubes, saddles of all shapes and sizes; they hung from the ceiling, they were piled against the wall and they were strewn across the floor. We followed Roger into the barn and Ben turned to me, clenched his fist and mouthed the words: 'Oh. My. God.' We were in bike heaven.

'How come you've got so many bikes?' I asked.

'It's just a hobby of mine really. I can't work because of illness, so I repair bikes. I don't really make any money from them but it keeps me busy.'

'So what sort of bike are you after?' he panted, clearly worn out by the 20-metre walk from his house.

'Whatever you can spare,' said Ben. 'We're looking for anything that's better than the scooter and BMX that we have.'

He patrolled the barn like a General, grabbing hold of the occasional bike and weighing up in his mind whether he could part with it, and whether it was suitable for our needs.

On his second lap of the barn he paused at a small, lurid pink girls' mountain bike.

'You can have this,' he said, 'but it's probably not the kind of thing you're... '

'It's perfect,' I said, before he had finished his sentence.

Despite its appearance, it seemed like a decent bike. All the various bits looked to be in place and it appeared to have several gears. It was slightly on the small size, but it was a huge upgrade from either of our other bikes.

'That's probably all I can offer you,' said Roger. 'All the other ones are either unfinished or I don't want to part with them.'

'You've been extremely generous to give us this one,' I said.

I looked up to see that Ben was over on the far side of the barn, tentatively stroking a very small racing bike.

'Ben!' I called over, 'Roger is going to kindly give us this pink mountain bike. Isn't that great?'

'Yeah, that's wicked. Thanks so much,' said Ben not taking his eyes off the racer.

'I guess we had better head off now, and try and find somewhere to stay,' I said.

'Yep, I guess we should,' said Ben, who had now straddled the racer and was leaning forward pretending to be on a downhill.

Roger walked over to the bike and started fiddling around with the brake cables. It was a 1970s junior Sirocco Falcon. It had 5 gears and the handlebars were covered up with multi-coloured tape. It was basically a racing bike for a child, but it had a certain retro charm.

'Oh, go on,' he said. 'You can take that one, too.'

'Are you serious?' said Ben.

'Well, you caught me in a good mood, and I've had both of these bikes sitting around for a while now,' he said.

'Well I hope you can put ours to some use, so that we can at least go some way to repay the favour,' I said.

Roger chuckled to himself.

'I might be able to pass the scooter on to someone,' he said, 'and I'll probably be able to get some useful screws and bearings off the other one, but that's about it. Good luck to you both. I'll put some air in the tyres for you and they should be good to go.'

We had travelled about 14 miles on the scooter and BMX. This may not sound like a lot, but I had never felt more drained in my life. The energy it takes to propel a scooter with foam wheels up a Cornish hill, or pedal a miniature BMX over a long distance, is immeasurable.

Our thigh muscles were burning, our knees were bruised from catching the handlebars on the BMX, our heels were completely blistered from wearing the rigger boots and our backs were aching from being in such unnatural positions. With hindsight, it would have been far less painful and probably quicker if we had walked from Land's End.

After just a few seconds on our new bikes we felt like we had been born again. We decided to alternate the bikes regularly, as they were both very different but each had their advantages. The pink girls' mountain bike – or 'Pinky' as we imaginatively called it – had a comfy seat, 12 gears and decent brakes. It was rather small, though, and the fat tyres meant it was quite slow. The racer – or 'The Falcon', as it became known – only had five gears, a seat made of the hardest material known to man and handlebars that were about a foot lower than the saddle. It had nice slick road tyres, though, and seemed faster than Pinky.

I did the first shift on Pinky and Ben started on The Falcon. We decided to attempt another 10 miles or so, to try and make up for the time we had spent in St Ives playing in boats and chasing deaf kids.

For the first time since setting off, we suddenly felt like we were making progress towards John O'Groats. The road had opened up in front of us and we could feel ourselves eating away at the 1000-mile route that lay ahead.

We had yet to establish a route for the trip. Seeing as we had to get everything for free, we weren't able to bring a route book or map. We knew at some stage we would have to ascertain how to get to John O'Groats, but in the meantime, we knew that if we roughly followed the A30, we would be heading in the right direction.

We had made it our aim to avoid A-roads as much as possible. They might be quicker and more direct, but they are no fun to cycle along and you don't get to see the country in the same way that you do via the back roads. We made an exception on this occasion, however, as we wanted to have covered a respectable distance. We joined the A30 just after the village of Lelant, and aimed to get to Camborne before dark. It was 7.30pm on a Sunday, and we had the entire A30 to ourselves. Not that you need both lanes of a dual carriageway when you are on a bike.

We reached the town of Camborne in good time. It was

still light and there was plenty of activity in the town centre. By activity, I mean there were groups of people hanging around outside shops and loitering on street corners. Camborne was once the centre of the Cornish mining industry and one of the richest mining areas in the world. It has recently been the target of a huge regeneration project to breathe new life into the town.

We decided to try and find somewhere to stay first, and received two rejections in quick succession from a hotel and then a pub.

'I suppose we had better start looking for a barn,' said Ben dejectedly.

'We've only been trying for ten minutes,' I said. 'We knew this wasn't going to be easy. I'm sure we can find somewhere to sleep. Besides, I don't think they tend to have barns in town centres.'

'That's true. I guess it doesn't matter too much where we end up. At least I've got a sleeping bag now.'

'YOU'VE got a sleeping bag?' I asked angrily. 'I thought it was both of ours.'

'Well we can't really both use it and I have been carrying it all day.'

'Fine, whatever. You have it, Mr Selfish.'

A man swigging a can of Special Brew started laughing at our pink bike. He swayed and dribbled as he spoke.

'Noice boike,' he spluttered.

'Thanks,' I said. 'Do you know anywhere we could stay tonight for free?'

'There's a pub up there called the Veeeeervan Aaaarms,' he said, pointing in three different directions. 'They have cheap rooo… ooo… ooms.'

'Unfortunately we can't spend ANY money at all. We're on a challenge to get to John O'Groats without spending

61

anything.'

'Oh,' he said. 'That sounds stupid. Well, you could ask at the Veeeeervan Aaaarms anyway. Tell them Big... ig... ig... Mick sent you.'

The Vyvyan Arms was a big corner building on a junction at the top end of town, and we wheeled our newly acquired bikes around to the car park at the back. This was the first time we would have to leave them unattended, and we suddenly realised that security was a slight concern. The BMX and scooter that we'd had before weren't worth stealing, yet they had been stolen. Now we had bikes that *were* worth stealing.

Pinky had a bike lock wrapped around underneath the saddle, but we didn't know the combination. Ben guessed 4856. I guessed 1234. Neither worked.

We tried again.

Ben guessed 1111 and I guessed 2199. Again, neither worked. This continued for sometime, until we realised it was futile. With a bit of effort, we managed to untangle some of the bike lock from around Pinky and then loop it over the Falcon's saddle, too. To the casual passer-by it appeared that the bikes were locked together.

The resident DJ was just setting up his kit when we entered the Vyvyan Arms, and there was a table of men huddled in the far corner. The lady behind the bar was in her forties, quite short and had the biggest breasts we had ever seen. We didn't technically *see* them, but we got a pretty good idea of their size by the fact that she seemed to be resting them on the bar to stop herself falling over.

'Hi there, are you the landlady?' Ben asked.

'Yes, I suppose I am,' she said, as if she had only just realised it.

'We were wondering if there is any work we can do here in

exchange for somewhere to sleep.'

'We're good at cleaning, washing-up, decorating, and we don't need a bed. All we need is a roof,' I added.

'Errrr... errrr...hang on,' she said. 'I'll have to check with my husband.'

Scotty, the landlord, was an intimidating looking guy. He was built like a prop forward. He had long blond hair that was tied back in a ponytail and he had tattoos down the length of both arms. To contradict his menacing biker image, he wore a t-shirt with a huge picture of Taz, the Tazmanian Devil cartoon character, adorned across the front.

'I hear you're looking for somewhere to stay tonight for free,' he said. 'We're fairly quiet tonight and I doubt we'll have any more guests arriving, so I'm sure we can sort you out with a room.'

'Are you sure? There must be some work we can do in return?' I asked.

'I don't think so,' said Scotty. 'As I said, we're very quiet so there's not much needs doing. I'll go and check that your room is ready. What can I get you both to drink in the meantime?'

'Let me get those, Scotty,' said one of the locals who had been eavesdropping. 'Sounds like you two need it.'

'Right you are, Colin,' said Scotty. 'The next round's on me, though.' Colin, like most of the other men, had been in the Vyvyan Arms for most of the day. They insisted that we join them, and we told them the story of why we were in Camborne.

Scotty and Billy – his wife – showed us to the room, where we were given a choice of beds. The room had two single beds and a huge four-poster bed. Ben and I were not quite ready to share a double bed just yet, so we opted for the singles

We both sank back onto the beds and lay there in silence for a few blissful moments, letting the feelings of relief and comfort pass through us. We still had our beers downstairs to finish, so we washed our faces in the sink and returned to the bar.

After our beer, Scotty offered us some food, but we decided that we didn't want to abuse his hospitality and so walked into town to try and find some food elsewhere.

'I fancy a Chinese,' said Ben.

'Sounds good to me,' I said.

We soon reached Tse House, a Chinese restaurant on the high street. We could see through the window that the place was quiet. For a normal person, this is usually considered a bad sign, but for us it was ideal. We had grown more confident about asking for things, but we still preferred to have as small an audience as possible.

We entered through the beaded curtain and approached the teenager behind the counter who then told us to speak to the manager.

Becky Tse, the manager, was frantically stacking glasses behind the bar. We apologised for bothering her and explained what we were doing, and asked if we could do any work in exchange for some food. She nodded throughout, but didn't look remotely interested.

'Ok. Eat in or takeaway?' she asked when we had finished.

'But we don't have any money,' I repeated in case she had not understood us.

'It's ok. Eat in or takeaway?' she said.

'Oh… thank you… eat in then please,' I said.

'Two chicken chow meins?' she asked, and pointed to a table over in the far corner.

'Whatever is easiest and cheapest for you,' said Ben.

'TWO CHICKEN CHOW MEINS,' she shouted through the curtain into the kitchen. 'Five minutes,' she said to us, 'I bring it over to table.'

'Thank you so much,' said Ben, 'Is there any cleaning or

washing up we can do in return?'

She smiled for the first time.

'No,' she said. 'Five minutes. I bring it over to table.'

And so she did. Two huge plates of steaming Chicken Chow Mein were soon sitting in front of us and we gratefully devoured every last noodle.

We returned back to the Vyvyan Arms where the disco was in full swing. By that I mean that the lights had been dimmed, and the DJ had started his set. The dance floor was empty, though, and the lone table of regulars were still the only people in the pub.

We spent a few hours chatting to the locals, playing pool and being bought drinks. At about 11pm, we went to bed, stuffed full of Chinese, a little drunk and completely knackered.

Harry Mann's farm, Zennor

Harry and Caroline, Zennor

Speedboat hire, St Ives

In a speedboat, St Ives

Ice creams, St Ives

Roger Badcock, Lelant

Scott, Vyvyan Arms, Camborne

Resident DJ, Vyvyan Arms, Camborne

66

Day 3
The lawnmower man
Camborne to Nanstallon - 48 miles

We ate our way through a huge pile of toast that Billy had made for us, drank a teapot full of tea, and ate several bowls of cereal each. The local paper had an article about a couple of horrific road accidents, and it made me think about how potentially dangerous our trip could be. We had dodgy bikes, no helmets, and little experience of cycling. I mentioned this to Ben and we both agreed to try and shake off the carefree attitude we'd had for the first two days. We also agreed to try and find helmets.

We said our goodbyes to Scotty, Billy and the resident DJ who was still in the pub, dressed in the same clothes that he had been wearing the night before. Ben gave them a frisbee that we had found by the side of the road near Lelant. It was all we had in the way of a gift, but they seemed really touched.

'We'll leave it here behind the bar to remind us of your visit. It's been so lovely to have met you both,' said Billy. She then gave us a couple of green t-shirts that they had been given from a brewery. They became our new Sunday Best, which we decided to save for the evenings, and not to wear whilst cycling.

We followed the old road to Redruth, which ran directly parallel to the A30, and we then cut back towards the coast.

We were on a steep descent into the village of Porthtowan when I saw a crane over to the right.

'Look at that crane!' I shouted to Ben who was in front of me. I have no idea why I decided to point out the crane to Ben, as it was not in the slightest bit remarkable, and I wasn't aware that Ben had a particular fascination with cranes.

'What?' called Ben, who was unable to hear properly because of the speed we were going. He slammed on Pinky's brakes and she skidded to a stop. The Falcon, however, had yet to be tested on a downhill.

I applied the brakes. They squeaked. Nothing happened. There was no time to avoid Ben and I crashed into the back of him catching my leg on his rear wheel cog. I was then thrown forwards and landed with my balls on the crossbar.

My leg was bleeding slightly, but it was nothing serious, and after a slight readjustment, I decided my balls would recover, too.

'There was a big crane just back there,' I said to Ben.

'Oh, right. Thanks for that. Are you alright?'

'Yeah, I'm fine thanks. I think we need to get The Falcon's brakes looked at.'

'No shit, Sherlock.'

Porthtowan is a pleasant village that is home to one of Britain's most popular surfing beaches. It apparently has some 'sick breaks' and 'phat tubes', whatever that means. Again, the village was once an important mining spot, but it now relies heavily on tourism. In case you were wondering, the name Porthtowan is derived from the Cornish words 'porth' and 'tewynn' meaning *'Cove of Sand Dunes'*. You will sleep tight now.

Just on the outskirts of the village we passed Porthtowan Garage. Now, I'm no bike expert, but we figured if we borrowed a spanner and tightened a few nuts here and there The Falcon would be cured.

'Wheel it in and I'll take a look at it,' said John the mechanic when we asked to borrow a spanner.

'The brakes are gone,' he said. 'I'll do my best to tighten them up, but they're pretty much finished.'

He tightened some nuts, lengthened some cables and shortened some others. He then dribbled oil from one of those old-fashioned oilcans with the ridiculously long nozzle, over various bits of The Falcon's anatomy. I could almost hear it purring. The Falcon, that is, not the mechanic.

The road out of Porthtowan was stupidly steep. For the first time since getting our 'real bikes' we got off and walked. We didn't feel guilty about it. When it gets to the stage that you are cycling uphill at the same speed that you would walk, there is simply no point in busting yourself.

Once we had made it to the top of the hill, the terrain levelled out and the cycling became easier. The sun was out so we took off our t-shirts. We still had limited clothing and we decided that the less we sweated onto our clothes, the better.

I was still commando at this point, as I had attempted to wash the salty sea water from my boxer shorts in the sink at the Vyvyan Arms and have them dry by the morning. I had succeeded in the washing part, but failed miserably in getting them dry. I'd hung them out of the window at night, naively expecting them to dry by the light of the moon. I then tied them to my rucksack so that they could dry during the day.

Going topless with my suit trousers left my lower half rather exposed. The bailer twine had not really helped, and in order to stop the trousers falling down completely, I had to roll the waistband over several times. This caused them to hang extremely low, revealing a view of pubic hair. Now I'm sure that this is a mental image that you didn't want formed, but I feel that it is my duty to paint as accurate a picture as possible.

The road between Porthtowan and St Agnes was banked with high hedges, so despite cycling along the coast, we only had occasional glimpses of the sea.

We had planned to have lunch in St Agnes, but we reached

the village by mid-morning so stopped for a short rest instead. The tracksuit bottoms that Ben had been given by Les-the-coastguard were unnecessarily bulky, and they constantly billowed out behind him like a wind sock. He decided to take evasive action and went to borrow a pair of scissors from the chemist on the high street. He emerged soon after in a pair of big baggy shorts and a tracksuit bottom leg on each arm for no other reason than he thought it was funny. It was a little, so I had a go at wearing them, too.

I was very envious of Ben's shorts, but didn't feel that I could do the same to the suit trousers. What if I had another wedding to go to on route, or a job interview? I would need to look my best, so I decided to roll the legs up to make them feel like shorts. Albeit, thick heavy woollen ones.

Ben had 'misplaced' his water bottle somewhere since Camborne. We were still using the bottles that John from the airport had given us, and we were filling them up at every opportunity.

'I'll go and get a bottle of water from the shop,' he said as he strode off.

'Can't you just find an old bottle and fill it up from somewhere?' I called after him.

'Nah, I'll just get a new one from the shop up here.'

He returned empty-handed.

'What a complete and utter idiot,' he said.

'What happened?'

'I went in there, right, and explained what we were doing and asked for a bottle of water and he said, 'Bring money like the rest of us. You're expecting people to pay for your 'oliday.' What a tosser.'

'But don't you think you were being a tosser by going off and expecting to be given a new bottle of water?'

'It's only a bottle of water, for Christ's sake,' he said.

'I know. That's the point. Water is something that we can get anywhere, and you could find an old bottle easily. You were being arrogant asking for something just for the sake of it.'

Ben curled his lip and considered that perhaps I was right.

I shared my water with Ben and we topped it up from an outside tap in the pub car park. We asked someone to point us in an easterly direction, and they told us to head towards the villages of Perranporth and then Goonhavern.

Ben and I first met in the summer of 1998, when we worked together at Althorp - the home of Earl Spencer and the resting place of Diana, Princess of Wales. We worked as wardens when the estate opened its doors to the public for July and August in the year following Diana's death. We spent our days smiling at visitors, answering questions and messing around with walkie-talkies. I seemed to be the only person on the 14,000-acre estate that appreciated Ben's odd sense of humour and we hit it off instantly.

There was a piano in the staff room which Ben spent every lunch hour playing. The older members of staff adored him, whilst the rest of the staff – including the managers - all found him a little bit weird. I worked a total of four summers at Althorp. Ben was not asked back after the first year.

Perranporth was a busy little seaside village. Its bustling high street was crawling with coach parties who were stripping the shops bare of their souvenirs.

It was lunchtime and there was an unmistakeable smell of Cornish pasties in the air. We soon found the source; Berrymans Bakery with a queue stretching out the door. They were clearly popular pasties, and we decided it was worth the embarrassment and possible humiliating rejection, to join the queue and ask for a freebie.

The young girl who served us was very smiley and didn't really understand what we were doing, but she checked with her manager and then gave us two huge pasties. We pushed our bikes further up the road to where we found access to the beach and we sat and ate our delicious pasties in the sand dunes.

There was another uphill section out of Perranporth, where we followed signs to Goonhavern until we became distracted by a signpost for *The World In Miniature*. We couldn't resist.

The World in Miniature was, well, the world, but in miniature. Most of the world's most recognisable landmarks were there to see, in reduced sizes. They had the Leaning Tower of Pisa, the Statue of Liberty and the Egyptian pyramids, to name but a few. We had an enjoyable world tour in about 20 minutes. It was almost as good as the real thing.

The manager of the place, Donna, was particularly generous and she piled us high with more pasties, sausage rolls, pick 'n' mix and energy drinks (which provided Ben with a new drinking bottle). We asked her for directions east, following the scenic route, and she reeled off a list of villages for us to look out for. These included: Fiddlers Green, Kestle Mill, St Columb Major, Withiel and Nanstallon. It felt like we were characters in a Charles Dickens novel. Actually, it didn't feel like that at all.

We borrowed a spanner from the workman who was busy repairing the miniature Buckingham Palace, and we raised Pinky's saddle. Neither bike was comfortable to ride, but the saddle on Pinky had been especially low and was particularly painful on the knees. Raising the saddle made a huge difference.

The Falcon's chain jammed as Ben tried to overtake me at speed on one of the many downhills. It was wedged between the main gear cog and the frame but he was able to freewheel for another half a mile before we had to pull over.

Conveniently, at the bottom of the hill was *The Lappa Valley Steam Railway*. We seemed to be doing an unintentional tour of Cornwall's most popular tourist attractions.

The Lappa Valley Steam Railway was miniature, as it seemed were most tourist things in Cornwall. We tried in vain to free the trapped chain, but no amount of yanking would release it. We decided the only way to release it would be to loosen the back wheel.

I queued up at the ticket office and they directed me towards the train driver who was just emerging from the train. He had a big white beard and every inch of his face was covered in oil and soot. He looked like a black Captain Birdseye. He happily leant me an adjustable spanner and I returned to Ben who was already tucking into his pick 'n' mix. We had agreed that we would save it until we were really desperate. It seemed that we were really desperate as I too grabbed my bag and started shovelling handfuls of sweets into my mouth.

It was the first sugar we'd had since the airport and our bodies certainly were wilting in its absence. I had started to get the shakes a few hours before, and I could feel the instant effect of the sugar. I have never tried heroin, and never plan to, but I can't imagine that it's any better than the rush we got from that pick 'n' mix.

We lay on the grass, completely sugar-stoned. Donna from *World in Miniature* must have given us at least a kilogram of pick 'n' mix each, and in about 30 seconds we had eaten half of it. After fixing the wheel and returning the spanner, we continued onwards with the sugar still racing through our veins.

We spent the rest of the day cycling along lanes that were so quiet that grass grew in the middle of them. It was lovely and peaceful, but extremely tough going. Despite swapping bikes regularly, alliances were beginning to be formed. Ben clearly favoured Pinky, and I preferred The Falcon - despite Ben claiming it was physically impossible to ride it up hills. Cycling uphill on The Falcon was an art that Ben never mastered. In fact, he didn't cope much better on Pinky, and she was supposedly a 'mountain' bike.

'These bloody hills!' Ben shouted, getting off to push yet again. 'Why can't we stick to the A-roads?'

'The A-roads have hills too, you know.'

'Yeah, but not like this. This is ridiculous. We've not seen any flat ground in two days.'

'But it's nice and quiet. Surely you'd prefer to be cycling along these country lanes than the busy A30?'

'No way. At least we'd get somewhere on the big road.'

'That's if we didn't get hit by a lorry. Besides, it's not about how quickly we do this trip, it's about seeing bits of the country, too.'

'I think I've seen enough already!'

We stopped talking for a few minutes and I thought he had calmed down, until I heard a shout of 'FUCKING PIECE OF SHIT' behind me. I turned to see Ben throwing Pinky into the hedge. She fell back out again and landed at his feet, where he gave her a kick.

This seemed to clear his system, as he seemed slightly happier afterwards. The hills smoothed somewhat, and we felt like we were making progress again.

Half an hour later, we were lost. We had been covering the distance but we had no idea if we were going in the right direction. It was a while since we had seen any of the villages that Donna had mentioned, so we stopped at a farm to ask if they had a map.

'Sorry, I was KILLIN' chickens,' shouted the lady, after we

74

had been wandering aimlessly around her farmyard for some time. She was in her early thirties, with bleached blonde hair. Her hands were covered in blood that she was wiping on her trousers. 'What can I get you? Is it chickens you're after?' she said, pointing to a sign on the gate. *Fresh Meat – For Sale.*

'Actually, we're a bit lost. Do you possibly have a map we could have a quick look at, please?'

'I think someone left one 'ere once. I don't have no need for a map,' she said and climbed into a caravan, which seemed to be her house.

'There you are,' she said, handing us a road atlas dated 1988. 'I can't read so good, so you'll have to work it out for yourselves.'

'Whereabouts on the map we are now?' I asked.

'I think somewhere around here,' she said, pointing to a bit of the map miles from anywhere.

'Nanstallon! That's one of the places that Donna mentioned,' I said.

'Yeah. Looks like we're going the right way then, Ben.'

'So if we keep going in this direction for about eight miles, we should get to Nanstallon. It looks quite big on the map, so we should find somewhere to stay there.'

Ben sighed.

Soon afterwards, we were at a crossroads and lost again.

We turned right and the grass in the middle of the road began to get to knee height, and it was obvious that no amount of traffic had been down there in some time. We tried one of the other turns instead. It led into a field. So, by a process of elimination, we figured the third and final option had to be the right way.

The chain jammed on The Falcon, yet again. This time it was on a long uphill. Again, we were unable to free the chain by hand, so I pushed the bike to the top of the hill, and then freewheeled down the other side.

We stopped at a cute little cottage at the bottom of the hill. We were in the middle of some woods, and we half expected Little Red Riding Hood to open the door. Unfortunately, the lady who answered looked more like the Big Bad Wolf.

Not only did she provide us with a spanner, but she gave us a Kit Kat each, which we swallowed whole as the rush from the pick 'n' mix had started to wear off. We asked if we were going in the direction of Nanstallon.

'Sure you are,' she said. 'You can either go up this hill, which is really long and steep and I wouldn't recommend it. Or, you can turn left just there and then take the long way round, but if you go that way there's a really long and steep hill which I wouldn't recommend.'

'So we can go either way, but you wouldn't recommend either?' I asked.

'Not on a bike, noooo.'

'But we are on bikes.'

'Well I wouldn't recommend it.'

As it turned out, we had been up far steeper hills already that day, and we made it to the top without breaking sweat. It was worth it for the long descent into the village of Nanstallon, which turned out to be a huge disappointment. Not that there was anything wrong with the village, but because we had hoped for it to be full of restaurants and hotels offering free accommodation. The stupid place didn't even have a pub.

We stood near the church wondering where to try first. It was 8pm, so we still had plenty time to find somewhere to sleep, but it was late enough to mean that people would not want to be disturbed.

A man wearing an *ER* t-shirt had been mowing the grass at the church. I mean *ER* the TV series - he wasn't a doctor.

After loading the mower into the back of his car, he wound down his window and asked if we needed any help.

'There's a farmer down the road there who might have a barn you can sleep in,' he said after hearing the shortened version of our story.

Ben chuffed. He wasn't in the mood for another barn.

'Although, last time he let people stay they burnt down one of his barns, so he might be a bit suspicious. Good luck,' said the lawnmower man as he sped away. He continued up the lane, and we stood there debating what to do.

'There must be a campsite somewhere near here,' said Ben after a while. 'Surely they'd have an old tent lying around that we could borrow?'

'Excuse me,' I said to a man who had just got out of his car with his dog. 'Do you know if there's campsite near here?'

'Gee, I think the nearest campsite is over near Bardmin?'

He was American.

'Pardon?'

'Bardmin.'

'Where?'

'Bardmin.'

'Where's that?'

'You know, the big moor.'

'Oh, Bodmin. Yes, sorry.'

Just then, the lawnmower man reappeared in his car.

'My wife says you can kip at our place,' he said. 'Get your bikes. You'll have to follow me, as I live up the other end of the village.'

The lawnmower man's name was David, and he lived with his wife Annie.

'We're really sorry to trouble you,' said Ben, after being introduced to Annie. 'This is extremely kind of you to put us up.'

'Well we shall bond as best we can under the circumstances,' said Annie, grinning from ear to ear. 'What would you like first, a cup of tea or a shower?'

'Well if you can bear us being smelly for a while longer, then a cup of tea would be lovely, thank you,' I said.

We sat at the kitchen table and drank tea and ate biscuits. We explained why we were homeless in their village, and they seemed reassured to learn that they had not taken in a couple of tramps for the night.

David, as we discovered, was more than just a lawnmower man. He was a former council chief executive, who had been responsible for the clean-up operation following the floods at Boscastle in 2004. A flash flood washed away parts of the village, but a successful redevelopment program - led by David - restored much of it by the following year.

He was smug, in a very amiable way. He'd had a busy career, which he was proud of, and now he was equally proud of his retirement and the fact that he did very little all day.

'I do the crossword, and mow the church lawn a couple of times a week and that's about it,' he said.

Annie was lovely, although slightly neurotic. She was probably about 60 - but looked a lot younger - and from the moment we arrived she had been worrying about what she could cook us for dinner. We insisted that we didn't need feeding and that we still had some pick 'n' mix, but she was having none of it. None of our insistence, I mean, not our pick 'n' mix. Although she was having none of that either.

'Right. I'll sort out some sort of pasta dish,' she exclaimed, jumping up from her seat. 'David will show you to your room. Have a shower and then dinner will be ready in about half an hour.'

David showed us to the attic room, which we accessed via a

secret door, a bit like Narnia, only not. It was a big white room with a double bed in the middle of it.

'I'll leave you both to it. The bathroom is at the bottom of the stairs,' said David as he left.

'So who's having the bed, and who's having the floor?' I asked Ben.

'Well I'm sleeping in the bed, and if you've got issues then you can have the floor, otherwise we can share.'

'Fine, we'll share. But don't try anything funny.'

Annie had created a monster dish of spaghetti and tomato sauce. This was no Dolmio (other pasta sauces are available), but fresh tomato sauce made from organic tomatoes grown in their own garden, flavoured with onions and garlic grown in their own garden, garnished with basil grown in their own garden, served on plates fired in their own kiln and with cutlery made in their own forge. I lied about the plates and the cutlery, but they were very proud to show how self-sufficient they were. Not that I blame them. I grew some cress once and I still count it as one of my greatest achievements in life.

The food was delicious. It was the sort of meal that cyclists should eat. I wonder how many Tour de Frances Lance Armstrong would have won on a diet of Cornish pasties and pick 'n' mix.

We ate seconds. And then thirds. And then huge slices of fruitcake, presumably made from a selection of fruits grown in their own garden.

'Do you have any socks?' asked Annie randomly.

'Yes, well, we've got a pair between us,' said Ben. David, who had been sitting quietly at the other end of the table, spat his wine across the table.

'A pair between you?' he laughed. 'My god!'

'We can't have that,' said Annie. 'I'll go next door and get some socks from our neighbour.'

'What about MY socks?' asked David.

'Your feet are too small, darling. Bill next door is a size 11.'

David didn't have a chance to defend his inadequate feet as Annie had already left through the front door. I didn't examine David's feet particularly closely, but he didn't look like the type of person that would have had especially small feet. I'm sure we would have comfortably fitted into any socks that he had, but Annie had been adamant that we needed bigger ones.

She returned with six pairs of the biggest socks I had ever seen in my life. If they'd been hung on the fireplace at Christmas, even the most generous Father Christmas would have struggled to fill them.

'Annie dear, they're going to Scotland, not Iceland,' said David.

'Yes, but it can get very cold up there at night. They'll appreciate them.'

'We do indeed, thank you very much. And please thank your neighbour, too,' said Ben with a grin.

'Oh, I didn't even tell him I was taking them. He's over 90, and was fast asleep.'

After dinner, Ben entertained David and Annie with an impressive piano recital and then we headed up to bed.

'What the hell are we going to do with all these enormous socks?' asked Ben when we got back to our room.

'I have no idea. I guess we'll have to wear a pair each and try and stuff the rest in our bags somehow.' We took it in turns to pick a pair and I ended up with the best of the bunch; a pair of knee length ski socks adorned with pictures of sheep wearing Christmas hats.

Annie had kindly offered to wash our boxer shorts, and the

pair of socks that we had been sharing for three days. She was concerned we would catch some sort of fungal infection, and she was probably right. This meant that I had to sleep in my suit trousers and Ben slept in his shorts. I enjoyed Ben's company, but our relationship was a long way from naked bed sharing.

On the road above Porthtowan

Me above Porthtowan

Ben above Porthtowan

Pharmacy in St Anges where Ben borrowed scissors

Donna, The World in Miniature

Berrymans Bakery, Perranporth

Annie and David, Nanstallon

82

Day 4
A new hero
Nanstallon to Okehampton - 52 miles

We woke before David and Annie, so had a shower each, and then spent 15 minutes rearranging our bags so that the socks would fit.

Yet again, our hosts insisted that we have breakfast so we gladly accepted. Annie gave us our clean and dry boxer shorts and socks and introduced us to their chicken Diamond Lil. Home grown eggs, too.

We looked at a map over breakfast, and for the first we had a sudden realisation of just how big Great Britain was. We had been on the road for three days yet we had covered only a tiny fraction of the island. We still had nearly 900 miles between us and the top of Scotland and it was incredibly daunting. Even with our new bikes we had only managed 48 miles, and if there was any hope in us reaching John O'Groats within three weeks, we were going to have to significantly pick up the pace.

Outside, David was doing something to our bikes.

'I noticed that the handlebars on this pink one looked really uncomfortable,' he said.

'Yeah, they are a bit,' said Ben.

'Well I think I have fixed them.'

We walked over to him and noticed that Pinky's handlebars had grown into huge sponges. He had taken a section of foam pipe insulation from the pipes in his garage, and cut them into handlebar-sized pieces, which he had then taped onto the bike. The Falcon also had a big bath sponge taped to its seat, with the intention of making it more comfortable.

'Thanks, David. They look... err... great,' said Ben.

'Yeah, they look loads better,' I said suspiciously.

We gave our thanks to Annie and David and left Nanstallon. David had suggested following a route known as the Camel Trail for a few miles. The Camel Trail was a stretch of old railway that had been converted into a path for walking and cycling. It had two parts; one stretching from Padstow to Bodmin, the other section stretching east towards Camelford, which was the direction we were heading.

We joined the path just after leaving Nanstallon. It was a pleasure to cycle along, considering it was the first piece of flat ground that we had cycled along since the car park at Land's End. Accompanied by a chorus of birds, we wound our way through forests and along the bank of the river Camel.

'Excuse me, is this the way to Camelford?' I asked an elderly walker, who was walking in the opposite direction to us, with a lady who appeared to be his daughter.

'Yes. It's just a few miles further down the trail,' he said. 'Is that where you are heading?'

'For now, yes, but we're on our way to John O'Groats,' said Ben.

'Oh really? I walked from John O'Groats to Land's End a few years ago. I'm actually mentioned in the museum at Land's End, as I'm the oldest person to walk the route. I'm just along the wall from Ian Botham.'

'And the story of the man who tried to push a pea with his nose the entire way,' I added.

'Yes, that's right. The stupid idiot,' he said.

Reg Savill was the only person we had spoken to since setting off that morning, and it turned out that he was a Land's End to John O'Groats record holder. What were the chances?

He was 74 when he completed the trip and he had walked the entire distance on his own. Fairly early on in his trip, he had a chance meeting with a man named Gil Campbell who was out driving in his campervan. He had noticed Reg walking along the side of the road looking languid, and offered him a lift to the next town. Reg declined the offer, but asked if the man could drop his rucksack at the next B&B along the route. Not only did the man oblige, but he also did the same every day, all the way to Land's End. They had been close friends ever since.

'He truly was a lifesaver,' said Reg. 'I honestly believe if it hadn't been for him I would never have completed it.'

'That's incredible,' I said. 'We've met a few of our own versions of Gil already on our trip.'

'And you'll meet plenty more. There are lots of them about.'

'So, it looks like you are still keeping yourself fit then, Reg?' asked Ben

'Well, yes, I used to be a Navy commando, so I was fairly fit. Until last year, I was doing my army training regime every morning; 100 press-ups, 100 sit-ups and 40 chin-ups. I had a hernia operation last year, so now I can only manage 20 chin-ups.'

Ben and I were both in awe. We had found a new hero. We wanted to hear as many of Reg's stories as possible, and so spent 45 minutes standing in the middle of the Camel Trail, being treated to tales from his journey.

'I ended up on a motorway one day, by mistake. I was walking along and I took what I thought was the correct road, but it turned out to be a slip road that led onto the motorway. The road was fairly quiet so I decided to keep walking, as it was too late to turn back. The police picked me up after a few miles and drove me back to where I'd joined it. I had to take a different route then, and ended up walking 38 miles in one day. I wouldn't recommend that.'

'Jesus, that's almost as far as we cycled yesterday. And you walked it!' I said. 'And any particular highlights of the trip for you?'

'The highlands in Scotland are spectacular. If you think it's pretty round here, just wait until you get to Scotland.'

'How far are you walking today?'

'About 12 miles. My wife and I try to do about 12 miles a day,' he said, pointing to the pretty young lady beside him. His wife? Nice one, Reg. You da man!

We left Reg with mixed emotions. We had been truly inspired by his achievements, motivation, and of course his young wife. If I can be half as fit as him when I'm in my late seventies then I'll be very happy. But on the other hand, it made us both feel that our challenge was somewhat inferior. We were fairly fit young men and we had bikes. He was nearly three times our age, and had walked every inch of his 868 miles on foot.

Camelford was a pretty little market town on the edge of Bardmin. I say *was* as I am writing this book in retrospect. It might be a shit-hole now, for all I know.

It was, however, home to some very strange people. We sat down on a bench in a square just off the main street. It was quiet, apart from a drunk over in the far corner, who was swigging from a bottle in a paper bag and shouting incoherent obscenities to passers-by.

It was almost midday and we were hungry again.

We were approached by an odd looking lady. She was about seven feet tall, mid sixties, with a mass of bright blonde hair. I thought she was a transvestite at first, and Ben thought she was a witch. She later became known, between the two of us, as Tranny Witch.

She had spotted me using my camera and had wandered over.

'What are you taking pictures of?' she asked.

'We're cycling to John O'Groats and we're just taking some photos along the way.'

'How interesting,' said Tranny Witch.

Her mouth started to foam in one corner, and the more she talked, the more it foamed. By the end of the conversation she looked like she had a marshmallow stuck to her face.

She turned out to be a very interesting (ish) lady and told us a story of a pilgrimage of sorts that she had undertaken a few years previously, when she and a group of others had walked to London. They had also relied on people to help feed them and provide them with shelter along the way. She said the reception they got from everyone was astonishing. Fortunately, she didn't set off in a pair of pants. That's something I don't want to even imagine.

'Remember you're not in England now, you're in Cornwall,' she said as she was leaving. 'Meur ras. Dyw genes.'

'I'm sorry, what was that?' asked Ben.

'That means *thank you and goodbye*.'

There was a butcher's opposite and we wandered over to try and fill up our water bottles.

'Ahhh, no problem,' said the lady behind the counter.

She asked us what we were doing and so we told her the story.

'You'll be wanting some lunch then, too. How about some chicken thighs?'

'That's very kind,' I said, 'but we don't have any means to cook them.'

'Oh, I see, fair enough. How about a couple of pork chops then?'

'Errr, again, I think we'd struggle to find somewhere to cook them for lunch. Thanks anyway.'

'Hmmm, so I guess bacon wouldn't be any use either then?

How about some ham?' she asked, not wanting to be defeated.

'Some ham would be brilliant, thanks. I'm sure we could get some bread from somewhere.'

'There are some cookies for you there, too,' she said, handing us a carrier bag containing ham, cookies and our water bottles.

I discovered that in 1988 Camelford's water supply was accidentally contaminated when 20 tonnes of aluminium sulphate was poured into the wrong tank at the local water works. The long-term effects on the residents are still under question. All I can say after meeting the locals is that it explains an awful lot.

There was little chance that we would have successfully navigated ourselves to John O'Groats without the aid of a map or route book. Asking random strangers 'which way is Scotland?' was proving fruitless. We realised that we needed a more organised approach to navigation.

'THE LIBRARY!' I shouted.

'What about the library?'

'We could borrow a map or a route book from the library. It solves all our problems. It will make getting to Scotland a hell of a lot easier, and we don't even have to spend any money.'

'Genius,' said Ben.

The library didn't loan out maps, nor did it have a vast selection of Land's End to John O'Groats route books but it did have one – *Bike Britain*, by Paul Salter. This was to become our bible over the following three weeks.

Borrowing the book proved far easier than we expected. Despite having no identification, we were able to charm the librarian with our smiles. We promised to return the book to our local library after we had finished and for it to be transferred back to them.

The book was perfect. It detailed a route from Land's End to John O'Groats following mostly minor roads. It was spread out over a 21-day schedule. The only problem was that Camelford was on Day 2 of the book. We were halfway through our fourth day, and had the slight handicap of children's bikes. We needed to get cracking.

It was going to be a long afternoon, so we decided to try and do a few more miles before lunch. The town of Launceston was a few miles up the road so we set off with the aim of stopping there for a break.

The route followed the busy A39 out of Camelford, and then cut away from the main road and carved its way through the countryside towards Launceston.

Just before reaching Launceston, the road dropped sharply into the town. We soon discovered that despite all his kindness, David had actually converted Pinky into a death trap. The foam on the handlebars was so thick that it made it impossible to squeeze the brakes enough for them to work effectively. Ben, who was riding Pinky at the time, had to swerve around a bus that had pulled over, swerve back to avoid a head-on collision with oncoming traffic, weave in and out of a queue of cars that had backed up at a narrow intersection, before eventually coming to an abrupt stop against a wall.

'What the fuck was David playing at?' screamed Ben. 'Was he trying to fucking kill me?'

We both laughed.

'Yeah, stupid David. What a fucking tosser!' I said. 'He took us in for the night, gave us dinner, a hot shower, a comfy bed, delicious breakfast, and then he went and fucked our bikes up. What a knob!'

Launceston seemed to be a town of two parts. One part – the crap part - is at the bottom of the hill, with nothing but a couple of shops and some featureless streets. The other part – the less crap part - sits on the top of the hill dominated by the impressive Launceston Castle.

There was no charge to visit the area of grass just inside the outer walls of the castle, so we sat on the bank and ate ham and stale bread that Ben acquired from a nearby baker. We had the remains of our pick 'n' mix for pudding. The view from the castle was stunning, and the 'crap part' of Launceston - that I had shunned just moments before - looked particularly beautiful from up high.

Ben talked about his anger from the day before, when he had thrown Pinky in the hedge.

'What you saw was only about 10% of the rage that was inside of me,' he said.

'Seriously? I thought you were just joking around.'

'Noooo, that was all real.'

'Were you pissed off with me?'

'No, I was getting pissed off with myself. I hate holding people up.'

'You weren't holding me up. I like it when you get off and walk, as then I can get off, too.'

'Well anyway, I'm feeling better today.'

The Cornish Stannary Parliament launched *Operation Chough* in 1999, which resulted in the removal or defacing of English Heritage signs from many of Cornwall's tourist attractions. One of which was Launceston Castle. The reason being, as Tranny Witch had pointed out, was that they weren't in England, they were in Cornwall. A court case ensued, and charges against the Cornish Stannary Parliament were eventually dropped after they returned all the signs and paid compensation to English Heritage.

Cornish or English, it was still a beautiful place. The castle itself only costs a few pounds to visit and looked to be well worth a trip.

'Shall we see if Launceston has got a Police Station? They might have some proper bikes lying around that they can give us?' asked Ben.

'What do you mean? We've got proper bikes, haven't we?'

'Yeah, I mean bikes to get us to John O'Groats.'

'I thought that's what these were?'

'What? Yeah, right. Very funny. These are just temporary things until we get something better.'

I was confused. I had thought that we were going to take Pinky and The Falcon all the way to John O'Groats, but Ben had different ideas. They weren't the best bikes in the world, admittedly, but they were doing the job. People had surely done the trip on worse bikes in the past.

'Ok,' I conceded, 'let's try the police station.'

Launceston Police Station was situated on the outskirts of town, fortunately in the direction we were heading. A smiling bald man manned the desk.

'We do get stolen bikes in occasionally, but if they're not reclaimed then they get sent to Torquay,' he said.

'How far is Torquay from here?' asked Ben.

'Oooh, I would say it's about 70 miles or so.'

Ben looked at me. 'That's not too far,' he said. 'It's probably worth a try.'

'Are you serious?' I asked, in shock. 'You want to cycle 70 miles out of our way, to somewhere that may or may not have bikes that are better than the ones we already have?'

'No?'

'No!'

Ben looked dejected.

'Is there a tip in Launceston?' he asked the policeman.

'Yes, follow this road down for half a mile. Right at the roundabout then it's on the right.'

'It must be here somewhere,' said Ben after we had taken every possible exit from the roundabout and still not found it.

'Do you really think the tip is likely to have bikes better than the ones we already have?'

'They might. It's worth a try.'

'Are you hoping that Lance Armstrong might have been holidaying in Cornwall and needed to get rid of a couple of his racing bikes? It's 3pm already and we want to do another 30 miles today.'

'You do. I don't,' snapped Ben.

We eventually found the tip. They had an exercise bike, half a Raleigh Chopper and a fold-in-half shopper bikes with no wheels.

'It doesn't look like they have anything,' accepted Ben.

'That's surprising.'

'What did you say?'

'Nothing.'

'What's your problem with upgrading our bikes?'

'My problem is that we've got bikes, and we've just spent the last TWO HOURS trying to get bikes, and we've covered about a mile.'

'But if we can get better bikes, then we'll be able to cycle more miles each day and we'll get there quicker.'

'Why do we need to get there quicker? It's not a race.'

'No, but these bikes aren't even comfortable to ride. You seem to like to suffer. They are not even adult bikes, they were made for children. I don't understand you!'

And so it went on.

I could see Ben's point. If we had got better bikes, we

would have made better progress, and the cycling would have felt less painful. The truth was, I was secretly falling in love with The Falcon. Yes, it was far too small for me. Yes, its handlebars were hacking my palms to pieces. Yes, it had the hardest saddle ever invented, and because of the position of the handlebars I was swiftly becoming a hunchback. Riding a stegosaurus to Scotland would have been more comfortable. But there was something about The Falcon that was winning me over. It was partly the added challenge of completing the trip on an inadequate bike; I imagined that it would perhaps make me feel more of a man.

I was also intensely aware that our trip was all about stripping things back to basics. People have been cycling the length of the country for years, on far crapper bikes, and just because we were living in the 21st century did not mean I needed a 21st century bike.

The first recorded 'End to End' cyclists were two Leeds policemen, who completed the trip on penny-farthings in 1882. It took them 14 days. If the trip could be done in two weeks on a penny-farthing, then I could sure as hell do it in three weeks on a child's racing bike.

Reaching the Devon county sign was a pivotal moment, and it caught us completely by surprise. We just turned a corner and there it was. *'Devon'*, it said, as you would expect it should.

We had cycled across an entire county. We had been warned that Cornwall was the worst bit, and so felt a real sense of achievement having successfully conquered it. We took an obligatory picture of the two of us at the signpost, for which I had to run back through a nettle patch to get in place before the self-timer fired.

From then on, it promised to be easy. The contours of the land would level out, and we would be in John O'Groats in no time.

Or so we hoped.

Devon had other ideas, however, and presented us with a huge big sodding hill straight after welcoming us. It stretched on for about six miles until just before the town of Okehampton, where it allowed us a brief downhill to gain its forgiveness.

It wasn't the best start. We had only been in Devon for a couple of hours and already thought it was shitter than Cornwall.

Okehampton looked like Devon's answer to the Wild West. Its main high street - which is called Fore Street, as many in Devon and Cornwall are for some reason – was unusually wide. Imposing flat fronted buildings banked each side of the road, and we half expected a gunslinger to swagger out from a dusty saloon. Only this was Devon, and there were no dusty saloons, or gunslingers for that matter. Instead, a blue-rinsed granny hobbled out of Specsavers.

The town is right on the northern edge of Dartmoor, and is considered one of the gateways to the national park. The main A30 used to pass straight through the town centre, which explains why Fore Street is so wide. A bypass was built in 1988 and the town now enjoys a little more peace and quiet from the traffic.

We arrived in Okehampton at about 7.30pm and decided to ask at The White Hart Hotel - a huge hotel on the edge of town - about the possibility of doing some work in exchange for somewhere to sleep.

The manager's name was Glyn - a small bird-like lady.

'So what you're saying is that you'll do some jobs for me around the hotel, and in exchange I'll give you some dinner and somewhere to sleep,' she said with a strong Yorkshire accent.

'Well, yes, but you don't have to feed us.'

'But you don't have any money or food.'

'No, that's true.'

'So if you have something to eat, and a bed for the night, I can write you a list of jobs and you'll do them. Is that right?'

'Yes, that's right.'

'I have to say this is a first, but, ok, take a seat and I'll write a list of things.'

This was more like it. Good honest work in exchange for board and lodging. She returned with a handwritten list.

Remove ALL leaves from car-park
Clean out bin room
Wash outside of hotel

The White Hart is probably the biggest hotel in Devon - possibly the world. And we had to wash it.

Glyn gave us a tour of our duties and described exactly what she wanted doing.

'You see these leaves on this path? I want every leaf picked up. EVERY LEAF... You see all these leaves all over the car park? I want every one of those picked up. EVERY ONE. This bin room needs sweeping, and clearing up, and the bins need wiping down... Take a large bucket with some soapy water – NOT TOO MUCH SOAP – and wipe down the black bit all the way down to the floor... Leave THAT bit, the council own that, so they can do it... Wipe down all the door frames and window frames, and that should just about do it.'

It was dark by the time we started.

As we scraped up huge piles of soggy leaves with our bare hands, it was obvious that they were all coated in urine. It was clear that people stopped to relieve themselves on their way back to their car after a night on the beers. Don't drink and drive, kids. In fact, if you're a kid, don't drink at all. Or drive for that matter.

The bin room was rank, too. It looked like foxes had been at the bins, as the contents were strewn across the floor. We scooped up eggshells and rotten vegetables with a shovel and put it all into black bin bags. As I knelt to reach under a big wheelie bin I managed to get rotten egg all over my suit trousers. The smell lingered with me for several days.

Whilst cleaning we met Arek, a Polish chef who had been in England nearly a year. He began working in the kitchen in the main restaurant, and then helped set up a pizzeria at the back of the hotel.

'My name iz Arek. I come from The Poland. My English izza not so good. I learn English for tree manths.'

'Your English is very good,' I said. 'It's almost better than mine and it's definitely better than Ben's. So, do you like living in England?'

'Yessa. I come to England and see English people they only eat steak and kidney pudding, chips and graaavy. I think I want show English people something new, something different, so I cook them pizza. So we bring piiizzas, 11 manth ago, to England. Is gone down very well.'

Pizza? How groundbreaking. Ben and I had to ask Arek what it was as we had never heard of pizza before. Apparently it's some sort of radical food that consists of a dough base, baked with tomatoes, cheese and various other toppings. They're going to become very popular in the UK, thanks to Arek. You heard it here first.

We told Arek why we were washing the hotel, which amused him greatly. We explained that Glyn was giving us a bed for the night and some food.

'I cook you piiiiizza!' he shouted.

'I'm not sure that's what Glyn had planned for us,' said Ben.

'Is ok. I speak her. I cook you piiiiizza. You come find me after and I cook you piiiiizza. Then we go uppa to my house abovva hotel and we drink beers from The Poland, ok?'

'Ok.'

Washing the hotel didn't take as long as we had thought. We slopped hot soapy water over the walls (with NOT TOO MUCH SOAP) and although we couldn't see what we were doing, it felt as though we were cleaning it.

It was 10.30pm by the time we had finished our chores. We had cycled 52 miles on children's bikes, had to scrounge our lunch and then spent 2 ½ hours cleaning a hotel. We were in need of our piiiizza.

Not only did Arek manage to wangle us a pizza each, but he also poured us both a pint, after Glyn had stated categorically that he should only give us squash.

Arek was slightly crazy. He made a big show of making our pizzas; tossing the dough in the air and catching it on his head. At one point he tied two tea-towels around his head leaving only his eyes visible. He then grabbed hold of the young assistant manager and held a kitchen knife to his neck. The other Polish kitchen staff found it hilarious. The young assistant manager, who looked like a work experience student, did his best to smile but was quietly shitting himself.

Arek's pizza was great. Not particularly revolutionary, but it was very tasty all the same. At about 11.30pm he closed up the restaurant. We had been the only guests. Apparently Devon was not quite ready for pizza.

As promised, Arek got some Polish beers and we headed up to his flat above the hotel. His friend Oukash came too but hardly spoke a word all evening.

Arek had lived in England for just under a year. He had ended up in Okehampton because Oukash – his friend from home – had come to England before him and had encouraged him to come over with the promise of work.

At about 12.30am we tried to leave.

'No, no, no,' said Arek. 'I stay and drink beer with my English friends.'

'But we've cycled a long way today and we've got to cycle a long way tomorrow,' I pleaded.

'Polish people, they stay up and they drink and they talk. I talk here and I drink here with my English friends. Here we stay and talk and drink and talk.'

It was 3am when we finally crawled back to our room, having stayed and talked, and drank and talked.

Reg Savill - Land's End to John O'Groats
record-holder

Glyn, White Hart Hotel, Okehampton

Arek making pizza

Butchers in Camelford

Devon, obviously

Arek, Okehampton

Late night beers with Arek and Oukash

Day 5

Mrs Rogers

Okehampton to Walton - 81 miles

I felt like I had been in a car accident. We had stupidly requested an alarm call at 6.45am with the intention of having an early start. My body felt like it belonged to someone 50 years older.

Again, I had foolishly tried to wash my boxer shorts late at night and have them dry by the morning. Again I had failed.

Glyn, the manager, was at the reception when we went downstairs.

'Good morning. Dave will sort you out with some breakfast in the dining room, and then I'll do an inspection to see if you did your jobs properly. Then I'll decide whether you can have your bikes back.'

She didn't look like she was joking.

Dave was in his sixties and clearly wanted to be anywhere else, other than serving breakfast in a hotel in Okehampton.

'Morning, Dave. Sleep well?' asked Ben

'Too well. That's why I was late this morning. So what will it be? Two full Englishes?'

'Sounds perfect. Thanks.'

During breakfast, the ketchup bottle exploded when I opened it. It covered my t-shirt, face, suit trousers, the table, the surrounding tables, the old couple on the next table, the ceiling and the window. Ben, who had somehow escaped unmarked, howled with laughter.

'Everything alright?' asked Dave when he came to offer us more tea.

'Errrr… I kinda covered the room in ketchup,' I said. Dave took one look at me and then began laughing and pointing.

'Ha ha, look it's all over your face and clothes.'

'Yes. I know.'

'How strange. I wonder how that happened?' he said, with the smirk of someone who knew exactly how it happened. He handed me a napkin, picked up the ketchup bottle and walked off.

It didn't take a genius to work out that he and the other kitchen staff probably had something to do with it. A couple of teaspoons of baking soda would have probably done the trick. I could hardly blame them; they had cooked and served breakfast to a couple of dirty, non-paying guests. I probably would have done the same thing.

After breakfast Glyn led us round the hotel checking we had completed the jobs to her standard. In the daylight it was clear that we had missed most of the leaves.

'It must have been really windy last night, because this car park was spotless when we finished last night,' I said.

This seemed to do the trick, and she seemed happy enough with our efforts. There were also several patches of the outside of the hotel that looked like we had failed to clean. We made sure that we were deep in conversation with Glyn whilst she checked these, and we managed to distract her sufficiently to get her seal of approval. We passed with flying colours and she allowed us our bikes back.

Arek was still asleep when we left.

We were both feeling like death. A combination of the Polish beer, the lack of sleep and the fact that we were cycling to Scotland on tiny bikes had started to take its toll. For the first few miles of that morning, neither of us enjoyed the ride. The road climbed yet again after leaving Okehampton. Devon was just one big fat hill after another, and we still had 2 ½ weeks and nearly 900 miles to go. It was demoralizing.

We were following what was once the main road between Cornwall and Somerset, before the A30 was built parallel to it. It was satisfying to hear the distant buzz of traffic on the very busy A30 that many End to Enders follow from Land's End all the way to Somerset. The road we followed, however, was completely deserted, and it didn't take long for us to get back into the spirit of the trip.

We gradually warmed to Devon. Its hills became less severe, and the countryside it offered us was breathtaking. Our route led us through the tiny villages of Belstone Corner and Coleford, which were little more than collections of houses. Dogs barked at us as we passed through these places, as though we were the first visitors in many years.

Quiet country roads are obviously a pleasure to cycle along, but they also have their drawbacks. As there are so few vehicles about, many of the vehicles that do use the roads assume that they are the only ones to be doing so. I turned a corner to be met with an oil tanker that was travelling in the middle of the road at a ridiculous speed. It would have vaporised me had it made contact. Fortunately, I managed to dive into the relative comfort of the hedge. I turned to see if Ben had survived, as he had been trailing slightly behind. There was no sign of him. I heard the screeching of the tanker's brakes and so feared the worst, but Ben soon emerged round the corner, looking like he had also taken refuge in the hedge.

Ben was becoming increasingly frustrated with me and The Falcon. Its chain had got into the habit of falling off at regular intervals for no apparent reason, and these occurrences were becoming more frequent. As if that wasn't irritating enough, its front wheel then fell off midway through the morning. It quite literally detached itself from the bike as I was cycling. Fortunately, I was moving relatively slowly at the time, trying to avoid a pothole, but when I pulled at the handlebars to attempt to hop over it, the front wheel stayed in contact with the ground and continued rolling. The bike's front forks then hit the ground and scraped along the road surface as I tried to regain my footing.

'I don't believe it,' said Ben. 'Is there anything else that can go wrong with the bloody bike?'

'Calm down. It's only a wheel. I'll get it sorted.'

'ONLY a wheel? Because it's not like wheels are important on bikes or anything.'

I flipped the bike upside down and reattached the wheel, tightening the bolts as best I could with my hands. It needed to be fastened with a spanner, though, or it was going to become a regular event. We were in the middle of the countryside and miles from anywhere.

'I'll just take it easy until we pass a house or garage or something, and we'll borrow a spanner there,' I said.

'But you might be dead before we get there.'

'At least you won't have to keep stopping for me then.'

'That's true.'

Just as I was climbing back on my bike, I saw Ben running off down the road, waving his arms at a passing campervan.

'Excuse me! Excuse me! Can you stop for a second?' he shouted. The van pulled over, and I immediately saw what Ben had spotted. The campervan – a badly converted transit van – had three BMX bikes on the back, and another two on the roof.

'Hello. I'm really sorry to bother you,' said Ben, 'but I saw your bikes and thought you might have a spanner that we could borrow. The wheel has just fallen off one of ours.'

Max was a very cool, dreadlocked man in his early thirties. He happened to be a professional BMX stunt performer, who was on his way to do a show in Cornwall. The back of his van was like a bike repair shop. He had tools and parts of all descriptions, and he set to work immediately. After securing the front wheel, he tightened a few other bolts, and gave both bikes a spray of oil.

'There we go. As good as new,' he laughed.

'Thanks so much. I don't suppose you want to swap this bike for one of yours?' Ben joked.

'Unfortunately not. Mine are all specially designed stunt bikes.'

'So is mine,' I said. 'I can do this great trick where I detach the front wheel whilst I'm cycling along.'

'Ha! I'll have to try and put that one in my repertoire. Good luck with the rest of your trip, guys.'

We arrived in the village of Thorverton shortly before midday, having covered about 20 miles that morning. After our long breakfast, the ketchup incident, and Glyn's inspection, our planned early start had become 10am. We had made good progress, though – considering the issues with The Falcon - so decided to try for an early lunch, and then embark on a mammoth afternoon of cycling.

Thorverton is a relatively small village with an attractive little garden in the middle. Unlike usual village greens, this one was an actual garden. It had a stream running through it, flowerbeds, trimmed shrubs and a bench. We sat on the bench for a few minutes and assessed the two pubs that we could see and decided on The Thorverton Arms. We pretended to lock our bikes in the beer garden at the back and entered the pub.

A sporty looking lady was manning the bar. She was in her forties and gave the impression from the way she was rearranging the bottles that she was the landlady.

'What can I get you?' she said with a smile.

'Hello. Do you have any work that needs doing in exchange

for some food?' asked Ben.

'What do you mean?'

'We're on a mission to get to John O'Groats without spending any money and thought we might be able to help you out with some jobs, in exchange for something to eat.'

A large bearded man appeared behind the bar. He looked sporty too, in his own special way.

'There's some washing up you can do, if you want. One of the lads called in sick today so they could do with a hand back there,' he said, as though it was the most natural thing in the world for two people to walk in off the street and do the washing up. 'Then when that's done, I'll sort you out with some lunch.'

'Brilliant,' I said. 'Which way is the kitchen?'

The sink was piled several feet high with dirty pans and dishes, but between the two of us we figured we would have it all washed in no time.

'Then when you've finished all the stuff in the sink there are a few things behind you that need doing,' he said.

We turned around and every inch of the kitchen's serving station was stacked with plates, cutlery, pots, baking trays, knives and mixing bowls. On the other side of the carnage, we could just about make out two guys working away at the stoves.

'Hi, guys. I'm George and this is Ben. We're here to help you with the washing up in exchange for some lunch.'

'Cheers, dudes,' said the younger of the boys. 'We've been completely swamped and haven't had a chance to do any all day. We've been washing stuff up as we need it.'

'That technique has worked for me for years,' said Ben.

Their names were Ryan and Matthew. They looked about 17 and 19 respectively. They were both aspiring young cooks who travelled half an hour each day to the pub, because of the reputation it was gaining. It won the *Newcomer of the Year Award 2006*, but whether this was a national award, or a competition at the Thorverton Village Fete, I don't know.

They were putting a huge amount of effort and concentration into their cooking, but were still keen to talk and find out about our trip. They were making what looked to be posh cheese-on-toast.

'Sounds like a wicked thing to do, man. The whole length of the country? Jeez. Still, at least you're nearly there.'

'Actually, we started at Land's End.'

'Oh, shit. That's tough,' laughed Matthew.

We were given a brief instruction on how to use the steriliser. It was basically a machine that steamed off any remaining germs after washing. Ben decided it would probably double up as a dishwasher too and so piled it high with pots and pans. The thing ground to a halt after a few seconds, and we had to ask Ryan to help unblock the filter that had become clogged with rice and peas.

Each time we started to make inroads into the mountain of washing up, Matthew and Ryan were on hand to replenish the pile. They were somehow using up pans and plates quicker than we could wash them.

We were hungry when we arrived in Thorverton, and after over an hour in the kitchen, we were ravenous. We started to pick at the leftovers on plates that were being returned from the dining room; cold chips, salad leaves, half-eaten pieces of bread. Ryan and Matthew looked on in disgust.

The lunchtime rush eventually ended. It was 2pm on a Tuesday in September in the middle of nowhere. Where the hell had all these people come from, and shouldn't they have been at work?

We sat on one of the picnic tables outside the front of the

pub and Garth brought us a big glass of Coke each (other colas are available). He also brought with him two t-shirts. One was a green polo-shirt with the logo of a local brewery on it, and the other was a black polo shirt with Thorverton Arms written on the back, and TITS written on the front.

'It stands for *Thorverton Impotent Tossers Society*,' he said. 'That's the name of the pub's darts team.'

I'd had first dibs of the last t-shirts we were given, and so Ben had first choice this time. He picked the TITS one, unsurprisingly, and I was left with the slightly inferior green one.

The food was well worth every last grubby plate that we had cleaned and there was enough to feed the whole of Thorverton. We each had a huge sizzling lasagne, a giant bowl of chips, a garlic baguette and a side salad. Food tastes so much better when you've earned it, and we had certainly earned it. However, as far as it being a suitable meal to have midway through a long day's cycling goes, I wouldn't recommend it.

We ate absolutely everything. Even Ben, who usually has the appetite of a daddy long-legs, demolished the lot. We were so stuffed that we could hardly speak, let alone cycle.

A big, hairy black cat walked towards us from across the road, right opposite where we were sitting. At the same time a coach was tearing downwards through the village and there was the rumble of something big coming the other way. The cat was completely unfazed and paused in the middle of the road to clean its paws. The coach screeched to a halt, and so did the enormous combine harvester that emerged from the other direction. Both vehicles waited patiently until the cat had cleared the road, before continuing with their respective journeys. The cat then hopped up on to the picnic table where we were eating, discovered there were no leftovers, licked the plates then jumped down and went through the front door of the pub. When we took our plates through to the kitchen, it was asleep on one of the bar stools.

'He's one of our regulars,' said Garth. 'He comes in most days about this time.'

Spurred on by our titanic lunch, we decided to aim for a record-breaking day on the bikes. We hoped to do another 40 miles but it was 3pm by the time we set off, and our lasagne sat heavily in our stomachs.

After leaving Thorverton the road crossed the River Exe by a weir and then climbed gradually for a few miles. We passed through the town of Bradninch and the tree-lined streets of Cullompton without even stopping.

We were ripping up the miles. We were whooping Devon's ass.

We reached the town of Wellington by about 5pm, having covered 43 miles, which included a 10am start and a 2 ½ hour lunch. Taunton was only a few miles up the road so we continued onwards. All I knew of Taunton was the M5 service station Taunton Deane - one of my favourites on the M5. I knew that if Taunton was half as good as that service station, I'd be a happy man.

We followed the busy A38 between Wellington and Taunton. It was the first stretch of A-road we had been on since Camborne, and it made an exciting change. It was rush hour and the traffic was streaming in both directions, but we could feel the progress that we were making. The directions we followed took us on the A361 bypass around Taunton centre without us even realising.

Taunton Deane service station is still all I know about Taunton.

The sun was sitting low in the sky and we decided to try to

find accommodation at the next possible opportunity. The A361, however, had other ideas. The road soon straightened out into a never-ending passage across the Somerset moors. The rush hour traffic had dispersed and we were left alone in an eerie calm.

Ben had not spoken for about an hour and this was a clear indication that he was in a foul mood.

'You ok back there, Ben?'

No response.

'Ben?'

'Yeah, I'm ok. Just getting a bit pissed off with this cycling.'

'Yeah, me too. I'm sure we'll pass somewhere soon.'

'That's if we are still alive and not thrown into the moor by some sodding axe-murderer. This place scares the hell out of me.'

'I know. I thought it was just me.'

The light was fading, there was no sign of any nearby houses, and the boggy marshes on either side looked like the perfect dumping ground for a couple of dismembered cyclists.

'It's moments like this I wish you had your Disco Bike to lighten the mood,' I said.

Ben and I had cycled together just once before, but it was an experience that made me realise that he would be the ideal person to join me on the trip. Earlier in the year we had taken part in the British Heart Foundation's popular *London to Brighton Bike Ride*. Ben, for some reason, decided to convert his mountain bike into a 'Disco Bike' for the day. He cleverly mounted his iPod (other mp3 players are available) onto the handlebars as well as a large pair of speakers. To power this setup, he then strapped a car battery to the back of the bike, which was then wired, via a transducer, to the iPod. After testing his sound system the day before, he wasn't happy with the sound quality, so acquired a football-sized bass sub-woofer, which he also mounted to the back of the bike.

The resulting 'Disco Bike' was absolutely astonishing. From the comfort of his bike seat, Ben was able to blast whatever music he desired, across the surrounding countryside. Many of the other 20,000 cyclists were in awe of his construction, and we were surrounded for the entire 50 mile trip by swarms of Ben's groupies.

What Ben hadn't taken into account was the immense weight of his sound system. His bicycle was the same weight as a motorbike. Cornering became very difficult, and on a couple of occasions, he came very close to having a major accident.

'I would do anything for my Disco Bike right now,' he said.

We survived the moors and then crossed the Greylake Bridge at the King's Sedgemoor Drain, which, in case you were wondering, is a 14th century ditch that is used to drain the surrounding moorland.

We spoke briefly with two Scottish men who were fishing by the bridge. They had driven all the way from the north of Scotland to fish in a ditch in the middle of nowhere. Finally, we'd met two people more stupid than us.

'Aye, you could try the wee pub just there. That's where we're stayin'. They might be able to help if you ken whit ah mean,' said one of the men.

The pub was surprisingly busy considering we had not passed a house in hours and there seemed to be no other buildings beyond it.

'Brilliant, it's quiz night, too. Maybe if they've got somewhere for us to sleep, we can come and do the quiz later,' I said, rather optimistically.

It turned out that the pub only had two rooms and that pair of ditch-fishing Scottish idiots were occupying both of them. As tempted as we were to bundle the pair of them into the King's Sedgemoor Drain and take their rooms, we decided to leave them to their fishing and continue onwards to find somewhere to stay.

It was dark and we were completely unlit. We pulled over to the side of the road each time a car passed, which meant that progress was ridiculously slow. We eventually reached the village of Walton at about 9pm.

Just on the edge of the village was the sign for a campsite and we followed the lane up for half a mile until we reached Bramble Hill Camping Park. It was a lovely, peaceful looking campsite adjacent to a farmhouse. Surely a place with such a storybook name could not refuse two desperate young men.

'Hello, can I help you?' asked a very well-spoken lady. She appeared in her doorway with a look of terror on her face as though 70-odd years of life were about to come to an abrupt end at the hands of two strangely dressed, sweaty young scallywags. She had a big, styled, silvery white bouffant, a black dress and a white apron on. She looked like she had walked straight out of Jane Eyre.

'I hope so,' said Ben. 'Do you, by any chance, have an old tent that we could use or anywhere for us to sleep tonight, for free. We are travelling without any money.'

'I am sorry, I am afraid I don't. We are just a small site, and people bring their own tents. We don't have any spares for people to use. What are you doing out in the middle of nowhere this late anyway?'

'We're on a challenge to cycle to John O'Groats without spending any money. All of our food, accommodation, clothes and bikes have been given to us. We were hoping to find somewhere to stay, but we've not passed anywhere until now.'

'No, I am awfully sorry, there is very little around here. I would imagine that there are some campsites in Glastonbury, but you have left it a bit late to get there tonight. I am sorry I can't be more help.'

'Ok, thank you anyway. I'm sure we'll find somewhere,' I said as we turned to walk out of the door. We bowed our heads in disappointment and pulled the most pathetic, sorry, needy faces imaginable.

As an experiment of human kindness, this bike ride had to be undertaken by complete nobodies like us. Any form of celebrity brings with it recognition, which changes everything. I watched Ewan McGregor's documentary – *Long Way Round* – with great admiration. Ewan McGregor – of *Star Wars, Trainspotting* and *The Da Vinci Code* fame – goes the whole way round the world on his motorcycle, with his friend Charley Boorman. It was an extremely impressive feat, and I'm not comparing our own journey to his heroic adventure in any way, but the fact is that he is Ewan McGregor. Even people in Kazakhstan and Mongolia recognised him; I often don't get recognised by my own family. What I am trying to say is that when asking for favours from random strangers, you are at a distinct advantage if you are Obi-Wan Kenobi.

We might not have had the power to conduct any Jedi mind tricks, but these pitiable faces of ours were our secret weapon.

'Well... just a minute,' she said hesitantly. 'Is it just some shelter you are after?'

'Yes, anything,' I said.

'Well I might be able to help you out in that case. Follow me.'

She led us through to a dusty old outhouse, which had walls on just two sides.

'You can prop your bikes up against the wall there,' she said, and we then expected her to tell us we could sleep on the floor next to them. It was a lovely evening and we would have been more than happy to sleep there.

But she wasn't finished yet.

'And you can sleep in here,' she said, unlocking the door to a self-contained annexe. 'There's a bedroom upstairs and you can use the campsite toilet block, which is just across the yard.'

It was unbelievable. We had been seconds away from walking back out into the night with nowhere to go, and then suddenly we had been offered our own little flat. Downstairs was a kitchen, and upstairs was a large bedroom with a double bed and a mattress on the floor.

'I can't offer you any food, I'm afraid, but there's a pub about half a mile down the road where you might be able to get something.'

'Thank you so much, you're a lifesaver,' I said. 'What's your name?'

'Mrs Rogers.'

Mrs Rogers said goodbye, and we promised we would clean the campsite toilets for her in the morning.

'Check this out. We've got our own flat!' said Ben before diving onto the double bed. 'Bagsie having the bed.'

'I suppose you're having the sleeping bag, too?'

'Too right I am. I did carry it all day.'

'You are such a dick. Looks like I'm sleeping on the floor then. Can I borrow your towel, please?'

'Yes. Let's go and try and get something to eat,' said Ben. 'The pub will stop serving food soon.'

'Yeah. We might as well go straight there now. England are playing another European qualifier tonight. We'll hopefully catch the end of the game.'

'Yeah, wow, that'll be fun,' said Ben sarcastically, as he has no interest in football whatsoever.

'Good old Mrs Rogers,' I said as I followed Ben across the room towards the stairs.

'Yeah, I'm going to roger her in the morning,' said Ben, for

113

no apparent reason.

And then he froze.

He turned and looked up at me as if he had seen a ghost. I've never seen anyone look more petrified in my life.

Mrs Rogers was standing at the bottom of the stairs.

Ben was halfway down the stairs and continued to stare back up at me with a look as if to say: 'Help me, George. Say something to get me out of this terrible situation.'

I said nothing. Mrs Rogers finally spoke.

'I just wanted to show you where the light switch is for the downstairs kitchen. It is just here at the bottom of the stairs. Could you make sure you turn it off when you go out and before you go to sleep.'

'Yes. Of course. Err. Will do. Thank you, Mrs Rogers,' said Ben, still motionless on the stairs. She turned and left the outhouse, and closed the door behind her.

'Oh. My. God. What have I done?' said Ben, cupping his face in his hands.

'What the hell did you say that for? What possessed you to say you were going to roger Mrs Rogers?'

'Oh god, I don't know. I think I must have Tourettes or something. If I hear a name like that I have to make a stupid joke about it. Do you think she heard me?'

'She must've done. She was standing about ten feet from you. You idiot!'

'I know. Bollocks. Oh fucking bollocksy, bollocksy, bollocks.'

'I don't know why she didn't say anything. Or even chuck us back out into the street.'

'Maybe she didn't hear me. Or maybe she didn't understand what it meant? She's probably in her house now flicking through a dictionary. Why am I such a twat?'

'I've no idea, but you are. It was very funny, though.'

'There's nothing funny about it at all. That kind old lady has

114

given us a place to stay tonight and then I said I was going to roger her. Shit, that was the most embarrassing moment of my life. How did she come in without us hearing her? She was like a ghost. She must've melted through the wall or something. Let's get out of here.'

We followed the pitch-black country lane back down to the main road, and then saw the pub a little further down the road. We hardly spoke the entire way. Ben was still cringing about what he'd said, and I was being smug that it hadn't been me.

The Pike and Musket was fairly busy for a Wednesday. It was full of young people playing pool and shouting excessively loudly at each other over the noise of the jukebox. Several of them were wearing England shirts but there was no TV and therefore no football.

'Any idea what the score is?' I asked one of lads, who had just sent the white ball flying across the room.

'Nah, mate. They're showing it at the pub at the other end of the village.'

The girl behind the bar looked very young. She laughed at us before we had even spoken to her. She was clearly in awe of the fine specimens of masculinity that had just entered the pub. Either that, or baggy rolled up suit trousers, sweaty t-shirts and cut off tracksuit bottoms are not the latest trend in Walton, Somerset.

Had I mentioned we had reached Somerset by this point? Perhaps not. Well, we had conquered Devon and had reached our third county in as many days.

'Hello,' said Ben to the still grinning barmaid. 'We've cycled over 80 miles today on children's bikes, and we don't have any money to buy food. Do you have any leftovers whatsoever that you could spare?'

'How come you've got no money? Is it some sort of challenge?'

'Yes. We're cycling to the top of Scotland without spending any money. We started in just pants. All these clothes have been scrounged, too. That's why we're dressed like this.'

'I was wondering why you both looked so daft. I think they've just closed the kitchen but I'll go and speak to the chef and see if he's got anything. Grab a seat over there and I'll see what I can do.'

There were a couple of other people finishing up their meals but other than that, the restaurant part of the pub was empty. If only we'd been there the night before; Tuesday night is 'Curry and a pint night' at The Pike and Musket, if ever you are passing.

She walked over to us a few minutes later.

'The chef is going to cook you up something. I'll bring it out to you in a bit. Do you guys want a beer in the meantime?' asked the barmaid, who clearly fancied us. Looking around the room, we were definitely the best of a bad bunch.

'To Mrs Rogers,' I said, toasting my pint to Ben.

'Don't. I don't want to think about that. I still can't believe it happened. I won't be able to look at her in the morning.'

'She might be looking forward to it. You never know, she's probably getting herself ready as we speak. Putting a skimpy little number aside to wear in the morning.'

'You're sick, do you know that?'

'You're the one who said you were going to roger her in the morning.'

'Alright! Enough! Let's never speak of it again.'

'Ham, egg, chips and peas,' said Siobhan the barmaid, as she placed two huge plates of food in front of us. 'The chef heard what you were doing and thought it sounded very funny so wanted to spoil you.'

116

It was our best day's eating of the entire trip; a fry-up for breakfast, lasagne, chips and salad for lunch, and ham, egg and chips for dinner. We would not have eaten so well had we had our wallets with us.

Only an hour beforehand, Ben and I had been hungry, homeless, tired and argumentative with each other. And there we were enjoying a huge pub meal and a beer, before heading back to our own little flat for the night.

Life could not have got better.

'Just got a text from my mate at the other pub,' said one of the young lads in an England shirt. 'England won 1-0. Peter Crouch scored.'

Life got even better.

We cleared our plates and finished our beer. It was nearly 11pm by the time we scrabbled our way back up the dark lane to Bramble Hill Camping Ground.

Ben climbed straight into *his* sleeping bag and lay on the bed.

'Night, mate,' he said.

My suit trousers were damp from a day's cycling, so I decided not to sleep in them despite it being quite a cold night. I put on the gigantic ski socks instead that Annie had given us in Nanstallon and lay down on the mattress with two towels over me.

'Night, Mr Selfish,' I said.

117

Somewhere, near somewhere else

Ryan and Matthew, Thorverton Arms

Garth and Melissa, Thorverton Arms

Max - the BMX stunt man

Mrs Rogers, Walton

Mrs Rogers' flat

118

Day 6
Michael Eavis in a pair of hot pants
Walton to Bath - 27 miles

'Morning, George,' said Ben.

'Morning,' I said grumpily.

'Did you sleep well? I didn't wake up once.'

'No. I slept really badly. It was fucking freezing. I had to put on my suit trousers in the middle of the night, along with all my t-shirts and my cardigan and I was still cold.'

'Oh. Sorry. It's a shame you don't have your own sleeping bag. Still, it looks like it's a nice day today.'

'A nice day for rogering Mrs Rogers?' I asked.

'Please shut up. You said you would never mention that again.'

There was a queue of about five girls waiting outside the shower block, despite there being an empty cubicle.

'Is the shower not working in that one?' I asked.

'Yez, it eez, but a big animal eez in there,' said one of the girls in broken English.

'What sort of big animal? Is it supposed to be in there?'

'No! Eeeza animal with wings. It very scary. It go whoosh, whoosh,' she said, making dive-bombing gestures with her hand.

I was intrigued. A large, scary, winged animal had taken over a shower cubicle in the middle of Somerset. I had to investigate. I opened the door to the cubicle and peered cautiously inside. Whatever the beast was, it was hiding. Either that or it was a master of disguise.

I turned on the light and a moth started to dance around the light bulb.

'Is that the animal you are talking about?'

'Yez, close door. Ezza evil.'

'It's just a moth. Do you mind if I go ahead and use the shower?'

'You mad. But ok,' she said.

I had a shower, and then Ben did, and afterwards the girls were still queuing. I then caught the moth, using my BARE HANDS and the girls applauded me like a hero.

Mrs Rogers was in fine spirits when we went to report to her for toilet cleaning duties. She didn't seem to hold any resentment over Ben's comment the night before, and despite our offers, she would not allow us to do any cleaning to repay the favour.

We had high hopes for the day. We left Bramble Hill by 9am, which was a very early start by our standards. It was a bright, clear day and we both felt the most enthusiastic we had done since leaving Land's End.

'I reckon if we try and find something quickly to eat in Glastonbury, we could be in Bath in time for lunch and then who knows how far we might get by tonight,' said Ben uncharacteristically.

'Sounds good to me. I think we've turned the corner and started heading up the country.'

'That's a bit too deep and profound for this time of the morning.'

'No, I mean it literally. Since we left Land's End we've just been heading east but I think we've probably turned north now. Do you get me?'

'No, not really.'

We reached Glastonbury town centre in 15 minutes. Ben and I had both been to Glastonbury festival twice before but neither of us had visited the town properly. It was full of quaint little hippy shops, with hand-painted signs outside. Groups of people sat in the little square selling various bits of stuff or having a peaceful protest about something or other. The whole town had a really relaxed vibe to it.

We headed for the Glastonbury Backpackers, which sits on the main square. As much as we were enjoying soaking up the hippy ambience, we were bloody hungry.

It was 9.30am and loud music was playing in the bar area. There were a couple of people sitting around at tables, and an attractive Dutch-sounding girl was checking herself out. I mean, checking out of the hostel, rather than staring at herself in the mirror. The girl behind reception directed us towards the manager after hearing our request.

'What can I do for you two?' he asked.

'We're travelling the entire length of Great Britain and we're not allowed to spend any money. We wanted to see if you had any work that needs doing in exchange for some breakfast.'

'Sounds like a fair deal,' he said without hesitating. 'Are you doing an End to End trip?'

'Yeah, this is Day 6, and we've allowed ourselves three weeks.'

'You're heading north, I presume?'

'Unfortunately, yes.'

'You've still got a long way to go then. We get lots of End to Enders passing through here. Some of them do it in less than a week, but they're insane. But then you two must both be insane, too.'

'You're not the first person to suggest that,' I said.

'All the floors in here need mopping, as does the floor around the pool table and in the toilets. If you do that, I'll get the girls to sort you out with some breakfast.'

The bar area was fairly long, but it only took us half an hour to clean the floor. I say 'us', but there was only one mop and Ben gave himself the role of 'supervisor', which involved muttering 'you missed a bit,' every few seconds.

We sat on bar stools along the breakfast bar that looked out onto the square. Claire – the girl from reception - brought over two large cappuccinos, two fry-ups and a couple of newspapers.

We'd only been travelling for six days, but we both felt completely out of touch with what was going on in the world. I'm a news junkie. I can't go for an hour without checking the BBC website. I usually have the radio on, or the TV, and regularly read the paper, too. Since setting off from Cornwall, we had hardly seen a TV, had no radio updates, and I don't think The Internets has reached the South West yet.

I had thought I would suffer severe withdrawal, but I was coping just fine. In fact, I hadn't missed any of it. For the first time ever, I had no interest in what was happening in the world. The front page of both The Mirror and The Guardian announced something that David Cameron had said or done, but I didn't read it to find out what. Even the match report of England's win the night before received little more than a cursory glance. I had become detached from the real world and felt no urgency to rejoin it.

Whilst we ate breakfast, we read through the 'What to take' section in our route book – the excellent *Bike Britain* by Paul Salter - which lists all of the equipment that is required when attempting a Land's End to John O'Groats bike ride.

The list, which extends to several pages, differed just slightly to our own meagre belongings. Here is the list of everything you are supposed to take, alongside our actual possessions in italics.

Bike

Bike with racks – *inadequate bikes, no racks*

Panniers and handlebar bag – *rucksack and pockets*

Water bottles and cages – *water bottle, yes. Cages, no*

Cycle computer – *as if*

Small flashing LCD rear light – *Tony the Tiger reflector*

Clothing

Raincoat – *no*

Rain pants (with elastic cuffs or clip for right leg) – *bare legs*

Mid-weight fleece top - *cardigans*

Polypropolylene underwear (longs and tops) – *Union Jack boxer shorts (cotton, not polypropolyley, whatever that is)*

Hat – *baseball caps*

Gloves - *no*

2 T-shirts or cycle tops – *4 t-shirts each*

1 Pair of lightweight shorts – *rolled up woollen suit trousers for me, cut off tracksuit bottoms for Ben*

1 or 2 pairs of cotton socks – *3 pairs of ski socks each*

1 or 2 pairs of lightweight longs – *woollen suit trousers for me, no trousers for Ben*

1 or 2 pairs of cycling shorts – *rolled up woollen suit trousers for me, cut off tracksuit bottoms for Ben*

Cycle gloves – *what were the other gloves for then? Evening wear? No*

1 Pair of shoes – *old trainers*

Sunglasses – *no*

Reflector sash – *this isn't a beauty pageant. No*

Bicycle helmet – *no*

Tools

Pump - *no*

Puncture repair kit - *no*

Tyre levers – *spoons in picnic set*

123

Spare inner tube - *no*

Tyre patch or spare tyre – *spare tyre? Are you serious? Where would we keep it? Only the ones around our waists*

Spare spokes – *I have never broken a spoke in my life, nor do I know anyone who has. The only reason a spoke would break is because of the weight of all of this shit*

Spokes for the rear cluster side – *no. What or where is the rear cluster side?*

Spoke wrench – *no spokes to wrench*

Cluster removing tool – *eh?*

Chain breaker and spare chain links – *why would we want to break the chain?*

Spare brake and gear cables – *no*

Spare nuts and bolts (including rack bolts) – *KP nuts, does that count?*

Appropriate Allen keys – *who's Allen and why would we have his keys? No*

Wrenches, pliers, screw driver – *No, no and no*

Zip ties – *what for?*

Grease & lube – *what is this, some sort of kinky shit?*

Duct tape – *I knew it! No*

Small rag – *that's what trousers are for*

Miscellaneous

Bike lock – *yes, sort of. But not one that we could actually unlock*

Pocket knife with can opener – *yes, in the picnic set*

Small First-Aid and sewing kit - *plasters*

Plastic bags to wrap gear in wet weather – *what gear? No*

Camera and film – *It's the 21ˢᵗ century. Get with the program. Everything's digital, man. Yes.*

Toiletries and medications (including sun screen and insect repellent) – *toothpaste, toothbrush and soap. What more do you need?*

Maps – *route book, yes*

Compass – *no. Asking people for directions is far easier*

Personal documents – n*o. Like what?*

Water Purification tablets or filter – *this is Great Britain, not Ethiopia*

Camping
Tent - *no*
Sleeping bag – *yes, 1 between 2*
Sleeping mat - *no*
Small towel – *2 enormous beach towels*
Small torch - *no*
Plate and spoon – *6 plates, 6 spoons, 6 bowls, 6 knives, 6 forks*

Optional Extras
Waterproof overgloves and shoe covers – *Overgloves? As well as the evening gloves and cycle gloves? My god, no*
Matches and candle – *in case of a birthday party? No*
Stove - *no*
Fuel – *no stove*
Pot – *no stove and no fuel*
Rear view mirror – *it's a bike, not a car*
Bottom bracket removal tool and parts – *I don't know what a bottom bracket is, so why would I want to remove it?*
Light plastic sheet with tent to cover bike while camping – *awww, bless. No*
Handheld GPS – *No, that's cheating*

'Any idea what time it is?' I asked Ben after we'd been sitting and staring out into the square for what felt like hours.

'Errr... ,' he said turning to look at a clock behind reception, which I had not made the effort to look for. 'It's 11.30am. That can't be right.'

'Oh, cool, that means it's nearly lunch time. We've done two miles so far today. Somehow I don't reckon we'll make it beyond Bath today. And even Bath might be a bit ambitious.'

'Oh well. This day is a bit of a write-off. Do you fancy going and checking out Glastonbury Tor? I've seen it in passing loads of times but never been.'

'Yeah, sounds cool. I think we're due for a break.'

Glastonbury Tor was a bastard to climb.

It's a compact, but prominent hill overlooking the town, with a beautiful stone tower adorning the top. It was particularly tough because we had to carry our stupid bikes all the way up. If we had left them at the bottom, there would have been a chance that someone would have taken them. Our misery would have been confounded by the fact we would have been able to watch it all happen from the top, but been unable to do anything about it. It wasn't worth the risk.

The top of the Tor was deserted except for a strange looking man carrying a large wooden staff. He had long white hair and a beard and he looked like a character from *The Lord of the Rings*.

'Good morning, gentlemen. Or should I say afternoon,' he said, looking at his watch. 'Is this your first time up here?' He was either just being friendly, or had tried a really bad chat-up line.

'Good afternoon. Yes, it's our first time. What a great view,' I said, turning round and taking in the view for the first time. It was spectacular.

'It sure is. It's not a bad place to work.'

'Do you work up here then?'

'Well, yes. I'm a sort of unofficial tour guide.'

'Aha, was that tour guide or Tor guide?' I joked.

'Yes, tour guide, as I just said.'

He didn't get it.

'Cool. It must be a great place to spend your day? What's your name?'

'Rod.'

Ben sniggered.

'Why is that funny? That's my name. Rod,' said Rod.

'But you're holding a rod.'

'Yes, I am. So?'

We didn't push it any further.

'I can give you a tour and tell you some of the history of the place, if you want,' he said.

'That's very kind, but we don't have any money whatsoever to offer you I'm afraid,' I said.

'Oh, that's ok. Just join in on my next one then. You don't need to pay. I'm sure there'll be some more people here soon.'

Sure enough, a group of about ten other people did arrive soon after and Rod treated them to one of his tours. We lurked in the background hoping for some useful information, but it soon became clear that we would have learnt more about the Tor by guesswork, than from Rod.

'You see over there in the distance…' he said, 'just behind that big telegraph pole,' he paused while we all looked for a big telegraph pole. 'Sorry, not telegraph pole, I meant hill. You see that hill over there? Well that hill and the one next to it are known as the Bra Hills. Because they look like a big pair of tits.'

The rest of Rod's Tor tour was completely incomprehensible and we learned nothing of the place's history except that it had some connection to Jesus or maybe King Arthur. It didn't matter, though. It's a beautiful spot and it doesn't cost a penny to visit, whether you are a scrounger like us, or an honest citizen.

Seeing as we were in Glastonbury, we thought we should call in to see Michael Eavis, the legend behind the Glastonbury festivals. It would have been rude not to. Everybody we asked, even Rod, knew where Michael Eavis lived, and it wasn't long before we found his farm near the village of Pilton.

We followed the long driveway through the farmland and up to the house and made our way to the Site Office.

'Hello. Can I help you?' asked the lady on the other side of the small office window.

'Hello. This is going to sound a bit strange,' I said, 'but we're cycling to John O'Groats and as we were passing we thought we'd call in and see if we could say hello to Michael Eavis.'

'Oh. He's not here at the moment. He's out on the farm somewhere,' said the lady. 'And you just want to say Hello? Does he know you?'

'No.'

'And he's not expecting you?'

'Errrr, nope.'

'Can I ask why you want to see him?'

'Just to say hello really,' I said, realising that I was sounding quite odd. 'Is it worth us hanging around for a bit to see if he appears?'

'Not really. I mean, I'm not going to stop you, but he might not be back for ages.'

'I think we should hang around for a bit to see if we see him. We have come all this way,' said Ben as we sat on the grass outside and drank our water that the lady in the office had kindly topped up.

'We haven't cycled all this way to see Michael Eavis. We're on our way to Scotland, remember? But I reckon as we're here now we should hang on for a bit.'

'He'll be cool when he finds out what we're doing. He must get loads of crazy Glastonbury freaks who just come to see him cos he's, y'know, Michael Eavis. He won't mind chatting to a couple of normal blokes like us,' said Ben.

'Hang on. That's exactly what we are. We're just crazy

Glastonbury freaks who want to see him cos he's, y'know, Michael Eavis. We are just a couple of sad freaky stalkers, aren't we?'

'When you put it that way, yeah, we are. It's too late to leave now though. Isn't that him getting out of the red Land Rover over there?'

And there he was. He was wearing, what I can only describe as, denim hot pants. They were the smallest, tightest shorts that I have ever seen. To complement these, he was wearing a white vest (the kind typically worn by rappers and wife-beaters) which was skin tight and tucked into his shorts. As if this sartorial statement was not bold enough, he finished off the outfit with a pair of wellies. We had salvaged clothes from a lost property, the coastguard, old people, cyclists and farmers, yet we still fell short of Michael Eavis' eclectic mix. But somehow he pulled it off.

We walked over to him.

'Hi, Michael. My name is Ben and this is my friend George.'

'Hello, lads. Nice to meet you both,' he replied whilst walking towards the office, seemingly trying to get away from us as quickly as he could.

'We're cycling to John O'Groats without spending any money and we thought we'd call in, as we were passing,' continued Ben unfazed.

'Ok, good luck with the trip,' he replied as he reached the farm door.

We thought that was it. We'd cycled all that way. We'd covered all those miles. We'd slept in a barn, and endured hunger, thirst, aches and pains. We'd creepily arrived on the doorstep of our hero, like a pair of crazed weirdoes, and all we were going to get in return was a brief 'Good luck'. I made one last ditched attempt to engage him in conversation before he entered the house and was gone for good.

'So, can you reveal any secrets about who's going to be

headlining the festival next year?'

'Ha ha, nice try,' he said, pausing at the door. 'Did you say you were going to John O'Groats? Come with me, I've got something to show you.'

Now, normally when a man says a line like this to you (especially a man wearing a vest, wellies and hotpants) you should scream and run away as quickly as possible. In this case, seeing as it was Michael Eavis, we decided to go with our instincts and follow him.

He led us back past the office and around into the yard. Leaning up against one of the walls was a huge metal ring, about eight feet in diameter.

'A couple of lads passed through here about 25 years ago,' he said. 'They set off from Land's End, like you two, and had this huge wheel that they planned to push all the way to John O'Groats. I don't know why, but they thought it would be fun, I guess. Anyway, they came to the festival here and had such a great time that they decided they couldn't be bothered to go to John O'Groats and they never made it any further.'

'That's amazing. And this is the wheel that they were pushing?' asked Ben.

'Yep, it's been here ever since. It was a lovely looking wheel back then. A type of wagon wheel, I guess. All this middle bit was wooden but it's rotted away over the years and all that's left is this metal rim. They phoned me up a few years back and asked if I still had it. I told them the wood had gone, but they could come and pick up the rest if they wanted. I never heard from them again.'

We were best friends with Michael Eavis by this point. Or, should I say Mikey Boy, as he liked us to call him. After we chatted for a bit longer he told us we could call him The Mickster, and then a while later we got to call him Eavo. By the time we left, we had dispensed with names all together, and had established our own special handshake, that only Ben,

Eavo and I understood. We were inseparable.

After some long farewell hugs and a tearful goodbye we got back on our bikes and left his farm. In doing this we had surpassed the two losers with the big wheel.

It was 3pm and we had cycled a total of five miles in six hours. 1.2 mph was not particularly impressive progress. We had missed lunch and so pressed on to get to Bath before the end of the day. The A39 skirted around the city of Wells, which they say is a pleasant market town. I'll have to take 'their' word for it, as we didn't get to see it. The film *Hot Fuzz* was filmed mostly in Wells. FACT.

After Wells, there were several long uphill sections that turned our legs to mush. We were feeling the effects of a fry-up being our only source of energy for the day.

From high up on the hill when we first saw it, Bath looked like any other city. From the ground level, however, it was particularly beautiful.

Pinky and The Falcon reached record speeds as we screeched into the town centre at about 5.30pm, tired and desperate for lunch. I was ravenous, but Ben had other things on his mind.

'There's a policeman!' shouted Ben. 'I'll go and ask him if they have any bikes at the station.'

'But… uh… wait… can't we...'

It was too late. Ben had dropped his bike and was chasing a policeman up the street. After a few minutes of animated nodding and gesticulating he returned.

'That policeman says we could try the station down here. It's just down this road, turn right, then left, then right and then it's on the left. He says you can't miss it. Come on, we might as well go there now and have a look.'

'For new bikes?' I asked.

'No, to hand ourselves in. Of course for new bikes, you bellend.'

'Can't we try and get food first? The police station will still be there later, but I might not be if we don't eat soon.'

'Alright, but we'll definitely give it a try later, yeah?'

'Yeah, yeah.'

We wheeled our bikes up the main street on the lookout for somewhere to get food. We passed a bakery that had closed for the day, but there was a stack of refuse bags piled up outside. Ben and I had talked about dustbin-diving a few days previously, and this was our first potential opportunity.

Dustbin-diving, or 'freeganism' as it is now fashionably known, has gained a new lease of life in recent years. Freegans adopt an anti-consumerist lifestyle and an alternative way of living. They prey on the discarded waste of supermarkets, restaurants, shops and cafés and try to have minimal impact on the economy. Due to a combination of stringent hygiene laws and an increased desire by the consumer for food to be of the highest standard, the stuff that is thrown out is often perfectly edible.

Ben and I both had a bit of anti-consumerism in us and a keen desire to 'beat the system'. We started rummaging through the bin bags, one by one. They all seemed to be full of empty cake wrappers.

We dug deeper.

'Shit, a needle,' squealed Ben, holding his finger with a look of panic across his face.

'Fuck. Oh shit, you...' I started, before noticing his big grin. 'You idiot. That's not funny.'

We carried on foraging for a few minutes until Ben found a giant tub of egg mayonnaise. The pot still had its label on, but drizzles of egg were oozing from the sides.

'Hey, George, check this out. What do you think? It's best before tomorrow.'

'Yeah, cool, it looks… err… great, yeah.'

'You can have it if you want. I'm not a big fan of egg mayonnaise.'

'No, you have it. Finder keepers, losers weepers, and all that.'

'No really. Consider it a gift from me to you.'

'That's very kind of you, but I couldn't possibly accept.'

'Well I'll just leave it here where we found it, if you're not going to eat it.'

'Good plan,' I said. We were the world's worst freegans.

'To be fair, though,' I said, 'I'm pretty sure real freegans don't eat egg either. I think the word freegan probably comes from 'free' and 'vegan'.'

'Good point. Shall we try those bags then?' asked Ben, pointing to another pile outside the back door of a restaurant.

We were halfway through the first bag when a large, sweaty chef stepped outside his restaurant for a cigarette break.

'Oi! Get the hell out of my bins, you tramps. Go on, clear off,' he shouted. We scurried off like a couple of diseased rats. It's a hard life being a freegan.

'Shall we just try asking in Caffè Nero for some food instead?' asked Ben.

'Yes, that sounds much more civilised.'

We asked the lady behind the counter what the company policy was on leftovers, and she told us that any leftovers were bagged up and then put outside the following morning.

'How many sandwiches do you have to chuck out each day?' asked Ben.

'Very few,' she said, 'Maybe three or four packs. We're pretty good at ordering our stock so there's not much waste.'

'So if we came back in the morning and went through your

133

bins before the bin men got here, we could have some free packs of sandwiches?' I asked.

'Yes, I suppose so. Or I could just give them to you now. I'm closing in ten minutes anyway.'

This sounded like a much better idea. She scoured the chiller cabinet looking for sandwiches that had reached their best before date, and returned with three packs of sandwiches and a fancy looking salad. See, we were freegans after all. Albeit polite and sophisticated freegans. I don't mean to imply that freegans are impolite and unsophisticated, I just meant that... oh, never mind.

We sat on a bench outside Caffè Nero and ate our sandwiches.

'God, I'm starving. We've only cycled about 20 miles today. How come we're so hungry?' I asked.

'It's all that mental energy we've been using up,' said Ben.

'What do you mean?'

'Did you know that our brains use up a third of our energy?'

'Really? That would explain why you don't eat much.'

'Very funny, you idiot.'

'So...' I pondered, 'does that mean that you could go to the library for exercise?'

'Well, no, it's not going to give you big muscles.'

'No, but you could burn calories just by reading books and learning stuff?'

'Yes. I suppose so.'

'We could start a new diet craze. Forget Atkins or Dukan, the Ben and George Diet sounds way better.'

We sat for a while debating this until we remembered that we didn't have anywhere to stay.

We got chatting to three students (two female and one male) back on the main street. It took us a while to explain what our challenge was, as they had no idea where either Land's End or John O'Groats were. Pah, the youth of today! We told them we were looking for someone who would let us sleep on their floor.

'We can help!' exclaimed the blonde.

'Yeah, you can sleep on our floor,' added the brunette.

'Really? That's great. Thanks. Where do you live?' asked Ben.

'Bristol.'

'Oh.'

'But you could get the train there with us, and then you would be a bit closer to Scotland when you set off tomorrow,' added the guy.

'It's very tempting. But that would be cheating, I'm afraid. We've got to cycle all the way and we wouldn't be able to pay for the train fare. Thanks very much for the offer though.'

It's not often that two gorgeous girls stop you in the street and then beg you to go and stay at their house. But such was our dedication to the challenge that we waved them goodbye and set out to find somewhere to stay.

'Let's go to the pub,' said Ben, after we had been wandering the streets for another hour.

'You read my mind,' I said.

We parked our bikes just inside the doorway of a pub so that we could keep an eye on them. It didn't take long for us to register that it was a gay pub. I know it's not politically correct to stereotype gays and lesbians, but the clientele looked like, well, stereotypical gays and lesbians.

The barman, a young rosy-cheeked boy, listened to our story while he held his head with his hands.

'Are you ok?' I asked, after we had explained our challenge and that we were hoping for a free beer.

'Yeah, yeah, sorry. I'm just feeling like shit from last night.

Bit of a wild one, if you know what I mean,' he said with a grin as he coyly looked over to a group of guys in the corner who all raised their glasses at him. 'I only got up about ten minutes ago and I feel like absolute crap. Yeah, I can definitely sort you both out with a beer, though.'

'How long have you been going?' shouted one of the guys in the corner who had obviously overheard us telling our story to the barman.

'Six days,' I said.

'And how many miles have you done?'

'About 200.'

'And you reckon you're going to complete it in three weeks?' he laughed.

'Yeah. We'll do it.'

'No you won't, mate. You're fucked. You've only done 200 miles and you've got 15 days left. Mathematics says you're fucked.'

'We'll make it. We're a bit behind schedule but we'll catch up,' said Ben.

'It's not possible, mate. Mathematics says you are fucked.'

One of the women joined in.

'What the fuck are you doing drinking in a pub, when you should be cycling? He's right y'know. You're fucking fucked.'

The whole group erupted into fits of laughter.

Of all the countless people that we met during our 1000-mile journey, these were the only people who ever doubted we would complete the trip. They continued to mock us in a tongue-in-cheek way, and we gave as good as we got. Their comments echoed through our minds for the rest of the trip and we felt even more determined to prove them wrong. I sent Adam – the most vocal of the bunch, and the obvious ringleader – an email after the trip to revel in our glory. I didn't get a response.

The table of doubters bought us pint after pint. It felt like we were being groomed, had it not been for the fact that none of them offered us a bed for the night. There we were, two attractive, naïve, homeless, drunken men in a gay pub and we still couldn't find a bed for the night. We stumbled out of that pub at about 10.30pm and into another.

This one was full of underage Goths mingling in close-knit groups. We needed to work quickly because closing time was approaching and we still had nowhere to stay. Five pints of beer had given us extra confidence so we took it in turns to approach the various cliques.

'Alright, guys. We're not mental or anything, so don't be afraid. I don't suppose any of you have a floor that we can sleep on tonight?' asked Ben.

Blank stares.

'We're cycling to Scotland without any money and we need somewhere to stay tonight,' I added.

There was still no sense of recognition whatsoever from any of the faces. They all looked completely stoned out of their brains, and trying to comprehend anything that we said was far too taxing. We had exactly the same response from each of the different groups. The barman gave us half a pint of lager between the two of us, and we retreated to a table to decide on our next strategy.

'Did you say you were looking for somewhere to stay?' asked a husky voice over our shoulder.

'Yeah. We've got nowhere to stay tonight. Have you got any ideas?' I asked.

The voice came from a young man dressed in army combats and a black Guinness t-shirt. He had floppy blonde hair and a goatee beard that was so goat-like that I was surprised when words came out of his mouth, rather than a bleat.

'You might be able to stay at my place. I'll have to give my housemates a quick call, but I reckon they'll be cool with it.'

'That would be brilliant. Thank you. What's your name?'

'Max. Sorry, I've lost my voice,' he whispered, pointing to his throat. 'I'll just go and give them a call and I'll be back in a minute.'

Max returned a few minutes later.

'Yeah, they were cool with that,' he whispered, 'but they asked me to check that you're legitimate and not some sort of clever con people. I know it sounds stupid, but have you got any ID or anything?'

'No. We haven't got anything at all, I'm afraid. We set off from Land's End with nothing but a pair of boxer-shorts and everything we've got we have blagged from people along the way,' I said, trying to reassure him.

'Errr, cool, that sounds wicked, man. You really just started in just boxer shorts? Respect. Yeah, man, you both seem genuine, but my housemates did want me to check. There are some dodgy people about.'

'We completely understand. I'm sorry we haven't got any ID or anything. But I can promise you that we are 100% genuine. We wouldn't be asking random people unless we were really desperate,' said Ben.

'That's cool. You can stay at mine. I haven't got anything worth nicking anyway, so if you are con men then you'll be pretty gutted. I'll just go and finish my beer and I'll give you a shout when I'm leaving.'

By this point, Max's voice had almost completely disappeared, so the prospect of him giving us a shout was unlikely. We had left it late, but by 11.15pm we had eventually found ourselves somewhere to sleep.

We walked with Max back to his house, which was 20

minutes from Bath town centre. He spoke – well, whispered – to us about the course that he was studying at university, his dream to direct music videos and the fact that he had only lived in England for two years. His dad had worked for the military and Max had spent his childhood at various bases around the world. In the two years he had lived in Bath, he had already developed a strong South West accent.

Max was having relationship issues. Sarah, a girl we had met briefly in the pub, had been in floods of tears. She and Max were supposed to be an item, but then had got very distressed because she had seen a girl that she liked snogging another girl. It was a very complicated situation that Max failed to explain properly, but he had basically realised that his girlfriend preferred girls to him. Ben and I, being 'men of the world', gave him the best advice we could, and he seemed genuinely touched to have received guidance from us older, more experienced guys. Although, I have to confess that my experience with lesbian love triangles is unfortunately non-existent.

Max's two housemates – Sonnie and Mark – were still up when we got back. They were playing some computer game on a massive widescreen TV with gigantic speakers either side.

'Bloody hell, Max. I thought you didn't have anything worth stealing,' I said

'Ha, yeah, well I didn't think you'd get very far with the TV on your bikes. Speaking of bikes, do you want to wheel them through the kitchen and stick them in the garden?'

Like all other students, Max, Sonnie and Mark were completely incapable of washing up. Every single utensil in the kitchen was dirty and had either been piled in the sink or on the cabinets. It was exactly the same as my kitchen had looked when I was at University, but in the eyes of a mature man, well trained by a cleanliness obsessed wife, the whole place was deeply distressing.

Ben and I made them all a cup of tea as we started work on the kitchen. We worked our way through the carnage, piece by piece. We washed up everything, we emptied the bins - which had erupted all over the floor - and put out the recycling. Well, we assumed it was the recycling. Either that, or Max was hoarding for a massive papier-mâché session.

Back in the sitting room, the students were watching television. It was the first time since we started the trip that we sat and watched television. The familiar glow of the TV was enthralling and we felt a sense of excitement as though we had been released from solitary confinement. Two minutes of channel hopping later, we realised we had not been missing anything. Even the students were defeated, and switched the TV off with a frustrated sigh.

'I'll show you where you can sleep,' whispered Max.

Max's room was on the ground floor, adjacent to the living room. Its floor was piled deep with clothes, CDs, books and unopened gas bills.

'You can sleep on the floor. Just push some of that shit to one side. I've got a spare sleeping bag somewhere.'

We scraped at the floor with our hands until we had cleared enough room for two bodies. For some reason Max chose to sleep in a sleeping bag, too. There was no sheet on his mattress, nor pillowcase on his pillow.

'How come you're in a sleeping bag?' I asked.

'I've just never got round to buying any bedding. And I quite like sleeping in this. It makes me feel like I'm on holiday.'

'You're on a permanent holiday, mate. You're a student.'

'Yeah,' he coughed, 'that's true. Night, guys.'

I hardly slept at all.

The sleeping bag Max had let me borrow was a 5-season

one. If I had slept out in the snow in Antarctica in it, I would still have been too hot. In a small, double-glazed, centrally heated room in Bath, it was like sleeping in a kiln. I unzipped it most of the way down and let half of my leg lie in the comparatively cool air. Had I not been wearing my tight Union Jack boxer shorts, and been in a stranger's room, I would have just lay uncovered, but I felt it best for the wellbeing of Max that I covered up as much as possible.

I had to venture to the toilet in the early hours of the night, and Max nearly shat himself when he opened his eyes to see a half-naked man wearing novelty underwear tip-toeing across his room. After a few seconds he registered who I was, and he gave a little wave before covering his head with his sleeping bag.

The Glastonbury Backpackers

Ben - manager of The Glastonbury Backpackers

Rod, Glastonbury Tor

Michael Eavis, Pilton

Me, Glastonbury Tor

Students from Bristol, Bath

Day 7
The Severn Bore
Bath to Newent - 50 miles

Max had early lectures to get to, so we were out of the house by 8am. It was another sunny day and we planned to make up some miles following the easy time we'd had the previous day. Max's voice was still absent but he waved us goodbye and whispered that he felt he had made a couple of new friends, and that he hoped one day he could do something like we were doing.

That was part of the thrill of our challenge. If I had been Max and had met us, I would have been incredibly envious, and it was this sort of reaction that we got from countless people along the way. We were the lucky ones and we had nobody to be envious of.

Bath town centre was a flurry of people on their way to work. We called into a bakery where a girl named Suzie gave us two freshly-baked sausage rolls, in exchange for two smiles. We stood outside on the pavement and devoured them in seconds, despite them being the temperature of molten lava.

A very tall man approached us. He had a huge, white, bushy beard, and was smartly dressed in suit trousers, polished shoes, a shirt, cardigan and a panama hat. He was very unstable on his feet and stank of alcohol despite it being before 9am.

'Hold these, will you?' he slurred, handing me the leather bag he was carrying and placing his panama on my head.

'You're not going to undress are you?' asked Ben.

'Don't be ridiculous,' he spluttered, resting his hand on my shoulder to steady himself. He pulled a penny whistle from the bag and started to play. Despite not being able to string a sentence together, his fingers glided over the whistle like a magician. With the whistle in his mouth he came to life. He jigged on the spot like Michael Flatley, having been unable to even stand upright only moments before. It was quite extraordinary.

'I'm... an... Attt... Atttten... Attenborough, you know, as in... one of the Attenborough family,' he said, when he'd finished playing. 'Peter Attenborough, but people call me Peter... Peter... The... Potter. I'm a busker... and a potter. I make pots.'

'It's really good to meet you, Peter the Potter,' I said. 'If we had any money, we'd give you some, but I'm afraid we've got nothing.'

'Nooooo, that was a gift. A musical gift… for you. I could tell you needed it. Good luck… on your travels, wherever you are going.' And with that he swaggered off down the street into the morning bustle.

I looked up Peter a few weeks later, to try and discover a bit more about him. Despite our brief meeting, he'd had a big impact on both of us and he seemed a remarkable character. I was saddened to learn that he had died just a week after we had met him. He had fallen down some steps whilst visiting a friend in their basement flat.

He was, as he had said, a relative of Richard and David Attenborough, and had been one of Bath's best-loved buskers. His funeral took place at Bath Abbey and was attended by over 1000 people.

Ben reminded me that I had promised him that we could call into the police station to see if they had any bikes. Despite my best efforts to convince him otherwise, we made our way towards the main police station in the town centre.

'Hello,' said Ben to the clerk behind the glass in the reception area, 'Do you happen to have any lost or stolen bikes that you are trying to get rid of?'

I lurked in the background, cringing at Ben's audacity.

'Yes, we do have bikes, but any that are unclaimed are shipped off to Africa. If you can hold on a minute I will get the Lost-Property Officer to come and speak to you.'

I stood there open-mouthed. Not just because I had been proven wrong, but because there was such thing as a Lost-Property Officer. It was a job that had all the glamour of being a policeman, but without the hassle and danger of real criminals; just a collection of other people's possessions to keep an eye on. If I was a policeman, I would want to be a Lost Property Officer. I'm not sure there is much scope for promotion, though. Lost Property Inspector? Lost Property Commander? Chief of Lost Property?

The Lost Property Officer's name was Kevin. He was a lovely, smiling man, who would not have looked out of place in a cartoon. He explained that, yes, they did have bikes, but that they were all shipped off by a charity to Africa if they were unclaimed.

'Unfortunately we can't just give bikes away to the general public as the charity will lose out,' he added.

'Of course, we completely understand,' said Ben, and I turned to leave assuming that Ben would follow. He had other ideas however.

'But what about if we were to give you our bikes instead, and that way the people in Africa would still get their bikes, and everyone would be happy.'

Kevin looked confused.

'If you already have bikes, then why do you want different bikes?' he asked.

'Good question,' I said.

'We're cycling to John O'Groats and we only have a pink girl's mountain bike and a child's racer. We were hoping to upgrade them to something more substantial.'

'Well, I suppose that could work. I can't see it being a problem. Have you got your bikes here? Wheel them in and we'll go and see what we can find.'

We had been impressed by the expanse of Roger Badcock's bicycle grotto, but this was on a completely different scale. Roger's barn had been filled mostly with bicycle parts, and those bicycles that were intact were fairly basic looking; as both Pinky and The Falcon were testaments to.

Bath Police Station, however, had a row of about 30 bright, shiny bicycles lined up ready to go to Africa. Some of them looked almost brand new, as I assume many stolen bikes are.

'Your bikes look decent enough,' said Kevin. 'We might have to do some basic repairs to ensure they meet the safety standards before we ship them, but if you see something you like the look of here then I'll do you a swap.'

'Are you serious? Any of these bikes?' gushed Ben like an excited school boy.

'Yes, that's fine,' said Kevin.

Ben patrolled up and down the length of the shelter where the bikes were lined up, checking each one in turn. After a while he paused next to a gigantic silver touring bike. It was surely the biggest bike that had ever been built, dwarfing everything else in the row.

'What do you think about this one, George?' asked Ben.

'I think it looks, well, it looks very big. Are you sure you can reach the pedals?'

'Ha ha, very funny,' he said, although I had not been joking. 'Yeah, I love this one, Kevin, if that's ok.'

'No problem, let me just take these charity labels off. What about you? Which one do you want?' he asked me.

'Actually, I think I'm going to keep the one I've got,' I replied, almost apologetically.

'What? Oh come on, George,' said Ben, dumbfounded.

'This is our chance to finally get decent bikes that will get us all the way to John O'Groats. This is what we've been looking for.'

'No, it's what YOU have been looking for. I'm happy with The Falcon.'

'Don't be stupid. Is this some sort of childish sulk because you didn't want to come to the police station? Because if so then that's pretty pathetic.'

Kevin looked away to avoid getting involved in our argument.

'No, not at all. I've always been happy with The Falcon and I've always wanted to take it as far as I can, and I don't feel that I have yet.'

'But its stupid chain falls off every few hundred metres!' he barked.

'Hopefully it'll sort itself out and it hasn't slowed us down too much. Besides, it doesn't feel right sending a small racing bike to Africa. It wouldn't stand a chance on the roads out there. At least Pinky is a mountain bike and would be suited to the place. The Falcon would be destroyed in no time. Also, I doubt that it stands any chance of passing the safety tests, considering that the chain falls off, the brakes don't work and the back wheel is wobbly.'

'Alright, fine,' conceded Ben. 'But you'd better not start whinging that my bike is much better than yours from now on.'

'Don't worry, I won't.'

We thanked Kevin, and said our goodbyes to Pinky - which was neither emotional nor sentimental for Ben - and headed on our way.

'I can't reach the pedals properly when I'm sitting on the seat,' panted Ben about 30 seconds after leaving the police station. 'I have to stand up to be able to pedal.'

147

I tried my hardest not to sound smug but I couldn't resist.

'And you told me not to whinge. What did I ask you back in the station about the pedals? That bike looks ridiculous. It is the size of a horse.'

'Yeah, well, it could beat the shit out of your crappy little bike no problem,' said Ben, trying not to laugh. 'Ok, so it's big, and difficult to pedal, but it's a proper bike. I shall christen it The Horse.'

Cycling behind Ben was very amusing. The saddle was so high that when he stood up to pedal it was positioned in the middle of his back.

There was a Halfords (other car and bike shops are available) that we passed on our way out of Bath, so we called in to see if they could help us out with some basic bike repairs.

'What sort of things do you need doing?' asked Jason, the sales assistant and bike mechanic.

'You know, just a few minor things like the brakes not working, and the chain falling off. That sort of thing.'

After a few minutes tightening screws, and prodding cogs he gave his diagnosis.

'The chain is basically buggered. I've put some oil on it, but the rear derailleur has had it. It needs replacing.'

'Is there anything that you can do?' I asked, sounding like someone who had just been told that their beloved pet was going to be put to sleep.

'I'm afraid not. Derailleurs for bikes this old are really hard to get hold of these days. It might last a bit longer before it goes completely.'

'Ok, thanks, what about the brakes?'

'Well, they're basically buggered, too. The pads are so worn down that for you to be able to use them to stop they will have to be tightened so that they restrict the wheels from going round.'

I could hear Ben sighing behind me, but I was determined not to be defeated.

'Is it possible to tighten them enough so that I can at least slow down?'

'Yep, can do, but you won't be able to stop quickly.'

'Ok, that's fine.'

After Jason had finished with The Falcon, Ben asked if he could lower The Horse's saddle. It turned out that it was already at its lowest setting, which amused me greatly.

'Do you guys have helmets?' asked Jason as we were heading out of the shop.

'No, but we wish we did,' said Ben.

'Wait there a minute. I think I can probably sort you out with a helmet.'

When he had said 'a helmet,' we assumed he had meant 'a helmet each,' but it turned out he meant just the one helmet. Still, we decided to take it in turns to wear it, therefore making us significantly safer 50% of the time.

We headed out of Bath via Pulteney Bridge. Pulteney Bridge is one of only four bridges in the world to be lined by shops on both sides. In fact, it feels so much like a normal street that we suffered the embarrassment of asking someone which direction the bridge was, only to be given the reply, 'you're on the bridge, m'duck.'

Having successfully crossed the Avon, we then continued with renewed enthusiasm in what we thought was the direction of Scotland. 45 minutes later we were forced to retrace our steps to the Pulteney Bridge and try again. In the excitement of getting a new bike and a helmet we had headed west towards Bristol instead of continuing north.

We then took a wrong turn and ended up having to take a

lengthy detour around Colerne Airport and then through the sinister sounding villages of Slaughterford and Thickwood before joining the busy A420 for a few miles to correct our mistake.

We arrived in the village of Nettleton with high expectations of a long leisurely pub lunch, but were greatly disappointed to discover that the village didn't have a pub.

It did, however, have a well stocked Post Office.

Di, the lady who ran the Post Office, seemed overly excited by the arrival of two strangely dressed 'out-of-towners' to her shop. When we explained our mission she got even more excited and seemed to find the whole thing very amusing. We offered to help out in the shop in exchange for some food but she just laughed.

'Does it look like I need help in here?' she chuckled. 'You two just help yourself to any sandwiches or cakes that you want.'

'We don't want to take away your stock like that. Do you have anything that you were throwing out?' asked Ben.

'There's a couple of prawn sandwiches out the back that expired yesterday. I had one for lunch and I'm still alive,' she said.

'That would be perfect. Thank you.'

'At least take a cake and a chocolate bar each,' she said.

'Oh, go on then. If you insist.'

We sat at the picnic table outside and ate our gone-off prawn sandwiches, Eccles cakes and Snickers (other peanut, nougat and caramel chocolate bars are available). We were enjoying the peace and quiet of the Wiltshire countryside when I felt a sudden rush of panic through my body.

'OH SHIT! It's my mum's birthday tomorrow. I haven't got her a present. I haven't even sent her a card.'

'She'll understand, won't she?' said Ben. 'You can get her something when we've finished the trip. She knows you're not allowed to spend any money.'

'Yeah, but that's a bit lame of me, isn't it? I mean, we've managed to get accommodation every night, food, most meals, bikes, clothes and plenty of beer. I should have got a card, at least.'

'Well, we're at a Post Office. What better place? Why don't you go and ask Di?'

I went back inside and casually explained my predicament to Di without actually asking her for a birthday card.

'I can give you a card and a stamp,' she said before I had even finished speaking. 'Go and help yourself from the rack over there.'

Di was one of those rare gems of humanity that you occasionally come across. I could imagine that she was the pride of the village and knew everything about everyone. Not in a gossipy way, but simply because of her warmth and generosity. I researched Nettleton whilst writing this book, to try and establish what county it was in (it turns out it's in Wiltshire. To be honest, I didn't even realise we had passed through Wiltshire. I don't think I even knew where Wiltshire was). My search unearthed another interesting fact. I discovered that Di was awarded the accolade of *Best Village Shop/ Post Office in Britain 2007*. This was a pretty strange coincidence, considering it was the only Post Office that we visited on the entire trip, and also that Di's generosity and award-winning potential was so evident. I quote one of the judges, who sums it up far better than I could:

This is a hugely difficult category to judge because our village shopkeepers and sub-postmasters form the hearts of every rural community, but Di Bell is a very special lady who inspires real devotion from her customers. She received dozens of nominations from people of all ages, all

151

praising her warm nature and the fact that she is a lifeline who always goes above and beyond the call of duty. With the threat of closure looming over many Post Offices in the region it is the perfect time to emphasise that our branches are about the soul of country life, not just about stamps and car tax. Many of Di's customers said that the village would change for the worse without her, which is why I am delighted to honour her in this competition and raise the profile of our embattled Post Offices. Long may Di continue!'

'Why have you signed the card 'DW', you weirdo?' asked Ben.

'Oh, no reason, it's a long story,' I said coyly.

'Well we've got plenty of time. In fact, about 800 miles worth of time.'

'It's just something my mum calls me, that's all,' I said, casually hoping that would satisfy his curiosity. It didn't.

'I gathered that much, but what does it stand for?'

There was a long pause.

'Dordie Wardie.'

Ben erupted with laughter and nearly choked on the Eccles cake that he was eating.

'What the fuck? Ha ha. Dordie Wardie? My god, what is all that about?' he spluttered.

'When I was little, I used to call myself Dord because I couldn't say George properly. My parents carried on calling me Dord, and then for some reason over the years it gradually got extended to Dordie Wardie. That's what my mum, Dad and sister call me now.'

'Ha ha, that's ridiculous. Dordie Wardie! Your family are bloody weird.'

'Your mum must have a name that she calls you? What does she call you? Benny Boodles? Benny Wenny? Benji Bunny?' I probed.

'Ben,' he said.

152

'Oh.'

My mum received the card the following day, and Dordie Wardie received some serious brownie points.

We had been sitting on the bench by the Post Office for over an hour before we realised it was 2pm and we had only cycled ten miles. We continued through the quaint villages of Sopworth and Leighterton, before reaching the busy A46 which we followed to Stroud. We stopped briefly at a pub on the outskirts of Stroud because Ben was peckish for some peanuts.

'Do you really have to go and get peanuts? Can't you just wait until later when we can try and eat properly?' I asked.

'No, I really need something now and I think peanuts are the answer.'

'They won't give you any. This is a pub. Do you really think they'll just give you peanuts if you walk in and ask?'

'Of course. Why wouldn't they? We've not had any problems so far.'

'Yeah, but that's because we haven't really been asking for specific things, and we've been asking out of necessity rather than just because we fancy a snack,' I said, trying to justify my increasing frustration. 'Remember that time you asked for a new bottle of water?'

'That was because that bloke was an arsehole. Fine, well you won't want any of my peanuts when I get them, I assume?'

'No, I definitely won't.'

I waited outside the pub with the bikes, as I was too embarrassed to go in with him. Part of me hoped that he would come out empty-handed having suffered humiliation in front of a pub full of locals. The other part of me hoped he would emerge carrying peanuts, as I too was hungry. I promised myself that I would decline them anyway, just to make the point that I didn't need them.

He appeared a few minutes later with four bags of peanuts; two packets of salted and two packets of dry roasted.

'See, easy. The guy didn't even question it. He just handed me these,' said Ben with a smug grin. 'Do you want a couple of bags?'

'Yes please,' I said sheepishly. 'Thank you.'

Following a long slog up Scottsquar Hill we were then rewarded with a long downhill into the Severn Valley. We stopped for a rest on the M5 flyover. We had crossed over the M5 a couple of times previously – either side of Taunton – but hadn't yet stopped to watch the traffic. I understand that this may not seem like a pleasurable pastime, but there was something surreal about watching other people's lives continue at high speed. We had already become accustomed to living life at an incredibly slow rate, and we had forgotten what it was like to be able to get in a car and be at your destination a few minutes later. It was strangely satisfying to climb back on our bikes and continue onwards at our own leisurely pace.

It was almost dark by the time we reached the town of Newent. There seemed to be a selection of pubs and B&Bs in the town centre, so we both were optimistic about the prospect of finding some decent accommodation.

'I'm sorry, boys, but I'm completely full, what with the Onion Fayre and all,' said the landlady at The George Hotel.

'Onion Fayre? What's the Onion Fayre?' asked Ben, looking at me as though I would know.

'Why, it's the Newent Onion Fayre tomorrow!' she said. 'Why, it's the biggest day in the town's calendar. I thought that's why you were visiting.'

'Nope, we're just passing through. We didn't know about the Onion Fayre,' I said. 'It sounds fun. We're happy to sleep in an outhouse or garage if you have one?'

'I'm really sorry. Every inch of space is full of supplies and onions for tomorrow. There'll be about 20,000 people visiting the town tomorrow and 50,000 onions.'

'20 THOUSAND PEOPLE? FIFTY THOUSAND ONIONS?' I repeated back to her, assuming she had got her figures wrong. 'I had no idea that onions were so popular.'

'Neither did I before I moved here five years ago. It's the only one of its kind in the world and it's been going – in one form or another – for 800 years.'

'Blimey, it sounds like quite a party,' said Ben, trying his best not to sound sarcastic. 'Can you recommend any other places in town that might be able to help us?'

'I'm afraid you'll get the same response at all the other places in town. Everywhere books up months in advance for this weekend. Sorry, boys, best of luck.'

Once outside, Ben and I looked at each other with a mixture of excitement and dejection. We felt privileged to have arrived in the town on the most eventful night of the year, but we were also faced with the dilemma of not having anywhere to stay. If we continued onwards we would miss out on what the fayre had to offer, but, if we stayed put, we might spend the night on the street.

'We'll get something sorted here, I think. We haven't failed so far on the trip,' said Ben.

'I think that's the first bit of genuine optimism I have heard from you.'

'I know. It's the prospect of the Newent Onion Fayre. I can barely contain my excitement.'

We wheeled our bikes down the main street as we tried to establish a plan of action. When we reached the main square there were people unloading a giant trailer load of onions and stacking them under an old Tudor-looking building.

'So this is where it all happens,' said Ben.

'I guess so. That's a LOT of onions'

'We could see if they need any help setting up all the stuff and then maybe one of the workers will be able to offer us somewhere to stay,' suggested Ben.

'Sounds good. It's definitely worth a try.'

There were blank stares from the onion stackers as Ben pitched his proposition. They continued heaving sacks of onions to one another in a line from the trailer to the stack. There was still no response after Ben had finished talking. I tapped Ben's arm to suggest that we leave them to it, when one of the men at the end of the line spoke.

'So you set off from Land's End and you're cycling to Scotland without spending any money?' he asked as he continued to haul onions.

'Yeah, basically,' said Ben.

'Sounds very enterprising,' he said, smiling for the first time. 'You can sleep at mine if you want. I could do with a hand setting up in the morning.'

It really was as simple as that. We had been milliseconds from walking away and giving up on Newent and its onions, and suddenly we had been offered somewhere to stay.

We spent the next hour helping the guys unload the rest of the trailer of onions. The man who offered us a room was named Rob - a local farmer and the main supplier of onions to the festival. Rob was in his early forties, slim, good-looking and un-weathered - compared to some other farmers.

After we had finished stacking the onions he offered to buy us a beer at the pub across the square. Most of the other men looked like local farmhands, but one of them was distinctly different. He was in his early twenties and he had a continuous full-faced grin like a clown. His dress sense looked, well, how can I put this politely? Eastern-European. He was wearing a pair of those baggy coloured patterned trousers that were in fashion for about a week in 1988. He then complimented this with a shiny red bomber jacket and a yellow baseball cap. None of the other men had said a word to him all evening. He had been one of the links in the onion line, but was so ineffective that the other men tended to bypass him and give the sack directly to the person on the other side.

I smiled at him when he made eye contact and he took this as an invitation to come over and speak to us.

'Helllo-a. My name-a iz Rooballs,' he said.

'Rooooballs? Hi I'm George.'

'Roooooooballs,' he repeated, changing the emphasis slightly.

'Hi Roooooballs, I'm Ben.'

'I from Slovakia,' he said, shaking us both by the hand. 'You England?'

'Yes, we live in England,' I said.

At this point he got out a Slovakian to English phrase book from his pocket and started flicking through it. After a while he found what he was looking for.

'Girlder-feend!' he shouted excitedly.

'Girlder-feend? Sorry, I don't understand,' I said. Ben took a look at the word Rooballs was now enthusiastically pointing at.

'Ahhh, girlfriend,' said Ben. 'Yes, we both have girlfriends. Actually, George has a wife.'

'No, no, no. Rooballs. Girlder-feend,' he said, becoming even more animated. 'Girlder-feend England.'

'Oh, you have a girlfriend here in England?' I asked.

'Yes, yes. Girlder-feend England. London.'

'Very nice. So how come you're here in Newent?' asked Ben.

'Bus.'

'Yes, but why are you here when your girlfriend is in London?'

'Bus.'

'Ok.' Rooballs started flicking through his phrase book again.

'Telephoner,' he said, and started pointing at me erratically.

'You want to give her a call?'

'Telephoner,' he repeated, prodding me repeatedly in the chest with his finger.

'You want ME to telephone your girlfriend in London?' I asked.

'Yes, yes, yes. Telephoner girlder-feend London.'

'Errr, okay. Do you have a phone? What do you want me to say?'

'I show book. Telephoner,' he said, waving his trusty book and showing me he had 50p for the phone box which he was frantically pointing at through the pub window.

'Ok, ok. Let's do it,' I said. 'What's her name?'

'Jenny,' said Rooballs. Ben shrugged his shoulders at me, and followed me outside giggling away to himself. I was too nervous about what I might have to say to Jenny to find the situation amusing.

The three of us squashed into the phonebox outside the pub and he put the 50p in the coin slot and dialled a number that he had scribbled on a piece of paper. After a few rings an English girl answered. It was very noisy and she sounded like she was in a bar.

'Hello, is that Jenny?' I said.

'It's Jenna. Who's that? Sorry it's very noisy here. I can hardly hear you.'

'I'm with a friend of yours called Rooballs. He has a message for you, that he wants me to give you.'

'What's that? A message from who?'

'Rooballs. From Slovakia. He said you and he know each other?'

'Oh, yes. I remember Rooballs,' she said somewhat hesitantly. I was beginning to sense that perhaps she didn't regard their relationship in the same way that Rooballs did.

'Good, well he's got a message that he wants me to translate for you,' I said, whilst Rooballs hurriedly flicked through his phrasebook.

Rooballs pointed enthusiastically at a word that he had found. It said, 'potrestat', pokutovat', pret'ažit''. Translation: 'to punish'.

I gave Rooballs a quizzical look, but he nodded his head excitedly as if to confirm he definitely had the right word.

'Err, Jenna, he says 'to punish'. Does that mean anything to you?' By this point, Ben had turned away and had his forehead squashed up against the glass of the phone box. I could hear the muffled sobs of his laughter as he bit onto his fist.

'To punish? Punish what? I don't understand,' said Jenna.

Rooballs was busy searching the phrasebook for the next word, which would no doubt make everything clear.

'Oh hang on, he's going to give me another word,' I said. Rooballs fumbled with the book, but as he did the phone line went dead as Jenna hung up.

'I'm really sorry, mate. We ran out of credit,' I lied.

'We could call back?' I said, genuinely sad and confused that the only message he had managed to pass on to his alleged girlfriend was 'to punish'. Rooballs shook his head and pushed the door of the phonebox open.

'No more money,' he said dejectedly.

Back inside the pub I tried asking Rooballs what the remainder of his message was, but he didn't seem to understand. His sadness was soon comforted when I taught him how to flick a beer mat over with the back of his hand and catch it. He howled like a maniac.

'Right, lads,' said Rob, who had broken away from the other farmers and had come over to speak to us. 'My folks are having a barbeque down by the river tonight. I'm sure they'd be happy for you to come along.'

'That's extremely kind of you, Rob. But we don't want to intrude at all,' said Ben.

'I insist. You're more than welcome.'

'Thank you. That sounds great. But these are the only clothes we've got,' I said, tugging at my dirty suit trousers that I had been wearing continuously for seven days.

'Oh don't worry about that. It's just a bunch of old people having a barbeque in a field. It will be too dark for them to even see what you look like anyway. It's the annual get-together of *The Severn Bore Society*. It's going to be the biggest bore for 25 years tonight,' he said.

'Cool. What's the Severn Bore?' I asked.

'A pig isn't it?' said Ben, realising straight away that he had said something stupid as Rob was choking on a mouthful of beer.

'Ha, no, it's not a pig. You must have heard of The Severn Bore, no?' We both looked at him blankly. 'It's a wave that comes down the river,' he continued. 'Anyway, I'll tell you all about it in a bit. We need to get going if we're going to make it in time. Sling your bikes in the trailer outside and I'll be out in a minute.'

'Ok, brilliant, is Rooballs coming, too?' I asked.

'Errr, no, I've no idea where he's staying. He looks happy enough here,' said Rob.

We waved goodbye to Rooballs who was still flicking beer mats at the table in the corner. He grinned and waved back.

Rob's trailer was parked just outside the pub and we retrieved our bikes that we had pretend-locked to a nearby pillar. We were just about to put them into the trailer when I was suddenly hit by a dilemma.

'Hang on, Ben, isn't this cheating getting a lift somewhere with our bikes?'

'What do you mean? Do you seriously think we should cycle miles to Rob's farm, in the middle of nowhere in the pitch black?'

'No, I don't mean that. I mean that we said that we wouldn't use any other form of transport for our bikes, didn't we?'

'Yeah, but we also said we could do different things that were not on the route, as long as we rejoined the route where we left it. Like when we hired that speed boat in St Ives.'

'I know, it's just that Rob will probably have loads of other stuff to put in the trailer in the morning and we might have to leave the bikes at his while we come and help him, and then when we get them back and head off it means we won't have cycled the bit between here and Rob's house, wherever Rob's house is.' I was even confusing myself. Just at this moment, Rob and a couple of the other guys emerged from the pub.

'OK guys?' he asked, noticing that I was holding my bike in mid air.

'Yeah, everything's fine, it's just that, and this will probably sound really stupid to you but…' and I repeated my pedantic concerns about the authenticity of our challenge to Rob.

'That's no problem. I guess if you're going to do something as crazy as this bike ride, you might as well do it properly,' he said. 'Here's an idea. We put your bikes in the trailer, just for a few minutes and drop them up at Mike's house at the top of the street. You can then leave them at his. That's alright with you Mike isn't it?' Mike nodded. 'Then, in the morning, you can come and help me load up the trailer and come back into town to set up the rest of the stall. Then when you want to leave, you can wander up the road to Mike's house and pick up your bikes. Because his house is at the top of the street, you will have cycled past it already so you won't have cheated at all. How does that sound?'

Rob had become my new hero.

'Amazing. Thank you,' I said.

'Happy now?' whispered Ben as we climbed into the trailer with our bikes.

'Yes, very.'

After dumping the bikes in Mike's back garden, Rob drove us the ten or so miles to his farm on the outskirts of Gloucester.

He led us through the large farm kitchen, up the stairs and into a giant guest bedroom. A giant bedroom, I mean, not a room for giant guests.

'Rob, we were expecting a barn or something to sleep in tonight. Not one of your bedrooms. Honestly, we would be perfectly happy with the onions,' I said.

'Don't be silly, I'm more than happy for you both to stay here.'

As soon as he had disappeared, I dived for the bed.

'I'm having the bed this time,' I shouted.

'You bastard,' said Ben.

After a quick wash and change from one smelly t-shirt to another, we went downstairs to meet Rob.

'So have you guys really never heard of the Severn Bore?' he asked, when we were in the kitchen.

'After you mentioned it I realised I had heard of it before,' I said, trying to disguise my ignorance.

'I've never heard of it,' said Ben, without trying to hide his.

'Basically it's a wave that goes up the river against the current. It happens a couple of times a year maybe, but the one tonight is going to be the biggest in 25 years they say,' said

Rob.

'Cool. How do they happen?' asked Ben.

'Basically it's when there's a high tide and the level of the sea becomes higher than the natural level of the estuary. The water has to go somewhere so it sends a wave of water several miles up the estuary. People surf it sometimes. In fact this one guy earlier this year surfed over seven miles down the river. Anyway, we'd better get a crack on. If you grab as many of those bags of barbeque stuff as you can on the way out that would be great.'

After about ten minutes, we pulled into a field in the middle of nowhere. We could hear the distant chatter of voices and could make out the faint glow of a fire. We followed the light of Rob's torch across the boggy and uneven field to where a group of about 30 people were gathered around a barbeque the size of a pool table. It was the biggest barbeque I had ever seen, constructed from three oil drums, and giving off an immense heat.

Rob introduced us to his parents who were both in their seventies and extremely nice. They, in turn, introduced us to their friends, who then introduced us to theirs and within half an hour we knew almost everyone.

After a while, some of the men began to put meat onto the barbeque.

'Can we help at all?' I asked.

'Well, yes, you can both be in charge of the barbeque, if you don't mind,' said the old guy as he coughed on the smoke. 'There are a couple of pairs of tongs over there. Be careful because it's very hot.' This was the understatement of the century. I could feel myself carbonising as I stood there.

'Nice one, George,' said Ben sarcastically, when the old man had turned away, 'You've got us a job cooking in a volcano. Just think, two hours ago we were roaming the streets of Newtown, or whatever that place was called, looking for somewhere to stay, and now we're running a barbeque in a field for a big group of old people while we wait for a wave to come the wrong way down the river. How mad is that?'

'It's crazy. It's weird to think that if we had done anything differently today, like take an extra ten minutes for a break, or if we had been offered a room at that George Hotel, or if you hadn't suggested we speak to the onion stackers, then we would never have got to experience this.'

'Yeah, or we might still be roaming the streets of Newtown.'

'Newent,' I corrected.

'You knew what?'

'No, Newent. The town is called Newent. Not Newtown.'

'Well, whatever, I wouldn't want to spend the night roaming its streets.'

'Here you go, boys,' said the old guy, who had returned with two cool-boxes. 'We've got burgers, sausages, ribs, chops, steaks and chicken legs. You might as well cook it all. We don't really want to take any of it home.'

There was enough food to feed Gloucestershire.

We set about our task of cooking the biggest quantity of meat that had ever been seen in one place. I dread to think of how many animals must have died to create the mountain of bits that we were faced with.

There was no light other than the coals themselves, so it was virtually impossible to tell if the meat was cooked properly. We managed to borrow a miniature LED keyring from one of the old ladies (yeah, she was down with the kids). This worked well, but only if we held it about 4cm from the piece of meat that we were inspecting. This had to be done at lightning speed to stop the skin on our arms blistering. In reality, we didn't really need to check if the meat was cooked. The barbeque was so ridiculously hot that the meat was charcoaled within seconds.

We piled the blackened food onto huge plates in batches as we cooked it, and they were taken to a table where people began queuing to fill their plates.

'You're doing a great job,' said one lady as she passed us with a full plate of carbon. 'It tastes like a proper barbeque,' which was a polite way of saying that it was completely burnt.

After everyone had helped themselves, Rob came over and took the tongs from us.

'Great job, guys. You go and fill your plates and I'll keep an eye on the last few bits,' he said.

'IT'S COMING!' shouted one of the group members, soon after 10pm.

Everyone rushed towards the river that was now eerily lit by the moon. The river was completely still and the prospect of a 'wall of water' as we had been promised seemed incomprehensible. We were several miles inland and it seemed impossible that a wave could make it up that far, and I did start to wonder if it was all an elaborate joke. Rob had also said that we would hear it long before we would see it. But, apart from the building excitement and chatter of the old people, I could hear nothing. Even a ripple would have made this lot gasp. My expectations were set very low.

Just then I heard something.

It's hard to describe the sound it made. Imagine the sound that a big wave makes when it breaks near the shore, but instead of this being followed by the lull as the water recedes, the noise just continues. Like one big, continuous wave. This, as you've probably gathered by now, is exactly what the Severn Bore is.

The river was fairly narrow at the point where we were standing, and we were only a few metres away from the water's edge. When the bore finally came into sight it exceeded all of my expectations. I couldn't help but gasp in amazement like the rest of the group. It was, literally, a wall of water almost two metres high travelling up the river. It was slower than I expected but far, far more impressive. For some reason, I had naively imagined that the wave would be on its own and once it had passed the river would be back to normal. What I neglected to realise was that this wave was being pushed by a continuous flood of water behind it. It carried with it huge tree trunks and branches that it had salvaged from the river bank on its journey. No surfers had managed to ride the wave this far, and to be honest I was slightly relieved. On this occasion it seemed that nature had won.

As the bore passed us, the water rushed up the river bank and flooded the field around us. I've never seen old people move so fast, as they all jumped for higher ground. Ben and I, who were too transfixed by the whole thing, failed to get out of the way and the fringes of the wave lapped over our feet.

The bore continued out of sight and the river quietened down, but still in its engorged form. The rest of the group headed back towards the barbeque deep in chatter, but we remained awestruck on the river bank. I can honestly say it was one of the most memorable moments of my life. I'm not sure how much of an influence the bizarreness of our evening had on the experience, but even on its own, the Severn Bore really is one of nature's great spectacles.

Our fortune was reinforced when the chairman of the Severn Bore Society told us that it was the best he had witnessed in over 30 years. I tried to think of something profound and meaningful to say to convey my emotions to the equally awestruck Ben.

'Awesome,' I said. 'Let's go and get some more meat.'

The group showed no sign of flagging as more and more

wine was drank, and more and more meat was eaten. They added to their generosity when the chairman made a short speech about our challenge, and presented us with a cheque for £50 from the society, for us to give to the charity of our choice.

I don't remember leaving the barbeque. I just remember waking up later with Ben tugging at my shirt.

'Come on, mate,' he said. 'You can't sleep on Rob's dining table. It's time to go to bed.'

Max, Bath

Jason, Halfords, Bath

Di, Nettleton Post Office

Wiltshire, obviously

Unloading onions, Newent

Day 8
Newent Onion Fayre
Newent to Ludlow - 46 miles

I woke up with my head pounding and my brain trying to piece together which bits of the previous night were real, which were drunken imaginations and which were dreams.

We conducted our daily routine of choosing the least rank of our t-shirts to wear for the day. On this occasion, though, it was 6am and ridiculously cold so we ended up putting on everything we owned. Rob was already busy in the kitchen when we went downstairs.

'Help yourself to cereal. The kettle's on.'

'Oh my God, look at this. Weetabix GOLD!' said Ben excitedly diving at a cereal packet.

'What the hell is Weetabix GOLD? Have you had it before?' I asked.

'No. I didn't even know it existed. I bet it's amazing,' he said as he lined three of them up in a bowl.

'They look like normal Weetabix.'

'Yeah, but I bet it's all in the taste.' There was a brief pause while Ben poured milk over his Weetabix GOLD, and most of the tablecloth.

'Oh. My. God,' he spluttered. 'It's the best cereal, ever. If you thought Weetabix was good, then you wait until you've tried Weetabix GOLD.'

I had to see what all the fuss was about.

'It tastes just like normal Weetabix, but with really nice milk,' I said.

'That's fresh out the dairy this morning,' said Rob as he joined us at the table with a teapot.

'Oh,' said Ben, 'I think you're right. I've just added some Corn Flakes too and they taste like the best Corn Flakes ever.

And these aren't even Corn Flakes GOLD. Just normal ones.'

'Do Corn Flakes GOLD even exist?' I asked.

'I doubt it, but they should bring them out, if they're anywhere near as good as Weetabix GOLD.'

'Hang on, but you just said… oh never mind.'

I later discovered that Weetabix GOLD was discontinued.

It was still dark when Rob drove us down the lane to his farm shop. This was not just a tiny stall selling onions; it was a vast food emporium, complete with bakery, butchery, cheese counter, gift shop and any vegetable you could ever want.

'I thought you just grew onions?' I asked.

'No, we grow all sorts here. Not everything in here is from this farm but most of it is.'

Rob was not content with just running a farm and a farm shop, he was also a local entrepreneur; always on the lookout for a new venture to keep him busy. I don't think it was even financially motivated, as many of his projects seemed to be charity schemes.

He ran Halloween trailer rides each year called *'Frightmare'*, which included a visit to the pumpkin patch, a haunted hayride and a trip to a ghostly cottage. He also organised train rides, Easter egg hunts, birthday parties, Santa's grotto and farm tours. My personal favourite was the Living *Pizza Field*. Rob had created a huge round field, and then divided it up into 12 pizza-like slices. Each slice of the field grew ingredients used to make a pizza, including wheat, onions (of course), garlic, tomatoes, sweet corn, olives, herbs and even cows, chickens and pigs. The idea was that children could go and learn more about where food came from, and how it is created. Having the field set out in the shape of a pizza made it easier for them to relate to. Children then got to cook a homemade pizza in Rob's specially created pizza kitchen with a traditional wood-fired pizza oven. It was the work of a genius.

We piled the pickup and trailer high with crates of vegetables, fruit and eggs. We then had to balance ourselves and the produce whilst standing up in the back of the pickup.

As we continued back up the track, the sun was rising and had cast its morning glow over the fields. At this point, an ostrich began running alongside the pickup truck. It was like being in Africa. Sort of.

Newent town centre was bustling when we arrived; stallholders were frantically getting their stuff ready, fairground rides were being assembled, gazebos erected, stages built, PA systems tested.

Rob left us in charge of transforming a pickup and trailer load of vegetables into an attractive and presentable market stall. Ben honoured himself with the title of *Director of Vegetable Aesthetics* and gave me the title of *Chief Vegetable Arranger*.

I soon established that this involved Ben pointing to where each pile of vegetables should go, and instructing me to do all of the actual lifting. I'm pretty sure Ben didn't make physical contact with a single vegetable during the entire operation.

Without wishing to boast, I soon discovered that I had a natural talent for vegetable arranging. It's a skill that I had never had the opportunity to fully realise. Sweet corn husks were stacked like a brick wall, carrots and leeks were laid out in majestic fan shapes, and bags of onions were elegantly suspended from hooks under the archway. Ben nodded approvingly and barked orders about more onions here, and fewer parsnips there.

When our work was done, we set off to see what else the Newent Onion Fayre had to offer. We were interrupted by the sound of a town crier's bell.

'Oyez! Oyez! Oyez! Good people of Newent, you are gathered here today for the Newent Onion Fayre. Shortly, our guest of honour Würzel – from the rock group Motörhead –

will be performing on the main stage.'

What was that? Würzel, from the heavy metal group Motörhead, was going to be performing at the Newent Onion Fayre? It was all very surreal.

What I also liked was the way the town crier had referred to the 'main stage,' as if there were many different stages. There was in fact just the one, and the word 'stage' was a little generous. It was a trailer with a gazebo on it.

When the town crier had finished his address we went and had a chat with him because he looked lonely.

William Chapman was well into his eighties but a lively character who had fully embraced the role of Town Crier, which he had held for many years. During the ten minutes that we spoke to him, we learnt about his time in the Royal Army Medical Corps and his career as a paramedic. He told us that he was one of the oldest Town Criers in the country and, get this, the oldest Town Crier IN THE WORLD to have a Blue Peter badge. Yes, you read that correctly. He was the oldest Town Crier in the world to have a Blue Peter badge. He even showed us the badge, which was pinned to his costume.

This seemed a bit weird to me at the time. Blue Peter has been going for 50 years, but even if William had got his badge during Blue Peter's first year he would have been well into his thirties. What sort of grown man sends drawings into Blue Peter?

'I think guests who appear on the show also get badges,' said Ben, when I voiced my concerns to him later. 'They're not just for kids who send in drawings.'

'Ok, good. That's a relief,' I said.

I discovered later, that, like Peter the Potter in Bath, William had died peacefully in hospital, aged 87, a few weeks after we had met him. It was very sad to think that two such vibrant and colourful characters had passed away so soon after our journey. It was a real privilege to have met both of them, and each made their mark on our trip in their own unique way.

I would like to make it clear that we had nothing to do with the death of either of them.

'Oyez! Oyez! Oyez! Good people of Newent, please welcome to the stage... ' said Willium, pausing to look at his script, '...Würzel.'

Suddenly, Newent was transformed. One minute it was full of grannies filling their shopping bags with onions, crocheted toys and unwanted tombola prizes. The next, all the dad-rockers, and emos had come out of the cracks and completely packed the town square in front of the stage.

Würzel emerged sheepishly through the flap at the back of the gazebo and picked up his guitar. He was a wispy little man wearing blue jeans and a Motörhead t-shirt, despite leaving the band in 1995. His hair was grey and scraggly and gave credence to the story that he was given his nickname after his resemblance to the scarecrow Worzel Gummidge.

He was joined on stage by a drummer and bass-player and he muttered a brief 'Hi,' before launching into a very entertaining ten minute rock 'n' roll instrumental. He then left the stage with an awkward wave and the masses began to disperse. Then a voice came over the PA system that gave one of the most surreal announcements I have ever heard:

'Würzel will be signing autographs at the Swan Rescue stand in about half an hour.'

It was time to leave Newent.

We gave our thanks to Rob for our unbelievable time in Newent, and he thanked us for our hard work, and gave us both a cup of his wife's 'world famous' onion soup and some bread.

On the way out of town, we called into a greengrocer and asked the lady if she had a couple of old bananas that she could spare. We both felt the need for some fruit or vegetables (other than onions), to help our bodies recover from the shock of the meat feast we had eaten the night before. After she had heard about our challenge, she got so excited that she filled a carrier bag with grapes, apples, pears, peaches, plums and bananas.

'This should keep you going,' she said. 'Good luck, guys.' We ate as much of the fruit as we could, and then hung the rest of the bag from The Horse's handlebars. Ludlow was 50 miles away, and we set our sights on getting there by the end of the day.

Soon after leaving Newent our route crossed the M50 and into Herefordshire. My knowledge of English counties was, and still is, awful, but the bike ride did fill in few gaps for me. For example, the realisation that Herefordshire is not just a misspelling of Hertfordshire. Ask me to name all 50 US states and I could give it a good go, but ask me anything about English counties, or any British geography for that matter, and I am completely clueless.

We reached the town of Bromyard at about 2pm and stopped by a pub on the edge of town. The large beer garden was packed full of people and there were Morris Dancers performing.

As they were prancing around and hitting their sticks, Ben invented his own Morris Dancers' song which he sang along in perfect time to the music and the click of their sticks: 'I'll bash yours, you bash mine. Let's play willy games.'

It was such a childish comment, and one that had come completely out of the blue, but it was several minutes before I stopped laughing.

'It's just not right is it? Grown men dressed like that, frolicking around with their bells, sticks and stupid clothes.

They give me the creeps,' he said.

'I agree. It should be made illegal.'

It turned out that Bromyard was hosting its annual Folk Festival, and the different Morris dancing groups were having some sort of 'dance-off' to see who the best was. In our eyes, there were no winners, only losers.

A pig roast was being served, and we decided to try our luck at getting some lunch. We joined the long queue of people and Morris Dancers (yes I know, Morris Dancers are human beings, too) and waited our turn.

'What can I get you?' said the agitated lady who was serving.

'Hi, we're cycling from Land's End to John O'Groats, and we... ' began Ben before being interrupted.

'Oh, not this, I haven't got time for this,' she said angrily. 'Do you want any food or not?'

'Well, yes, but we don't have any money. Is there any work we can do in exchange for a bread roll or something?' said Ben, trying to win her over.

'No, there are all sorts of health and safety issues. I can't have you helping back here. You'll have to try elsewhere.'

We were forced to do the walk of shame past all of the smug-looking Morris Dancers.

We had a very similar response from four other places that we tried in the town centre, including a butcher, a newsagent, a baker and a café. It was not just that we were being refused food - as this was to be expected on our challenge - it was that we were being looked at with genuine disdain.

On previous days, the responses had always been jovial and enthusiastic, even when they had been unable to help us. In Bromyard, however, there was a definite feeling of suspicion and distrust.

'I think our luck has expired,' sighed Ben after our fourth

consecutive rejection – a new record.

'I wonder whether it's us, or if it's Bromyard?' I asked.

'Definitely Bromyard. This place is full of miserable people.'

'Maybe. Although, we're both looking particularly rough today. Neither of us have shaved in over a week, we didn't get much sleep last night, and our clothes smell really bad.'

'But we've still got our charm and wit, haven't we?'

'Maybe that's flagging, too,' I suggested.

Our indictment of Bromyard was spared by the kindness of one lady. Just when we were about to write-off an entire town, the lady behind the counter in Loafers Patisserie was a ray of sunshine, in an otherwise overcast town. This is a metaphor, by the way; the whole town was actually very sunny when were there. She giggled away self-consciously as we told her of our challenge and then gave us each a French-bread pizza and a pasty.

We sat on the pavement outside Loafers and ate our lunch. Just as we were beginning to warm to Bromyard, and regret being so critical of it, we witnessed one of the most shocking and horrible sights that it is possible to see in this world; a giant procession of all of the different Morris Dancing groups, joined together in one long terrifying Morris Dancing snake. And they were dancing towards us.

We scoffed down our pasties, jumped on our bikes, and left Bromyard as quickly as we could.

A lady from nearby Bishop's Frome, named Violet Eveson – the granddaughter of a local hop grower – died in 1993 leaving £47million in a trust fund for local improvements. At the time, this was considered the largest ever single donation to a charity in the UK. This is not particularly relevant. I just wanted to highlight that there are (or at least *were*) other nice

176

people in the Bromyard area, other than the lady from Loafers Patisserie.

We were soon out of Bromyard, and then out of Herefordshire and into Shropshire. We cycled through the village of Collington and the market town of Tenbury Wells without stopping and reached Ludlow at about 5pm.

Our visit coincided with yet another festival. The streets were packed with revellers for the Ludlow Food Festival - our third festival in 12 hours. There was obviously a buzz of excitement associated with each of these festivals, which was great to experience, but the downside was that accommodation became so much harder to find.

We asked at nearly a dozen hotels, pubs and B&Bs in town, but were told by each of them that they were full. Our offers of help were also unwanted as each establishment had ensured they were fully staffed to cope with the influx of people to the town.

Ludlow is a quaint little town, dominated by the impressive Ludlow Castle. The town has almost 500 listed buildings, and boasts some unique medieval and Tudor architecture. Its links to gastronomy do not end with the Food Festival either; until recently, it had more Michelin-starred restaurants than any other town in the UK.

We passed a house on one of the cobbled backstreets with a sign in the window which said: 'ACCOMMODATION'. I knocked on the door.

A lady in her late sixties answered the door. She had bright white hair and a big smile. We explained that we had seen the sign in her window, and that we were looking for somewhere to sleep.

'Well, I do have a spare room. But I very rarely have anyone staying. I don't advertise, and nobody tends to walk this way,' she said.

We made it clear from the outset that we had no money, and that we did not want her to feel under any obligation to let two strange men into her house.

'Well, it's always nice to have company, so if you're really desperate then I'd be very happy for you both to stay,' she said. Ben and I looked at each other. There was a short pause before we turned back to the lady, and said, in perfect unison:

'We're desperate!'

The lady's name was Monica, and she had lived in Ludlow for nearly 30 years. We wheeled our bikes around to the back garden, which was a storey lower than the front of her house, as it was built onto the steep Ludlow hillside. She showed us to our room and then asked if she could get us anything for dinner.

'That's very kind of you,' said Ben, 'but we're intruding enough as it is. We'll be able to get some food in town, hopefully. We've become pretty good at getting stuff for free.'

'I bet you have, if you've survived this far.'

'Is there anything we can get you?' asked Ben, realising that it was a bit of a stupid question considering that we had no money.

'Actually, yes, it would be great if you could pick up some milk for breakfast.'

'Ok… of course… no problem,' said Ben.

Monica gave us a key to the front door and we set off to hit the town.

'How are we going to get milk? Are we going to have to shoplift, or find a cow to milk?' I asked.

'We'll sort something out. I was only being polite. I didn't expect her to actually ask us to get anything. Ludlow, baby!' said Ben.

We walked back up to the castle where the food festival

178

was taking place. Admission was £5, but there was nobody manning the gate so we nipped inside to have a look, just as the last few stalls were packing up their things.

We had arranged to meet our mums and girlfriends for lunch in Shrewsbury the following day, and although I had successfully sent my mum a birthday card, I did not have any sort of present to give her.

Being a keen foodie, I knew she would love anything sold at a food festival. In a frantic ten minute begging spree I pitched my plight to the remaining stall holders in the hope of some freebies. Ben lurked outside in the shadows, embarrassed by my tenacity. I was rewarded with the following:

Two bottles of cider
A bottle of elderflower cordial
Dried cranberries
Pate
Pickled walnuts
Dried mixed herbs
Sweet chilli dipping sauce

In all my life, even at my most generous, I don't think I had bought my mum a better present.

'Holy shit! That's incredible,' said Ben outside. 'You're getting a bit too good at this blagging. How the hell did you get all that?'

'This is what happens when you're not there. I'm thinking of going solo.'

'You wouldn't last half a day without me. Anyway, your mum won't need all of that. Let's have some of it now for dinner.'

'Sod off! This is my mum's birthday present. How would you like it if I ate your mum's birthday present?'

'Well, it depends what it was. I bought her a CD this year,

so if you ate that I would find it a little strange, to be honest.'

'Well I would find it weird if you ate my mum's dried herbs.'

'What about the cider then?'

'I thought you were hungry?'

'I am, but your mum doesn't need two bottles, does she? And if we drink one it means you've got less to carry tomorrow.'

'How about we give a bottle to Monica as a present?'

'Ok, fine. Shall we just eat the pate then?'

'No.'

Two hours later, we found ourselves sitting in a pub just off the main square eating a plate of Paella and drinking our fourth beer of the evening.

We had got talking to a couple in the street named Andy and Alison and they had insisted on buying us both a beer after hearing about our journey.

Andy and Alison were a couple in their mid-thirties, having a romantic weekend away from their busy working lives in Bristol. Often when we recounted to people some of the experiences we had had along the way, their eyes would glaze over and they would wish they had never asked.

With Andy, however, he wanted to know absolutely every single detail of our trip.

'I think what you're doing is really life-affirming,' he said.

'Really? Thank you,' I said, not fully understanding what the phrase meant.

'Seriously, guys, I think it's just brilliant what you're doing. There must be some other way I can help you with your trip? What do you still need?'

'Thanks, Andy, I think we're pretty much fully kitted out,' said Ben. 'Besides, you've just bought us a beer. That's all we need.'

Andy wasn't going to give up that easily.

'I assume you both have helmets?'

'Well… yeah, we've kinda got one helmet that we take it in turns to wear,' I said.

'Ha ha…' said Andy, assuming we were joking and then realising that we weren't. 'My word, you're serious? You share a helmet? Well I do a bit of kite-surfing and I've got a spare helmet back at the hotel if one of you doesn't mind looking like a prat.'

'I don't mind looking like a prat,' said Ben.

Andy gave us directions, and we made an arrangement to cycle over to their hotel the following morning. He then bought us both another beer and managed to persuade the man behind the bar to sort us out with a plate of paella each.

Whilst we were eating, Andy and Alison were talking to other people in the pub about us, and after we had finished eating we were bought another two pints. We finally said goodbye and stumbled out of the pub at 11.15pm at the end of yet another memorable evening.

'DAMN!' shouted Ben as we staggered across the square. 'I nearly forgot. We haven't got Monica any milk yet.'

Getting free milk in Ludlow at 11.15pm is not an easy task. All the shops and restaurants had closed, and it was too late to knock on random people's doors. There were no cows about, either. We tried one of pubs on the main square but were told that the kitchen was closed. We then tried another pub, and we were met at the door by the landlady.

'Sorry boys. We're closing. Last orders have been served,' she said.

'Actually, we're trying to get hold of some milk. I don't suppose you've got any here that we can have?'

'Milk? How come you need milk? How much do you need?' she asked.

181

'It's a long story. Basically, we promised we'd get an old lady some milk, but we don't have any money and all the shops are closed. We don't need much. Only half a pint or so,' said Ben.

'Ok then,' said the lady, 'I'll see what I can do.'

She returned a few minutes later.

'The chef said they used up the last of their milk a few hours ago because it's been so busy. They've only got these, which they've been using for the teas and coffees.' She handed over a carrier bag containing mini UHT milk portions and a yoghurt pot. 'I thought you could maybe empty them into this plastic pot to make it look like real milk.'

'Perfect. Thank you, you're a lifesaver,' said Ben.

In Monica's kitchen, which was down a flight of stairs on the same level as the back garden, we emptied all of the milk portions into the pot. There were 25 little 12ml pots, which equalled 300ml – just over half a pint.

Rob, Newent Onion Fayre

Onions

Sweetcorn

Wurzel from Motorhead, Newent Onion Fayre

Ben at the Newent Onion Fayre

More onions

Day 9
Family reunion
Ludlow to Ellesmere - 45 miles

For the second consecutive morning, we awoke in a comfy spare bedroom with awful hangovers. It wasn't how we imagined our penniless voyage to John O'Groats would take shape, but we were more than happy with how it was unfolding.

Monica was already in the kitchen when we went downstairs.

'Thank you very much again for letting us stay,' said Ben.

'It was my pleasure. I hope you were alright with just a double bed. I don't want to presume you're gay,' she said, completely out of the blue.

'No, we're not a couple. Ben keeps trying to seduce me but I'm not going to give in to him,' I replied.

'Well, whether you're gay or not, it doesn't matter to me. Help yourself to breakfast.'

We sat at the table in Monica's kitchen for nearly two hours.

She had been a little wary of telling us too much about herself to begin with – and rightly so – but after she realised our good intentions, she relaxed completely.

She told us all about her life, and how she had been a nurse during the war, and had had a baby with a Canadian soldier at a very young age. She had regrettably given the baby up for adoption, as she felt she was too young to look after it. She then later came to Ludlow on horseback to visit friends who lived in the town, and had stayed there ever since.

In 2005 she received a letter from her daughter – then in her fifties – who had managed to track her down. The daughter lived in Canada but flew to Ludlow straight away as soon as Monica suggested it. The two have been extremely close ever since, and Monica has visited her daughter in Canada several times.

'That's incredible,' I said. 'And how does your daughter feel about being adopted? Is there any sort of resentment?'

'None at all. She completely understands how hard it was for me. Things were very different back then. And besides, she was looked after by an amazing family and as far as she's concerned, they are her parents, but she has definitely found a new friend in me and we are both enjoying getting to know each other.'

'That's really lovely. What about you? Do you have any regrets?' asked Ben tentatively.

'Yes, of course. Never a day went by when I didn't think about her, and how I had given her away. It changed my whole life. That's why I never married. I didn't ever feel anyone would ever be able to understand me properly. As I say, things were very different back then - it's what I had to do. We're making up for it now, though. She's coming over again next week with her family. She's got two children of her own. They think it is great having three grannies, as it means they get an extra present on their birthdays and at Christmas.' Her face was filled with happiness as she looked out of the window, her eyes welling up as she spoke.

'And what about her father? Has she managed to track him down? Are you still in contact with him?' I asked, eager to find out more.

'No, no. She did try, but I don't even remember his name. In fact, I don't even remember which soldier it was that got me pregnant. There was more than one Canadian soldier during that time,' she said with a smile. Neither of us quite knew how to respond to this.

'Oh, I nearly forgot. We got some cider for you from the

food festival last night,' I said, fishing it from my rucksack.

Monica was delighted with her cider and pleased that she had gone with her instincts and allowed us both to stay.

'I'm the one that should be thanking you. I feel like I've made two new friends,' she said.

After a lengthy search we found Andy and Alison's hotel – the glamorous-looking Dinham Hall Hotel.

'They've checked out already, but they left this helmet and this box of energy powder with me and said you would be calling past to pick it up,' said the man at reception. He handed over the kite-surfing helmet, which was basically a full crash helmet, but without the visor part, and half a box of powdered Lucozade (other energy drinks are available). If Ben was going to look like a prat in a crash helmet, at least he would be a prat full of energy.

'Mr and Mrs Jacobs told me about your challenge,' he said. 'It sounds like a great idea. The hotel would be happy to offer you both breakfast.'

'Thank you, if only we'd known. We've just filled up on cereal and toast at the place we stayed,' said Ben. 'Thanks very much for the offer, though. We really appreciate it.'

On the way out of the hotel we bumped into Andy and Alison in the street. Not literally. That would have been very clumsy.

'Ahhh, there you are,' said Andy. 'We thought we might not see you before we left. We were just having a last look around town.'

We thanked them both for the helmet and Lucozade, and Andy once again reiterated that he thought what we were doing was 'life-affirming.' The more we heard it, the more we liked it. He was pretty much saying that we were like modern day Mother Theresas.

It was 10.30am by the time we left Ludlow. Shrewsbury

was 25 miles away, and we were due there for lunch.

We covered those 25 miles in about two hours, which was one of our fastest sections of the entire trip. The route climbed gradually for the first eight miles along beautiful little country lanes, and we cruised through the villages of Culmington and Pedlar's Rest.

'Look, Pedlar's rest. We're pedlars. I think that means we should stop for a rest,' panted Ben.

'No, we're pedallers, not pedlars. Keep pedalling.'

The road eventually reached its peak a mile or so before the town of Church Stretton before joining an old Roman road, which traced alongside the busy A49. It was brilliant to cycle along; a deserted road stretching into the distance as straight as a runway. The A-road had stolen all the traffic and we were completely alone.

I cycled for nearly four miles no-handed. I know what you're thinking; 'my god, this guy is cool', and you would be right. On that short stretch of Roman road in Shropshire, I was the coolest god-damn mofo on the planet. That was, until my wheel caught a pothole and I nearly ended up in hospital.

I managed to grab the handlebars, but the bike had already been thrown off course and the front wheel had caught the grass verge. My right foot then slipped from the pedal and the bike skidded from underneath me and clattered down the street. I had somehow managed to remain upright and was completely unhurt.

Ben, who had been following just behind me, managed to skid to avoid hitting me and came to a stop alongside, where he proceeded to ridicule me for cycling no-handed.

Thankfully, The Falcon was also unhurt and we were able to complete the last few miles into Shrewsbury without incident. I kept my hands firmly on the handlebars the entire way.

187

We were not prepared for the cheers of six excited women as we cycled up Shrewsbury's main street. For a split second, we thought we had some groupies, until we recognised the embarrassingly loud whoops as being those of our families. Both of our mums, sisters, my wife and Ben's girlfriend had made the trip from Northampton to have lunch with us. We had only been on the road for nine days, but it was really uplifting to see their familiar faces again. They were astounded by our possessions, and took great pleasure in mocking The Falcon, Ben's helmet and my suit trousers.

We walked with them to a pub that they had spotted by the river.

'I bet you boys will enjoy having a proper meal bought for you,' said Ben's mum.

'Actually, I don't think we're allowed to let you to buy us lunch, I'm afraid,' I said. 'We decided that it would be against the rules to accept anything from friends and family.'

'Crikey, that's cruel. Who made these rules?' she asked.

'George did!' said Ben bluntly.

'The point was to rely on the generosity of members of the public, rather than friends and family,' I said.

'Yeah, but this is just one meal,' said Ben.

'It is, but I would still feel like we cheated if we get bought a meal. If you want, you can let them buy you a meal and I'll try and get food for free, like we have been doing.'

'It would be nice if we could all eat together, though,' said my sister.

'We'll try and work our charm in the pub,' I said.

After nine successful days of acquiring bikes, clothes, accommodation and countless meals for free, we were looking forward to impressing our loved-ones with our skills.

'So your family will all be paying for their Sunday roasts,

but you want yours for free?' said the lady behind the bar.

'Yes, I know it sounds very cheeky. We don't have to eat the same as them. Any food that you can spare, and we're happy to wash dishes or clean tables in return,' I said.

'We've got staff to do that,' she said angrily. There was an awkward shuffle of feet from our family behind us. Things weren't going quite to plan.

'Ok, I can probably sort you out with some bread and butter,' she said.

We sat and ate our bread and butter while the others all tucked into their Sunday roasts. It was cruel, but the sun was shining and we were both sitting in a pub garden by the river with our three favourite women. Things could have been worse.

'Here, I'm not going to be able to eat all of this. You boys have some,' said Ben's mum, pushing a plate of roast beef in front of us. Ben looked at me as though he was seeking approval.

'You eat it if you want, mate. I'm not going to have any, because it's still accepting help from friends and family,' I said.

'But these are just leftovers that will go to waste.'

'Yes, but they are only leftovers because they are here having lunch because of us,' I said, trying to downplay how much of a stickler for 'the rules' I was being.

'My god, you're hard work,' said Ben. 'So it would be ok for me to eat leftovers from anyone else's plate in this pub, as long as they are not our friends or family?'

'Exactly.'

'He's a strict one, isn't he?' said Ben's mum.

'Tell me about it. It would be more relaxing going on a bike ride with Hitler. The other day he was struggling up this big hill on his stupid little five-speed racer, panting away because it's such a crap little bike, and when he got to the top I suggested

189

he consider looking to upgrade his bike to something better to make the cycling easier. He just cycled past and panted 'THIS WASN'T SUPPOSED TO BE EASY'. It's like he wants to suffer as much as possible.'

The entire table burst into laughter. I could do nothing but join in. I tried desperately to think of a reason to justify my behaviour, but I knew Ben was right. I think a part of me did want to suffer, in the sense that the harder the challenge that we faced, the more of an achievement it would be to complete it.

Cycling from Land's End to John O'Groats is a great achievement in itself. Doing the journey unsupported is even more of an accomplishment. Completing the trip without spending a single penny is an impressive feat, and riding a completely inadequate bike the entire way took it to the next level.

Perhaps I was being slightly masochistic, but then isn't anyone who undertakes a physical challenge? That's the whole point of it being a challenge; pushing yourself mentally and physically beyond your comfort zone.

I think Ben also felt slightly threatened by The Falcon. He didn't just want me to get a better bike to speed things up; he wanted me to get a better bike to put us back on level terms. He saw The Falcon as something that would upstage his achievement.

I didn't see it that way at all. It was simply a personal challenge of mine to keep The Falcon for as long as I could. I had wanted Pinky to make it all the way to the top of Scotland too, but Ben traded her in at the first opportunity.

Ben was not particularly fit or athletic. The closest he got to physical exercise was walking to the pub at the end of his road. For him to even attempt to cycle 1000 miles was remarkable in itself. He didn't need an inadequate bike to make it even more impressive.

We said goodbye in the car park, which was surprisingly emotional. Not because of the car park, you understand. Being reunited, albeit briefly, with our family had given us both a sense of security and familiarity. The thought of going back into the unknown was suddenly quite daunting.

After they had left, a lady in a long, floaty dress came running across the car-park towards us, as we were climbing onto our bikes. She was in her early twenties, slightly hippyish and very giggly. She was clutching a huge sandwich bag full of chocolate bars and sweets.

'Hello, sorry to bother you,' she said. 'I hope you don't mind, but I overheard your conversation in the pub and I gather you are cycling to John O'Groats, but you're not allowed to spend any money?'

'Hi. Yes that's right,' I said, a little shocked as it appeared we had our first ever stalker.

'Don't worry, I'm not stalking you. My car was parked in this car park too, and I wanted to give you this bag of sweets. I thought it might come in handy.'

'Thank you. That's amazing.' I said, as she ran back across the car park. The bag was stuffed full of fun-size chocolate bars, flapjacks and sweets. Ben and I gawped at it like a couple of children at a tuck shop.

'You're welcome. Good luck!' she shouted back.

We ate several bars there and then to make up for our measly lunch and then agreed to ration the rest over the next few days.

I hope what I am about to tell you fills you with as much anger and disappointment as it did me.

Let me set the scene for you. It is Christmas Eve, almost three months after we completed the trip (Dammit! I hope I haven't spoilt the ending for you). Ben and his family have been invited to my parents' house for dinner. We all had a great evening and drank way too much when the conversation turned to our bike ride. Someone mentioned the day that we all met in Shrewsbury and then Ben and I reminisced about the hippy girl and the bag of sweets. At this point, my mum burst out laughing and then quickly put her hand over her mouth.

'What's so funny?' I asked.

'Nothing. Just laughing about what fun we had that day,' she said.

'Why did you laugh when I mentioned the hippy girl?'

'Did I?'

'Yes. You did.'

'Oh, no reason.'

She laughed again and then bit down on her fist as though she had just put her foot in something. Metaphorically, of course; my mum's carpet is very clean.

'Well, about that bag of sweets. I kind of gave it to the girl to give to you,' she said.

'You did what?' I said, not believing what I was hearing.

'I brought all of those chocolates with me to give to you, but when I heard how seriously you were taking 'the rules' I thought I would give it to somebody else to give to you.'

'When? How? I still don't understand.' I could feel an anger bubbling up inside of me.

'I saw her in the car park before we left and recognised her from the pub, so while you were all chatting I told her what you were doing and asked if she could give you the sweets when we had left. Sorry, I thought you would appreciate it.'

'Of course we appreciated it, but that's because we thought it was from a random, good-natured stranger, not my own mum,' I said, angrier than I had spoken to my mum since being a teenager.

'I thought you would recognise the chocolates as being the same ones I normally buy?'

'What? Snickers? Yeah, mum, because you're the only

person in the world who would buy them?'

'They weren't Snickers. They were Racers – Aldi's own-brand Snickers.'

'Well you're not the only person in the world who shops at bloody Aldi, either.'

There was an uncomfortable silence around the room and some awkward noises from Ben, who was caught between wanting to agree with me and not wanting to criticise my mum.

I know her intentions were good, but I did feel that she had undermined everything we were trying to achieve. She just laughed and said I was being dramatic, but if I had slipped her some carbs during one of her freaky diets, or sneaked some sugar into her tea during lent then I would be officially disowned within minutes. Mums don't always know best.

So there you have it. We failed. The whole challenge completely corrupted by an innocent bag of sweets provided by my own mum. I can assure you that until that moment on Christmas Eve, neither Ben nor I had a single clue that our challenge had been tampered with. If you can forgive us this one mistake, I can promise you that it was the first and last of such instances on the trip.

The novelty value of cycling in thick woollen suit trousers had worn off soon after leaving Land's End, and nine days later I had grown to hate them with a passion.

I had rolled each leg up as far as my knee, which did help aerate my lower leg, but the disadvantage was that it created a tight, thick band of fabric that rubbed and chafed, and completely sealed in the top half of my leg. In a sense, my leg was cooking in an enclosed bag of hot sweat. I appreciate that this is not the nicest of descriptions, but it's the only way I can convey the discomfort.

To make matters worse, as the trousers were about eight sizes too big for me and had to be tied with bailer twine and rolled over at the waist band several times, they cut into my flesh like the string on a joint of pork. In the blistering sun, my exposed love handles had become pork scratchings.

Despite the discomfort, we had an easy afternoon's cycling with the terrain rarely altering from its even plateau. The mood was sombre, though. We both agreed that meeting our families had been a bad idea, in hindsight. It was great to spend time with them, but it had broken our focus. After nine days without such contact, we had become used to not knowing who we would meet each day, where our next meal would come from and what sort of experiences we would have. Having that brief experience back in normality made us both feel far more isolated and lonely than we had before.

'I tell you what,' said Ben, 'it's made me more determined than ever to get to John O'Groats as soon as possible.'

'Me too. It's depressing to think that they will all be back home now, sitting on the sofa, drinking tea, making whatever they like for dinner. Here we are, sitting on a grass verge by the side of the road in the middle of fuck-knows-where not having a clue where we're going to sleep tonight.'

'The weird thing is that from what they were all saying at lunchtime, it sounds like they are all very envious of what we're doing and would prefer to be here than at home on the sofa.'

Fortunately, this moment of despondency only lasted about two hours. As we started to devour the miles through the charming Shropshire countryside, things suddenly felt much better.

It was clear that accommodation would be hard to find as civilisation was almost non-existent. The village of Little Ness was, as you would expect, very little, and Stanwardine-in-the-Fields should be renamed One-house-in-a-Field.

About 20 miles beyond Shrewsbury we reached the small town of Ellesmere. It was 7.30pm and just on the outskirts of town we passed a narrow-boat marina.

'Why don't we try to blag a boat for the night?' suggested Ben, coming to a stop by the gate.

'Surely the boats in the marina will be full of people? Let's just head into the town and try and find somewhere there,' I said.

'Oh go on, it's worth a try. There might be some empty boats.'

'Alright,' I sighed.

There were several boats tied up in the marina but no sign of life either on land or water. Ben knocked on the door of a house that seemed to double as the marina's office.

'There's nobody in. Let's go,' I said.

'Hang on. Give them a chance. Look, someone's coming.'

A small man with a trimmed silver beard and cropped grey hair answered the door. He looked identical to Mr Hankey - my GCSE Media Studies teacher. What? You mean you don't know what Mr Hankey looks like? That's a shame, because this man could have been his twin brother.

'Hello?' he said questioningly.

'Hello. Sorry to bother you, but are you in charge of the marina here?' asked Ben.

'Uh huh,' he nodded.

'Great. We're cycling the length of the country without spending any money at all, and we were wondering if there is any chance of us sleeping in a boat tonight.'

'Why do you want to sleep in a boat?'

'That's what I asked him,' I said.

'Well we've been going for nine days now and we've slept in B&Bs, people's houses, barns, all kind of places. When we saw this place we thought it might be fun to sleep on a boat.'

The man screwed up his face and pressed his palms against his forehead.

'Lads, lads, lads. It's nearly 8pm. I'm just having dinner and settling down in front of the telly and then you two scruffy buggers turn up on my doorstep.'

'I know, we're really sorry. We'll try our luck in town. Sorry for bothering you,' I said.

'No, no, no, it's ok. I do want to help you guys out,' he said, looking slightly less miserable. 'I'm just working out how I can.'

He paused for a moment.

'Alright. I think I can sort you out with a boat for the night.'

The sun was setting as Neil – the marina manager – walked us along the bank of the marina. It was a really beautiful moment. The perfectly still water reflecting a perfect orange sky, and we were being given our own boat for the night. Ben had raised the bar yet again.

'Climb aboard!' said Neil. 'I'm going to have to drive her back to the other end so I can hook you up to the mains.'

'Don't worry about that, Neil. We don't mind not having power. We just wanted somewhere to sleep,' said Ben.

'Nah, don't be silly. You won't be able to fully appreciate life in a narrow boat without electricity.'

As well as being a marina for privately owned boats, Blackwater Meadow Marina also had a fleet of hire boats, one of which Neil had let us have for the night. He kept apologising profusely that it had not been thoroughly cleaned.

I had never been on a canal boat and I was utterly shocked when I climbed down through the hatch. I am not exaggerating when I say it was more luxurious than my own house. It had a lounge area with a flat screen TV, DVD player and hi-fi; a dining area with seating for several people; a fully-fitted kitchen that included a dishwasher; a bathroom with an actual bath, and two bedrooms – one of which had an en-suite. It was arguably the most lavish accommodation of the trip.

Ben claimed the double room, as the boat idea had been his, and I took one of the single beds in the other bedroom.

After giving us the tour of the boat, Neil disappeared back to his house and returned with a bottle of red wine, four cans of beer, some teabags and half a pint of milk.

'I'm afraid my cupboards are empty at the moment,' he said, 'otherwise I would have offered you some dinner, too. The town is only a five minute walk down the road, so I'm sure you'll find something easily enough there.'

Neil had become a leading contender for the 'nicest person that we met' award. This award didn't exist, by the way, but if it had then Neil would have been a leading contender.

We drank a can of beer each and walked the five minutes into Ellesmere town centre. I don't mean to suggest that we needed the Dutch courage just to venture into the town centre. Ellesmere is really not that intimidating.

We called into an Indian restaurant after being lured in by the smell. The young waiter told us we would have to come back on Tuesday to speak to the manager. It was Sunday. Waiting two days for the possibility of getting a free curry was a little impractical.

We had another rejection from a takeaway but then a kind man from the kebab house gave us a large portion of chips to share.

'If only we had some bread,' I said, 'then we could have chip butties and wine back on our boat.' That was a line I never thought I would hear myself say.

'Great idea. I'm sure we can get some stale bread from the Co-op over there,' said Ben.

Ben was not suggesting that Co-op is notorious for selling stale bread. He meant that shops that sell bread are likely to have surplus stock at the end of the day that they are forced to throw out. It was 9.30pm, by this point, and the shop was half an hour from closing.

'We don't tend to have too much bread left at the end of the day but I'll certainly look for you,' said the lady in Co-op, who had the face and manner of a friendly lollypop-lady.

'Here you go. Is this alright?' she said, holding out a small loaf of freshly baked granary bread. When I say 'freshly baked', I mean freshly baked a few days previously.

'That's perfect. Thanks very much,' I said. 'We managed to get some chips down the road, so we're going to make chip butties.'

'What a good idea. You certainly are on an adventure. Do you have any butter and ketchup?'

'No. Thank you. We'll be fine with just chips and bread,' I said.

'Don't be silly. You can't have a proper chip butty without butter and ketchup. Can you?'

'No, I suppose not.'

'Wait there, I'll be back in a minute.' She returned a minute later with a packet of butter and bottle of Heinz Tomato Ketchup.

'Wow, you're amazing. But how did you... ?

'Shhhhhh,' she interrupted, putting her finger to her lips, 'breakages.'

We had expected to see some element of generosity from the small independent establishments that we asked for favours at, but we had anticipated the opposite from the big corporations. We had assumed that the amount of bureaucracy involved in the larger supermarkets would restrict their ability to show generosity. However, we had been proven wrong on several occasions. It seems that even working for a large corporation allows some element of free will. And if rules can't be bent, then there will always be 'breakages'.

If, like me, you were curious about the origin of the word 'ketchup' (No? Just me?), I will fill you in. It is thought that the word comes from the Malay word *kēchap,* which was also a sauce. But rather than being tomato based, it was made from fish brine, herbs, and spices (not so great in a chip butty). In the 18th and 19th centuries the word was used as a generic term for all vinegar based sauces and it was not until the 20th century that the word became synonymous with the tomato sauce that we know today. Thank you, Wikipedia.

Back on the boat we each assembled two huge chip butties, and opened the wine. It was a lovely warm evening so we sat on the small deck at the back of the boat.

Before our trip started I imagined all sorts of possible scenarios of where we might spend each night and what sort of food we would eat. Sitting on the deck of a luxury narrowboat with two chip butties and a bottle of wine had never even entered my thought process. Sitting there with the bright, starry Shropshire sky and the gentle lapping of the water on the side of the boat, was the most content I had felt in a long time.

The boat felt like it was swaying a lot, but when I stepped briefly onto the land to check on the bikes the ground continued to sway. We moved inside at about midnight and made a cup of tea, to try and offset the half a bottle of wine and two beers that we had both consumed.

'What are you doing?' I asked Ben, who had been in the kitchen for some time.

'I'm just washing my pants,' he slurred.

'Ok. Why?'

'Cos they haven't been washed for days.'

'So you thought that midnight on a canal boat would be the best time to wash them? Have you not learned from my mistakes? How are you going to dry them?'

'You'll see. You'll see.'

I sat there with a cup of tea in one hand and the remains of my beer in the other and listened to an Elvis Costello CD that we found in the cupboard. I was disturbed by a familiar humming noise.

'Are your pants in the microwave?'

'Yep, they sure are. Two minutes should do it.'

'That's genius,' I said, jumping from my seat and joining Ben in the kitchen.

It was very odd to stand and watch a pair of Union Jack boxer shorts rotate on a microwave plate. It's not something I had ever done before, nor something I can ever imagine doing in the future.

DING.

'They're done!' said Ben excitedly.

He took the boxer shorts out of the microwave.

'Shit!' he said, throwing them to me. 'They're bloody hot.'

'Arghh,' I said, catching them, 'and they're not even dry. It's like an extreme version of those hot towels that you get in an Indian restaurant. Except, I'm not washing my face with these. What's this brown stain on the arse?'

'That wasn't there before!' shouted Ben.

'It's a burn mark! You've burnt your pants and now you've got a permanent skid mark on your arse.'

Andy and Alison, Ludlow

Somewhere near Bromyard

Neil, Blackwater Meadow Marina, Ellesmere

Monica, Ludlow

Day 10
A Welsh puncture
Ellesmere to Up Holland - 58 miles

We were greeted in the morning by Neil with a huge pile of toast and jam. After a long, leisurely breakfast on deck, we were on the road by 10.30am.

'What the hell? How come the road signs are in Welsh? When did we enter Wales?' said Ben, skidding to a halt.

'Hang on, I'll check,' I said, pulling the day's directions from my pocket.

It was too difficult to cycle whilst holding the route book, so each morning I would write down the instructions for that day onto a scrap of paper which I then kept in my pocket. This whole process took at least ten minutes.

'It says here: *Between Ellesmere and Penley, the tour briefly enters Wales – the first indication being the road signs'*. Well they were right about that. Yes, it appears that we are in Wales.'

'Cool. England tick,' said Ben.

'Yes, but we'll be back in England soon. We can't get to Scotland through Wales, you div.'

'Yeah, I knew that. I was just saying.'

We were just about to set off when I looked down and noticed a huge thorn sticking out of The Falcon's front tyre.

'I think we've got a slight problem,' I said, pulling out the thorn and holding it up to Ben.

'Oh, bollocks. Is it flat? What are we going to do?'

'It's completely flat. I guess we just walk and ask at the first house that we see if they have a puncture repair kit.'

'Why did you have to go and get a puncture in the middle of nowhere?'

'I didn't choose to get a puncture here did I?'

'No, I'm just saying that your wanky bike has caused us no end of problems.'

'It's a puncture, for god's sake. It could have just as easily happened to your mighty bike.'

'But it didn't, did it? It happened to that pile of crap.'

'You're being a bit unreasonable. We've cycled nearly 400 miles and this is our first puncture. That's pretty good going, isn't it? It's just a puncture. It's no big deal.'

Half an hour of walking later we reached a group of three houses. There was no answer at the first house. Or the second. Eventually, after a few minutes, a man with a smile that filled his entire face answered the door of the third house. He laughed when he saw us, as though he had been expecting us.

'Hellooo,' he said, 'have you come to look round the house?'

'Err, no,' I said, 'Sorry to bother you. Are you expecting people?'

'No, no, it's fine. How can I help you?'

'We're on a bike ride and we've got a puncture. I don't suppose you have a puncture repair kit and a pump that we could borrow?'

'Oooh, that'll be the thorns,' he said. 'They're cutting the hedgerows today and there are thorns all over the road.'

'I told you it wasn't my fault, Ben.'

Ben was too busy staring in disbelief at the man who had answered the door. Despite living in Wales, he had a distinct Yorkshire accent. His animated face was full of character, including a unique triple curved dimple on his chin. I can only assume that this was the result of a lifetime of smiling and laughing. He looked like an affable gargoyle, and I half expected water to spurt from his mouth.

'I think I've probably got a repair kit in the garage. I'll go and have a look for you. Everything's a bit disorganised at the moment as I'm in the process of moving,' he said, pointing to the *For Sale* sign at the end of his driveway. 'I've got someone coming to look around any minute now. That's why I was a bit confused when you came to the door. My name is Peter, by the way.'

Peter was a genuine character. He emerged from the garage with an unopened puncture repair kit and a hefty tyre pump.

'Here you go,' he said. 'I knew I had one somewhere. Not sure why, as I've not owned a bike since I was a child.'

Peter had lived in Wales for 15 years, and was planning to move to a smaller house just over the border in England. During the ten minutes that we spent repairing the puncture in his driveway, he didn't stop laughing. It was very refreshing, and was the perfect antidote to Ben who moaned incessantly about The Falcon. He confidently claimed that he could remove the inner tube from The Falcon's tyre with his bare hands and that 'tyre levers are for losers'.

'Why don't you just get a couple of teaspoons out of the picnic set? It would be much quicker,' I said.

'No, I can do it. It's easy. Just you watch,' he said, gritting his teeth and turning slightly purple as he pulled and tried to prise the inner tube from the tyre.

'You look like you're struggling. Why don't you just give me a couple of teaspoons? I could've had it off by now.'

'Hang on!' he snapped, turning blue. 'What use are teaspoons going to be anyway?'

'To use as tyre levers. What did you think?'

He continued to exert himself, so I reached into his rucksack and took out a couple of spoons while he wasn't looking. Ten seconds later, the inner tube was out and I hadn't had to turn blue.

'Oh, I didn't think it would be that easy,' said Ben.

'Have you ever actually repaired a puncture?' I asked.

'Well no, but I know they are annoying.'

Being brought up in the country, I was used to having punctures and so was fairly competent at repairing them. Ben, on the other hand, was a puncture repair virgin. He watched, in genuine admiration, as I set to work.

'How long is it going to take?' he asked.

'Five minutes.'

'Five minutes? I thought we were going to be here for bloody hours. I didn't realise it would be so quick.'

'I wondered why you were so miserable.'

Peter stood over to one side, watching us and laughing the entire time.

'You two are like a married couple,' he said.

Just as we were packing up, the estate agent pulled into the driveway with some prospective buyers. Their faces looked slightly bemused at the sight of two strangely dressed men and their possessions strewn across the driveway.

'We'll get out of your way. Thanks so much for all of your help, Peter. Good luck with the house move,' I said, as we frantically squashed everything into out rucksacks and pushed our bikes down the road and out of sight.

'I'm very impressed by your bike mechanic skills,' said Ben.

'Thanks. I can't believe you've never had a puncture in your life.'

'We don't get many thorns in London. Actually, I did get a puncture once, but I couldn't be bothered to repair it.'

'So what did you do?'

'I just bought a new bike instead.'

After Peter had mentioned the hedge cutters, it became very obvious that the road was covered in thorns. Just to be on the safe side, and to keep Ben happy, we pushed our bikes for half a mile until the road was clear.

After just five miles in Wales we crossed back into England, and the county of Cheshire. It was very fitting that although it made up just a tiny fraction of our total route, Wales still made its mark on our journey by giving us our only puncture of the entire trip. And although we didn't meet any genuine Welsh people in Wales, the one Welsh resident that we did meet was completely unique; a fine ambassador for the country.

We passed through the town of Farndon, which hosts the National 24-hour Cycling Championship. The winners tend to rack up mileage of over 500 miles in just a 24-hour period. This is quite astonishing considering we were covering about 60 miles in an eight hour day. The prospect of doing three of these stints back to back, at three times the pace, was incomprehensible. I hate proper athletes. They make the rest of us just look rubbish.

We reached Chester and were a little disappointed to discover that its occupants didn't all look like the cast of Hollyoaks.

On the occasions that we passed through other town centres along the way, we had both felt a slight feeling of claustrophobia and a desire to get back into the countryside. This was partly because cycling in urban areas is so much more demanding, and also because people in towns tended to be more hesitant and suspicious of us. Chester felt different somehow. The town itself is very striking with its mixture of Roman, Medieval, Victorian and Tudor architecture. The streets were also packed with tourists walking the streets aimlessly, so we fitted in perfectly.

Chester was the last English town to fall to William the Conqueror, and it has the most complete city walls in Britain.

Two facts that I am sure you will be thrilled with.

Despite all of the history and culture on offer, we had hunger issues so called into Subway to try our luck. Craig, the friendly South-African manager, offered us a foot long sub and a drink each. We ate half there and then, and stashed the other half away to eat on the road. I mean that figuratively, of course; we didn't eat our food off the tarmac.

On the way out of town, we called into a bike shop called The Bike Factory, where a man kindly oiled our bikes and tightened Ben's brakes.

'The cycling's fairly grim between here and the Lake District,' he warned. 'You're heading right into the heart of all the industry around Merseyside. Be careful, because the cars don't have much time for cyclists around there.'

Just a few minutes after leaving Chester we were back in the beautiful countryside, with the ugly sprawl of the industrial Ellesmere Port visible in the distance.

'Maybe our route avoids all that ugly stuff,' suggested Ben.

'I hope so,' I said, 'but I don't think it does.'

'I desperately need some shorts,' I said to Ben. 'My balls are unbearably uncomfortable.'

'No kidding. I don't know how you've lasted so long in those ridiculous trousers. I only managed a couple of days in those tracksuit bottoms and they were quite comfy. You should've cut the legs off those long ago.'

Ten days of wearing thick woollen suit trousers had finally taken its toll and the sweating, chafing and itching had become excruciating.

'I probably should cut them off, but that wouldn't stop them being uncomfortable. I need some real shorts or my balls are going to disintegrate,' I said.

'Thanks for that mental image,' said Ben, 'I just sicked up a bit of my Subway.'

We reached the town of Frodsham, where the town sign proudly boasts its accolade of *North West in Bloom – Best Small Town 2001*.

Ben spotted a sign for Frodsham Leisure Centre and we followed the road towards it in the hope of finding some abandoned shorts. The Leisure Centre turned out to be a school, too. The main doors were locked, but we caught the attention of one of the ladies in the office who came to the door and opened it hesitantly.

'Can I help you?' she asked, looking us up and down.

'I hope so. Do you by any chance have a lost property?' I said.

'Have you lost something?'

'Not exactly. We are on the look out for some shorts.'

'Sorry, no. I don't have access to the lost property cupboard I'm afraid.'

She had not been particularly welcoming, but we could hardly blame her. We were a pair of strangely dressed men, on school property, asking to have a rummage through the lost property. It's no wonder she didn't welcome us in with open arms.

We sat down by a wall and tried to decant some of the Lucozade energy powder into our water bottles. The wind had picked up and the white powder blew all around us, like we were part of a very ugly snow globe.

The door was opened a few minutes later by a large body-builder sized man, wearing a running vest and shorts. He had a well tanned face and he gave us a stern look, as though he was about to beat the crap out of us. His running vest was a souvenir t-shirt for the *Coniston 14* road race in 1998. I liked that he, along with the rest of the town (*North West in Bloom -*

2001), was hanging on to the memories of the glory days.

'Can I help you with anything, gentlemen?' he asked in a threatening manner.

'Sorry, we're just leaving. We're just trying to fill up these energy drinks,' said Ben.

'Oh, is that what it is?' he laughed. 'The ladies inside could see you on the CCTV and they thought you were doing something with drugs. They asked me to come and check up on you.'

'Oh no. Sorry. It's just Lucozade, I promise,' said Ben.

'No worries. It's just that being a school and all we have to check up on these things. I think they thought you were going to try dealing to the kids.' He stepped from the doorway and walked towards us with his arm outstretched and a warm smile on his face.

'The name's Mr Smiddy. I'm the head of PE. You can call me Martin.'

'Thanks, Mr Smiddy. I mean Martin. Sorry to be a nuisance, we'll be on our way,' I said.

'You take your time. No rush. So, they said you wanted to look in our lost property? What's the deal, are you homeless or something?'

'No, not quite. We're cycling the entire length of the country without spending any money, and I'm on the look out for a pair of shorts, instead of these suit trousers.'

'That sounds pretty crazy. How come you didn't just wear shorts from the start?'

'We didn't have anything at the start. Just a pair of boxer shorts. We didn't even have bikes,' said Ben.

'You're kidding?' he said. 'So you managed to blag all of this stuff from people along the way?'

'Yes.'

'That's amazing. You guys are mad.' He shook his head, unable to take it all in. 'I can sort you out with some shorts.

Come with me. We'll see what else we can find for you both. You guys crack me up.'

He led us down a few corridors and into the PE changing rooms. It was the first time I had been in a school changing room in ten years and it was pleasing to discover the familiar smell of sweat, mud and Lynx deodorant.

Mr Smiddy unlocked the store cupboard and rootled around inside. (Incidentally, the word 'rootle' doesn't get used enough these days). After he had finished rootling, he emerged with his arms full of clothing and other random items.

'The only shorts I've found are for kids and they won't fit you. But don't worry I'll sort you out with some. Is any of this of use?' he said, emptying the contents onto one of the benches.

Never before had two grown men been so excited at the sight of a pile of other people's neglected clothing. Mr Smiddy watched on with his arms folded, delighted to see our excitement.

'A belt. Amazing,' I said.

'Wow, a Frodsham School t-shirt. Looks kinda retro.'

'Here you go, Ben. Sunglasses. You've been complaining about getting flies in your eyes.'

'You are a legend, Mr Smiddy. Can we really have these?' asked Ben.

'Of course, help yourself to any of that. None of it has been claimed all year. I'll go and try and get you some shorts.'

Mr Smiddy (it seemed wrong calling a PE teacher by his first name, especially as we were in the school changing rooms), reappeared a few minutes later carrying a pair of the skimpiest running shorts I had ever seen. They were made from a silky blue material and were slit at the sides to allow full leg movement.

'Wow, thanks. Those look... errr... airy,' I said. 'Where did you get them from?'

'These are mine, but you're welcome to have them.'

'That's very kind, but I don't want to take your own clothes. I can try and get a pair of shorts from somewhere else.' I should point out that this was a different pair of shorts to the ones he was wearing. I don't want you to think he had whipped off his shorts in front of us there and then.

'Trust me, I think my kids would be delighted to see the back of these. Go on, try them on.'

'I think I'll have to try them on later. I'm... errr... going commando at the moment.'

'You haven't got any pants, either?'

'Well, we've got one pair each, but mine are airing at the moment.'

'Pah, you two are something else,' he snorted.

Frodsham was paradise compared to what we were faced with next. Shortly after leaving the town, we joined the horrendous Runcorn to Widnes road which is basically a motorway that it is legal to cycle along. More vehicles passed us over the next few miles than the entire rest of our journey combined. I didn't count them all, so I can't be sure of this fact, but I think it is extremely likely.

There was a hard shoulder which should have made things safer, but this was littered with car fragments and broken glass. We thought we were over the worst of it, but then we saw the intimidating sight of Runcorn Bridge. The bridge is officially called *The Silver Jubilee Bridge* in an attempt to make it sound picturesque and quaint. It's not. It's absolutely terrifying.

The bridge itself would look quite attractive, if they moved to a different part of the world, painted it a different colour and closed it to everyone but cyclists. It is, however, pale green, situated in the middle of a sprawling mass of industry and used by over 80,000 motorists a day.

The bridge was opened in 1961 to cross the River Mersey

and the Manchester Ship Canal. It is the only route across, although swimming did seem preferable. We arrived at the bridge at the peak of rush hour and pulled over to the side of the road to plan our attack.

The northbound side of the road, which we were on, had an extremely narrow strip of pavement, no more than a foot wide, which seemed to serve no purpose whatsoever. The Falcon would have been sleek and narrow enough to glide along this, but had Ben attempted to cycle along it on The Horse, his handlebars would have taken up half of the left hand lane, too.

Our route book mentioned a 'pedestrian walkway' on the opposite side of the bridge, which was just visible. It was a tantalisingly wide pavement protected from the road by a metal crash barrier. The only problem being that between us and it were four lanes of relentless traffic.

Remember the computer game Frogger? Well, attempting to cross this stretch of road, at rush hour, with our bikes would have been harder than the final level of Frogger. And we didn't have the luxury of having three lives. There was no choice but to stay on the side of the road that we were on, and just go for it.

'Right, after this one,' said Ben, half-aboard The Horse. 'No, no, wait, after this one… No hang on, ready? After this one.' And so it went until eventually we both bounded onto our bikes in perfect synchronised fashion.

What followed was about five of the scariest minutes of my life. The lanes of traffic on the bridge are so narrow that there is no room for cars to give cyclists any freedom. On two occasions Ben's handlebars were clipped by passing vehicles. We lost count of the number of angry drivers who beeped their horns at us as though we were a real nuisance to them. We kept our eyes focused firmly on the road ahead and cycled as fast as we could.

Once clear of the bridge, we were greeted with more views of picturesque chemical plants and car-wrecking yards.

After another ten miles, the route eventually left the A-roads and re-entered the countryside. We passed through the villages of Eccleston and Crank as the wind started to pick up, and the landscape became more undulating.

Not since Cornwall had we had to dismount from our bikes because of a hill, but shortly before the town of Skelmersdale, Ben admitted defeat. I took this as a welcome invitation to walk, too.

'It's my calf muscles. They're really aching today,' said Ben. 'What's your excuse?'

'I don't need an excuse. I just can't be bothered to cycle up this hill.'

'That doesn't sound like you. Normally you like to suffer.'

'Yeah, well we've suffered enough for the past few hours.'

On reaching the top, we pulled into a field and collapsed in the grass for a break. Surprisingly, it was one of the most scenic views of the entire trip. We had a sweeping cornfield directly below us, which led to more fields and then in the far distance the murky sprawl of Runcorn and Widnes. The distant hum of traffic and industry was overpowered by the chorus of birds, and during the 15 minutes we lay there, not a single car passed.

'I'm ready for bed,' said Ben.

'Me too.'

As if to taunt our bed-ready souls, the first building that we came across, just a few minutes later, was a very upmarket looking hotel – The Lancashire Manor Hotel.

'Thank you, God. Look, it's destiny,' said Ben, pulling over.

'It's a bit out of our league, isn't it? We've not stayed in anything like this so far.'

'Worth a try isn't it? They might have staff quarters or something that we can sleep in.'

The inside of the hotel didn't match up to the charm of the exterior, but it was still far superior to anything else we had stayed in. The reception was empty, but a lady appeared from the back room after we rang the bell, and we gave her our now well-rehearsed speech. I won't bore you with it again.

'I'm sorry, we can't offer you a room, I'm afraid. We can offer you a discount, but the hotel is part of a chain and we can't just give free rooms like that.'

'You don't have to tell them,' joked Ben. 'We'll even clean the room afterwards. You won't even know we'd been there.'

'I'm sorry. I can't help. We wouldn't be able to let you do any work either, I'm afraid. There are all sorts of health and safety and insurance implications.'

We could sense that she wanted to help, so decided to use our secret weapon; the pathetic, helpless faces that won over Mrs Rogers.

'I can't authorise anything myself, but I'll give my area manager a call and see what she says.' She scurried into the back office and then returned a few minutes later.

'My manager wants to know if the hotel will get any exposure or media coverage if we let you stay. I mean, are you writing a book about it or anything?'

'Yes, yes, of course. I'm going to write a book about it,' I blurted. 'And I'll be sure to say how great this hotel is.'

'Ok, great. I won't be a minute,' she said, returning to the office.

'I didn't know you were going to write a book,' said Ben.
'Neither did I.'

We were both laughing when she returned.

'Right. I've got you a room for the night. Breakfast is 7am til 11am in the morning. Dinner is served until 9pm. What time shall I book you a table for?'

'Dinner?' Ben said.

'Breakfast?' I said.

'Yes. You've got dinner and breakfast on us, too. Shall we say 8pm? That gives you an hour.'

'Wow. Thanks. Yes, 8pm is perfect. Thank you.'

'They better have a swimming pool,' joked Ben as we walked to our room.

'Look at us!' said Ben throwing himself onto one of the beds in our room. 'We've blagged a posh hotel.'

'Don't you feel a bit guilty about the fact that we only got it because they think they're going to get publicity out of it?' I asked.

'Nah, course not. They'll forget about us in a couple of days.'

'No, I don't mean guilty about deceiving them. I mean don't you feel guilty about the fact that it's the first time we've got something just on the basis that they thought there was something in it for them? We are supposed to be testing people's natural generosity but the hotel was only generous because it thought it was going to get publicity.'

'Yes, I suppose you're right,' said Ben. 'You're the one who said you were writing a book. She did want to help us, though. I mean, she was a nice person but just couldn't do anything because of the bureaucracy.'

'I know. Don't worry, I'll get over it. It just feels a bit like we cheated, that's all.'

'Oh my god, this shower is fucking amazing,' I shouted to Ben from the bathroom two minutes later. 'I bloody love hotels!'

It didn't take me long to get over the guilty feeling.

215

She need not have bothered booking us a table. We were the only people in the entire restaurant.

Dinner was very nice but slightly uncomfortable. It was strange enough having a formal meal sat opposite Ben, when our conversation on the bikes was usually based around who could do the loudest fart. It was also slightly odd having a waitress that clearly wanted to be anywhere other than serving us.

In the hotel bar afterwards, Jaime-Lea - the waitress - was a completely different person. The moment her shift finished, all of her bitterness and antipathy vanished and she was great fun to talk to.

'So is it true that you both don't have a penny between you, and you've got all this way scrounging off of people?' she asked.

'Basically. Yeah.'

'Fair play to ya,' she said after necking a third of her pint of lager. 'Suppose you could do with a fuckin beer then?'

'Aww, thanks, but you don't need to buy us drinks,' I said.

'I know I don't, but I wanna. Anyways, Gav behind the bar's had bugger all to do all evening. Might as well give him something to do.'

Like the restaurant, the bar was completely empty.

'Is it always like this around here?' I asked.

'Yeah, pretty much,' said Jaime-Lea. 'We have conferences and weddings here sometimes, but it's dead most of the time.'

She took another sip of her pint.

'Stupid place to build a hotel, if you ask me,' she muttered. Jaime-Lea bought us another two pints, and Gav the barman bought us a fourth. I'm not entirely sure that either of them were actually paying for the drinks, as we didn't see any money go into the till. Still, it's the thought that counts.

'Haven't you got a home to get back to?' Ben asked Jamie-Lea.

'Nah, I live in a flat above the hotel. There's no escaping this bloody place. I'm here 24/7, even on my days off.'

She was almost asleep on the bar by the time we staggered back down the corridor to our beds.

I take huge delight in staying in hotels. It doesn't happen very often, so when it does I am keen to make the most of my stay. I watch TV in bed, just because I can. I flick through all of the different satellite channels, because we only have the basic ones at home. I drink as many of the different teas and coffees as possible. I even drink the herbal teas and have been known to eat the sugar sachets just because they are there. I use the flannels. I wear a shower cap. I use bubble bath and moisturiser. I wash my hair with shampoo AND conditioner. I dry my hair with the hair dryer. I sometimes even read the Gideon Bible.

On this occasion, however, I ignored every single one of these luxuries and climbed straight into bed and went to sleep. Because of the nature of our bike ride, each night's accommodation was unknown until late into each evening. The quality of our lodgings became insignificant. All we needed was some shelter, and whether this came in the form of a cow shed, a canal boat or a guest house, we were still as thankful. Things were stripped back down to basics; a posh hotel was no longer a posh hotel, it was simply somewhere to sleep at night. During our stay at The Lancashire Manor Hotel, the TV wasn't even turned on, the shower cap and moisturisers stayed in their packets, the tea and coffee tray remained untouched, and the Gideon Bible remained in the bedside drawer.

Our canal boat, Ellesmere

Craig, Subway, Chester

Peter, Wales

Mr Smiddy, Frodsham

On the road to somewhere

Ben attempts to navigate

Day 11
Singing for sandwiches
Up Holland to Milnthorpe - 67 miles

Jaime-Lea was serving at breakfast and she had reverted back to her zombie-like work persona. She did manage a coy smirk as she brought us both a coffee, but didn't offer anything in the way of conversation.

I discovered that the Lancashire Manor Hotel closed down soon after our stay. Not because of us, I should add. It was a sad, yet somehow predictable end. How such a big hotel had survived in such a random location for so long was a surprise in itself. Here I am giving them the write up that I promised and it's now all worthless. Having said that, I haven't given it the most glowing of reviews; drunken waitresses, thieving bar staff, a deserted restaurant, and its proximity to Runcorn. I do hope that the staff all found jobs elsewhere, though, and that Jamie-Lea found somewhere else to live.

Mr Smiddy's shorts were outrageous. They were verging on obscene and barely legal. Unlike most running shorts, these didn't have any sort of lining and were slit all the way up to the waist on each side. This meant that a section of my Union Jack boxer shorts at the top of each thigh was on permanent display every time I moved my legs.

They were incredibly invigorating, though. I felt free. I felt liberated. I felt naked. Compared to the suit trousers, they were incredible. I could feel the air on my legs - as well as more intimate places. I suddenly felt more athletic, too, like I had been wearing the trousers pre-competition to keep warm, and now I had changed into my proper sporting gear. My legs instantly felt stronger, my body felt more energized and I was raring to go.

Soon after leaving the hotel we found ourselves hopelessly lost.

We had reached the village of Up Holland and it appeared that there was only one road out of the village, which we had taken. It turns out there is an alternative road that we missed. It was four miles and a long uphill walk before we realised this.

Ben and I blamed each other, and so hardly spoke for the entire morning. When we did speak, it was to gripe about the navigation.

'But I don't understand how you could miss out such a crucial direction on the route,' said Ben.

'Well you can do the navigating from now on if you like. Do you think I enjoy spending bloody ages copying out the route onto a stupid bit of paper each morning?'

Ben paused.

'There must be a better way. Can't we just get someone to photocopy the page of the route book for us each day, so that we've got the exact directions and you still don't need to carry the whole book whilst cycling,' he said.

It was worrying that it had taken eleven days for two seemingly intelligent men to think of this simple idea. It was so ingenious, yet such a glaringly obvious solution, that until now we had both failed to think of it. It was a revelation. It was the answer to all of our problems. I felt like a new man.

'I suppose we could give it a go, if you want,' I said to Ben, not wanting to show him any gratification.

We reached the town of Garstang and Ben successfully got a photocopy of the next few pages from a local estate agent.

'Sorry for being in such a foul mood this morning,' I said. 'I was just getting really frustrated with the navigating.'

'No worries. I know that you've been really good at doing it all. I do appreciate it. I'm happy to give it a go if you want.'

'Sure. Lead the way.'

Five minutes later...

'Oh, bollocks to this! I bloody hate navigating. I preferred it when you were in charge,' he said, handing me the directions back.

We had covered the length of Garstang high street three times, and Ben still couldn't decide which direction we should leave by.

The local Co-op gave us a huge bunch of semi-bruised bananas and we set off again with me navigating, a reformed friendship, and a potassium overload. We joined the busy A588 and followed it all the way into Lancaster town centre with the aim of doing a spot of sightseeing.

The tourist information was surprisingly busy for a weekday in September. It seemed to me that Lancaster was not an ideal place for a tourist to visit, but I was prepared to be persuaded otherwise.

'Well there's the castle,' said the helpful lady in the Tourist Information, 'that's well worth a visit, but it's closed today. There's something going on in the Crown Court, I think.'

'The castle has a Crown Court?' I asked.

'Oh yes. It's still a fully functioning prison, too. Or you could... let me think... you could go to the Maritime Museum. I've never been but I'm sure it's wonderful. Or there's the theatre, although there won't be anything on at this time of day. What else is there? There's the cathedral, that's nice. Or the Priory Church. There's so much you could see. Oh, I nearly forgot, there's the Lancaster Leisure Park.'

'The Leisure Park sounds good,' said Ben, having started to drift off to sleep during her other suggestions.

'Yes, it is. It's a shopping village with a big antiques centre. I think there's a children's play area there, too.'

'Perhaps the Leisure Park doesn't sound so great after all.'

Lancaster Castle is fairly impressive to look at, but because of the fact that parts of it are still used as both a prison and a court, access to visitors is very restricted and it is not possible to visit the towers, keep, battlements and dungeons. It seems a shame that it is only criminals and suspected criminals that get to enjoy Lancaster's best tourist attraction.

'Shall we give the Maritime Museum a go?' asked Ben once we were outside.

'Are you serious?'

'Of course I'm not. I can't think of anything I would rather do less. Lancaster's rubbish isn't it?'

'Yeah, it is a bit, although if someone came to Northampton Tourist Information, the best advice they would get is to go to the Shoe Museum.'

'I know. Northampton's even worse. That's why I moved to London.'

'The shoe museum's actually quite good, though. Have you ever been?'

'No. I'd rather visit Lancaster's Maritime Museum.'

We wheeled our bikes down into the city centre. On the way we passed a busker who was playing a badly tuned guitar accompanied by a badly tuned voice.

'Even the buskers in Lancaster are crap. We could sing better than that,' said Ben.

'Actually, that's not a bad idea. We could do some busking for our lunch.'

'Yeah, very funny.'

'I'm serious. Why not? We don't need instruments; we could just sing and get people to give us food instead of money.'

'You're serious aren't you?'

'Yeah, why not?' I said, becoming increasingly excited by the idea. 'What about Christmas carols? We both know the words.'

'It's September.'

'I know. We would be being proactive.'

'You're mad. Sounds fun to me, though. Let's do it.'

We found an empty cardboard box next to a dustbin and opened it out to form one large piece of card. Ben then managed to borrow a marker pen from a confused shop assistant and we set to work designing our sign.

We needed to make sure people understood that we didn't want money. As tempting as it was to busk for money and then spend it on whatever we wanted, we had made it clear from the outset that we wouldn't use money at all, even if it was given to us. We settled on the following:

WE DON'T NEED MONEY
WE JUST NEED FOOD

We scrawled our message onto the cardboard in big capital letters and propped our bikes by a fountain in a quaint cobbled square just off the main street. There were lots of people sat around on the edge of the fountain and the steps of an adjacent building. What was more important about the location of our 'patch' was that it was outside a branch of Greggs.

It had seemed like a fun idea when I suggested it, but when we were actually standing in the middle of Lancaster town centre about to launch into an a cappella version of *O Little Town of Bethlehem*, I realised I was incredibly nervous. I used to sing in a band and was quite happy to stand in front of hundreds (tens) of people and sing rock songs, but the thought of busking suddenly filled me with fear.

Ben didn't hold back. He launched into the first verse like a seasoned pro. I was astonished by his voice. His speaking voice is slightly squeaky and irritating, and I expected his singing to

223

be a melodic version of this. I could not have been more wrong. He sounded like a posh old man, with years of experience singing with a church choir. He sang with an affected baritone voice that took me completely by surprise. The tone and volume were phenomenal. I did my best to compete, but I was no match for him.

Neither of us knew what followed the line, 'the silent stars go by,' so we just repeated the first bit again. Everyone just stared at us in bemusement.

'Why are you singing Christmas carols in September?' asked a lady who approached us.

'We are helping people get into the Christmas spirit early,' said Ben.

'Well I'm a devout Christian and I find it very offensive that you are singing carols so early. You should both be ashamed of yourselves. It's considered very bad luck.' And with that she put her nose in the air, turned and strode off up the street.

'She wasn't very Christian for a Christian, was she?' I said.

'Miserable cow. How can this be causing offence?' asked Ben.

'Who cares? If there is a god then I doubt he would be offended about us singing some of his hits too early in the year.'

'His hits?'

'You know what I mean. Christmas carols are HIS songs aren't they?'

'Well, no, he didn't write them. Do you think he gets royalties every time people sing them?'

'No, but he should. He needs a better lawyer.'

One little girl, aged about four, started dancing right in front of us before her mum grabbed her by the arm and led her away muttering 'silly boys.'

Our persistence eventually paid off.

'Do you not have anything to eat?' asked a smiling middle-aged lady.

'No,' said Ben.

'Are you homeless?' she asked.

'Not exactly, no. I mean, we are for a few weeks. We're cycling to Scotland without spending any money.'

'Oh. Ok. What sort of sandwiches do you like?'

'That's very kind of you, but we're not expecting people to buy us sandwiches. We thought people might have food that they don't want or are going to throw away,' I said, secretly delighted by the prospect of a sandwich.

'Well I'm going into Greggs to get my lunch, and I'm happy to get you both a sandwich. What do you like?'

'Aww, thank you,' said Ben. 'We'll eat absolutely anything. Whatever's cheapest.'

She returned with two packs of sandwiches (one ham and one cheese, in case you were wondering) and a loaf of bread.

'There you go. They said you could have this loaf of bread, too, as they were going to throw it out.'

'Thank you,' I said, 'that's really kind. What's your name?'

'Susan,' she said. 'Well you both seem like a couple of really nice boys, and I definitely believe that niceness brings about niceness. Good luck with the rest of your journey.'

Before eating the sandwiches we tried a rendition of Silent Night in German that I could still remember from primary school. A guy on a bmx, in his mid thirties, approached with a small paper bag from Greggs.

'Hi guys. You can have these two donuts if you promise to stop singing.'

'You've got yourself a deal. Thanks, mate,' I said.

Toby, the BMX man, was a really interesting guy. He was on a half-hour break between his two different jobs. He worked in a factory in the morning, and a restaurant all afternoon and evening. He was trying to save money to convert a room in his house into a recording studio. Ben, being a musician with a home-studio, stood and talked for ages about mixers and 8-tracks, condenser mics and digital samplers. I stood nodding enthusiastically for as long as I could, before leaving them to it and skulking off to sit on the steps of the museum that lines one edge of the market square. Unfortunately, it wasn't the Maritime Museum, otherwise I would have been in like a shot.

Ben joined me after a while and we tucked into the sandwiches. We were soon approached by a strange looking teenager with a mess of bright blonde hair, school blazer, untucked shirt and a half-undone tie. He was about 17 and was flanked by a couple of giggling teenage girls. He stood there with a huge grin across his face and a carrier bag in his right hand.

'We were eavesdropping on your conversation a few minutes ago,' said the boy, with a slightly camp, posh northern accent. 'We've bought you a bag full of food and stuff, but there's a condition.'

'Errr... ok,' I said.

'You both have to sing *Take on Me*, by A-ha.'

'Are you serious? You want us to sing that here? Now?'

'Yes.'

'I only know the chorus,' said Ben.

'Me too. Nobody knows the words to the rest of the song. We'll just do the chorus. Is that ok? What's your name?'

'Bob. Think of the sweets,' he said, pulling his mobile phone from his pocket and pointing the camera towards us. 'I'm gonna stick this on YouTube.'

'Evil bastard,' muttered Ben.

The end of the chorus climaxed in an ear-piercing wail as though a large Alsatian had grabbed our balls in its teeth. A group of pigeons that had been scavenging on the ground nearby all took flight on hearing our pain. Passers-by winced as they hurried past. Bob however still grinned and pointed the phone at us.

'That was perfect. I think you've earned this,' he said, putting the phone back in his pocket and handing us the carrier bag. It was stuffed full of cookies, peanuts, chocolate bars, fizzy drinks, jelly sweets, crisps and extra-strong mints. This was one of the biggest single acts of generosity on our whole trip, and it had come from a scruffy teenager. Our challenge never failed to throw up surprises.

'I think you'd better give me those donuts back,' said Toby - the BMX bandit - who had reappeared as if by magic.

'Huh? Ok. Why's that?' asked Ben, handing him the bag of donuts.

'The deal was that you got the donuts if you stopped singing, and I just heard you singing.'

'Oh shit, sorry mate. We totally forgot. This guy came and bribed us with a big bag of sweets if we sang to him. I thought you just wanted us to stop singing Christmas carols?'

'I'm just fucking kidding, guys,' he laughed, handing back the donuts. 'I'm not going to take your donuts away. Anyway, I don't think what you were doing counted as singing. It was painful.'

'Are you guys homeless as well, then?' said a voice from further up the museum steps to our left.

We turned to see a man in his early twenties, wearing a pair of old tracksuit bottoms, and large grimy puffer jacket. His eyes were red and tired-looking and a patchy beard covered his weathered face. His chapped lips clung tightly to a small rolled up cigarette.

'No. We're not homeless,' I said, sheepishly, realising the significance of the use of 'as well' in his question. 'Well, we don't have anywhere to stay today, but we do have homes to go to. Are you guys homeless?'

His name was Paul and he had been living rough for three years, on and off. We explained all about our trip and why we were busking for food. He seemed genuinely amused by it all.

'You must think we're real idiots doing this trip when we've got homes to go to. I hope you're not offended by it?' I said.

'Offended? Nah, not at all mate. I think what you're doing sounds wicked, man. It sounds much more fun that a week in Butlins or summit. Anyway, if you have to sleep in barns and stuff like you have, then it will make you appreciate how lucky you are when you get back to your houses.'

'That is so true. And just meeting you makes us realise how lucky we are. We worry when we miss a meal or if it starts getting dark and we've got nowhere to stay. You have to go through that every single day.'

'Yep. We sure do.'

'What is Lancaster like for homeless people?' asked Ben.

'It's pretty good. That's why there's so many of us. These lot are all homeless, too,' he said, pointing to a group of about eight people towards the other side of the steps. 'I come from Manchester originally, but I needed to get out of there. A mate told me Lancaster had good hostels and shit, so I came here about a year and a half ago and I've been here since. There are a few different shelters and places to get food. In fact, you guys could stay tonight, I'm sure. There are usually a couple of spare beds.'

'That's really kind of you, but I think we'd feel like frauds if we took up a bed in a homeless shelter,' said Ben.

'Alright, suit yourselves,' he laughed.

'It's been really good to meet you and I hope things get sorted out for you soon. You seem like a really decent bloke,' said Ben.

'Yeah, you both are, too. Not many people sit and chat to us lot like you do. Fair play to you both. Good luck getting to Scotland.'

'We're never going to get all this food into our bags,' said Ben as we walked back to our bikes. 'Why don't we give some of it to those guys?'

'Good idea. They deserve it much more than we do. We can get food whenever we want just by singing *Take On Me*.'

We squashed a packet of cookies, dry-roasted peanuts, extra strong mints and the drinks into our rucksacks and took the carrier bag with the remaining crisps, cookies and sweets to Paul.

'Here you go, mate. We've not got room for all of this in our bags. We thought you all might be able to help us out,' I said.

His face lit up.

'Thanks, guys. Much obliged,' he said.

On our way out of Lancaster we passed a bike shop.

'Why don't you see if they can do anything to fix The Falcon here? It's getting ridiculous. The chain is falling off every few hundred metres,' said Ben.

'Fine. If it shuts you up for a bit longer.'

We wheeled it into the shop and the man agreed to take a quick look at The Falcon's chain.

'Nah, I can't fix that. You're going to need a new rear derailleur,' he said.

'Here we go again,' muttered Ben.

'Do you have any of those?'

'Nope, not for a bike like this. I could try to order one, but they're tough to get hold of and it would take several days to arrive.'

'Is there anything that can be done to it, to make it last a bit longer?'

'Nope. It's properly broken.'

'I think it's time to start looking for a new bike, George,' said Ben smugly.

'I don't think we've really got time to start hunting for a new bike today. Why don't we just keep going and if we see somewhere that looks like a possibility along the way we can stop,' I suggested, with no intention of stopping whatsoever.

'But we're in a big town now. Surely this is the best place to try?'

'Yeah, but I'd rather get going. The chain's not that bad.'

'IT FALLS OFF EVERY FUCKING MINUTE!' he shouted.

'But I'm the one that has to put it on. It only takes a few seconds. I'm not slowing you down so why does it bother you?'

'It bothers me that you're continuing to ride such a piece of shit when we could get a decent bike,' said Ben as he cycled off.

'It was hard enough to get these bikes. The Falcon has made it from Cornwall to Lancaster so it can't be doing too badly.'

I climbed onto The Falcon and pedalled after him. The chain fell off straight away.

'Keep going!' I shouted. 'I'll catch you up!'

The route followed the busy A6 for half a mile before turning onto minor roads through the pretty villages of Nether Kellet and Over Kellet. We reached the small market town of Milnthorpe at about 6pm. I was confused as to why some towns are described as 'market towns' when others don't boast about the fact that they have a market. I did some extensive research (Wikipedia) and it seems that the phrase is a legal term originating in medieval times, which gives a particular settlement the right to hold a market. It doesn't mean they have to. But they can if they want.

It was 6pm on a Tuesday and there was no sign of a market in Milnthorpe. But it could have had one, you know, if it wanted to.

We reached the main square, which was also presumably known as the 'market square', as it looked like the sort of open space that could host a market, should Milnthorpe decide it wanted one. The square was deserted apart from a group of five teenage Goths squashed onto a bench. They snarled at us as we approached. Actually, it was more of a harmless giggle, but a snarl seemed to suit their image better.

'Yo, dudes,' said Ben, trying to be cool, 'do you know of anywhere in town we could stay tonight... for free?'

They all smirked at each other. Sorry, I mean growled. They all growled at each other.

'No. Why? Are you tramps?' asked one of them.

'No. We're cycling to Scotland and we're not allowed to spend any money,' said Ben.

'That's messed up, man,' said one of Goths.

'Yeah man, totally,' said Ben, sounding totally uncool.

'Can we stay with any of you guys?' I asked hesitantly.

'Nah, man, my pad is too small,' said the head Goth.

'You mean your mum wouldn't let you,' said one of the girls. 'You don't have your own pad.'

'Yeah, whatever. Nor does none of you.'

'Alright, homies. Keep it real. Word to your mothers,' said Ben, turning to leave. As he did, he caught his leg on the pedal of The Horse and stumbled a few feet before becoming entangled in the bike's frame and falling head-over-heels onto the cobbled pavement. Just seconds before, he had tried to be all 'down with the kids' with a group of teenagers and then, right in front of them, he had managed to spectacularly fall whilst pushing his bike along a pavement. As Ben lay crumpled in a heap with his bike on top of him, I looked on, unable to breathe as I was laughing so hard. The Goths howled with laughter. I mean literally howled. Like werewolves. At the moon. That's what Goths do, right?

'Alright, cheers for helping me out,' said Ben sarcastically when he was back on his feet.

'Sorry, I couldn't breathe.'

'Yeah, well I'll remember that. Quick, let's get out of here.'

The Cross Keys Hotel was an imposing building that stands on the corner of the main crossroads in the town.

Ian the manager was unable to offer us a bed for the night, but said that we were welcome to pitch a tent in the car park, if we could find one. He also offered us a pizza each if we came back later.

About 20 metres down the road, a lady was cleaning her front windows. The house fronted directly onto the street so we had to walk around her to pass.

'Excuse me,' said Ben, 'this is going to sound like a really strange question, but I don't suppose you have a tent that we could borrow for the night?'

'You want to borrow a tent?' she asked.

'Yes, it's a long story, but basically Ian from the hotel up the road said that we can pitch a tent in his car park if we can get one.'

She paused.

'Well, I have got a tent, but how do I know that I'll get it back?'

'I can promise you that we'll take great care of it and return it to you first thing in the morning,' said Ben. She considered this for a moment.

'Ok then. I don't see why not. Wait there, I'll go and see if I can find it.' She went inside and returned a few minutes later with a tent, and her husband, whose job it was to stand in the doorway and look intimidating, in case we had any doubts about returning the tent.

'I need it back tomorrow by 8.30am. That's when I go out to work,' she said.

'You've got a deal. Thank you very much indeed.'

'Hi Ian. We've managed to get a tent. Is the offer of your car park still open?' I asked in the Cross Keys, five minutes later.

'Blimey, that was quick. Where did you get that?'

'From a lady just down the road. She was the first person we asked.'

'I'm very impressed. You guys are good. Yes, of course you can pitch your tent in the car park. If you don't mind, I would prefer it if you could wait until it gets dark. It might be a bit weird if you're putting a tent up while everyone is still arriving at the pub. I'll bring you a couple of pizzas when I get a minute.'

'Aren't you going to be a bit cold in the tent?' asked Ben.

'Why? Are you claiming the sleeping bag AGAIN? I haven't used it once yet.'

'You can use it if you want, but it smells of me now.'

'I don't care. I nearly froze to death at Mrs Rogers' house.'

'Fine. You can have it then. But I'm warning you, it may have a few sticky patches in it,' he laughed.

'Oh, you're a sick fucker. Keep the bloody sleeping bag. I'm going to go and ask at that other pub across the road if they've got a blanket or something I can borrow.'

The pub across the road could not have been more

different. It looked exactly the same as it would have done in the 1950s; lots of brass, very few lights, and - judging by the three old men at the bar - probably the same occupants.

'I've got a duvet you can borrow,' said Chris, the man behind the bar. He was in his mid-thirties with spiked hair, pierced ears and a fluorescent shirt, straight from a 1980s disco.

'That would be perfect. Thank you. I'll drop it back in the morning if that's ok,' I said.

'You're welcome,' he said, pushing me in the shoulder in a flirtatious way. 'If you need anyone to keep you warm in the night, you know where to come.' The men at the bar laughed.

'Thanks, but I'm already sharing the tent with another man.'

'Even better. Threesome!' he laughed.

'I think I'd better sleep with one eye open tonight with you just across the road.'

'You'd better believe it,' he said with a wink.

When it was dark we started to put up the tent. I am rubbish at putting up tents. Even in daylight. There is only one person in the world worse at putting up tents than me, and unfortunately he happened to be in the pub car park with me. In darkness, we were completely incompetent.

Ben and I came very close to strangling each other during the tent's erection. Let me rephrase that, as it sounds like a sadomasochistic version of *Brokeback Mountain*. We came very close to strangling each other during the course of putting up the tent. There, that's better.

'What are you doing?' screamed Ben.

'I'm putting pegs in. What does it look like?'

'Don't bother pegging the inner bit. Just peg the flysheet.'

'But then the flysheet and the inner will touch and we'll get wet.'

234

'Bollocks. That's an urban myth.'

'No it's not! It's a fact. I've been in plenty of tents that have leaked.'

'That's because you're so shit at putting them up.'

'Why are you being so miserly with the pegs?'

'There's no point in using pegs for the sake of it.'

'Ok,' I said, and then pegged the inner tent anyway, whilst he was struggling to undo the zip.

After about 45 minutes, we had muddled the tent into some form of basic shelter. Thankfully there was no wind, and rain seemed unlikely. I had tried to attach the guy ropes just in case, but Ben had snatched them away saying, 'there's no way are we having guy ropes. Guy ropes are for gays. They should be called gay ropes.'

I will never get bored of the excitement of climbing into a tent. It is one of those moments that bring about extreme feelings of excitement and nostalgia. In the pitch black, we fumbled our sleeping bags, duvet and possessions into some sort of order and lay down to go to sleep.

Lancashire, obviously

Suzie, Lancashire Manor Hotel

Ian, Cross Keys Hotel, Milnthorpe

Garstang

Ben gets a photocopy of the route book

Day 12
The hitman
Milnthorpe to Carlisle - 50 miles

We awoke to the sound of drilling.

'What the hell is that noise?' asked Ben.

I undid the zip and poked my head out of the tent. Four workmen were drilling into the tarmac of the car park less than three metres from the tent. The guy with the drill acknowledged me with a raise of the eyebrows but carried on with his work.

'Some workmen are drilling just outside the tent,' I said to Ben.

'It feels like my head is going to explode.' It was all quite surreal. We went to sleep in a tent, in a pub car park and woke up in the middle of a building site.

'How did you sleep?' I asked.

'Brilliant. Didn't wake up once. How about you?'

'Not great. I had to fold the duvet in half so that I wasn't sleeping on the tent floor but then my feet poked out the bottom.'

'Oh well, you should've swapped for the sleeping bag. If you were given a four-poster bed and a feather duvet, you'd still whinge about how badly you slept.'

We took the tent down in record time and squashed it back into the bag, just as it began to rain. *There's nothing worse than a wet tent,'* or so my dad claims.

Ben returned the tent to the lady down the road, whilst I returned the duvet to my admirer in the neighbouring pub. Thankfully, he was still asleep upstairs when I called, so I left it with a lady who was cleaning the bar.

237

We then went to retrieve our bikes and say thanks to Ian.

'Why don't you both come in and have some breakfast in the hotel?' he asked as he unlocked the cupboard that housed our bikes. 'Just go and get a table whenever you're ready. Order whatever you want off the menu and tell whoever serves you that it's been cleared with me.'

We felt more than a little bit out of place in the hotel restaurant. The tables were full of well-dressed elderly couples preparing for a day's tour of the Lake District. We were sat at a table in the corner, unwashed and unshaven, wearing the same clothes we had been wearing for 11 days.

'What can I get you?' asked the waitress.

'I'll have the Full English, please,' said Ben.

'I think I'll go for the kipper and poached egg please,' I said.

'Kipper and poached egg? What the fuck?' questioned Ben when she had left.

'I just thought I would go for something a bit different. We've eaten so much crap this trip I don't think I could handle another fry-up.'

'You'll regret it. I'm not going to give you any of mine.'

Sure enough, I regretted it deeply.

For some reason, I half expected Ben to be the envious one, but it turned out there was no competition. For some reason I thought that *'Kipper with Poached Egg'* would be more than just a kipper with a poached egg. I don't know what I was expecting. Maybe two kippers. Or perhaps three. What is the collective noun for kippers? Anyway, I was given a kipper and a poached egg. Just like it said. It was very tasty, but I have never felt greater envy than I did at the sight of the plate of steaming greasy bacon, sausage, beans, fried bread, hash browns, mushrooms, tomato, egg and black pudding that Ben was served. I came close to crying.

Thirty seconds later I had eaten mine, and I then had to sit and watch Ben orgasm over his Full English. Not literally, of course. That would have been revolting.

We set off on our bikes, just before 9am, at the peak of rush hour. Rush hour in Milnthorpe consisted of an old lady on her way to the greengrocers, and a farmer tightening the straps on his trailer. Imagine how busy it gets if Milnthorpe decides to have a market. Because it can if it wants, you know.

Milnthorpe sits right on the edge of the Lake District. As soon as the buzz of that small 'market town' had faded, we were surrounded on all sides by *'the loveliest spot man hath never found,'* according to William Wordsworth.

It felt like we were on holiday. Technically, we *were* on Day 12 of our holiday, but this was the first time that we truly felt it.

For the next 15 miles we saw no more than half a dozen cars. The rain had stopped, but the air was still damp with thick low-lying cloud. It made the scenery look even more spectacular. Dry stone walls weaved their way across fields before being swallowed up by the mist. Eerie derelict stone barns were partly visible, and sheep moved like ghosts across the hillside.

There is also something poignant in the fact that much of what makes the Lake District so beautiful is man-made. I don't mean the sheep and the clouds - I'm pretty sure man didn't make those. I mean the stunning dry stone walls, the derelict barns, and the picture postcard villages that punctuate the area. The landscape itself is obviously spectacular, but it is man's additions that really give it its character.

We passed through the villages of Brigsteer and Underbarrow which seemed to both be asleep. I paused momentarily to look at the directions.

'Why do you have to keep stopping to check we're going the right way?' asked Ben. 'There is only one road in the Lake District and we are on it.'

'If there is only one road, then how come we are at a junction?'

'That road up there doesn't count. That's someone's drive. It's got to be down this way.' He set off down the hill through the village and I folded up the directions and followed him without double checking.

'This doesn't seem right, Ben,' I said, a few minutes later.

'You hate it when I'm in charge don't you?'

'Well, yes. Especially when I'm the one with the directions and your sense of direction has been proven to be shit.'

'That's not true. I've got a great sense of direction.'

'Yeah, you're like a homing pigeon,' I said sarcastically.

'Well you're like a homo pigeon.'

I studied the route.

'You know that road that you said was someone's driveway?'

'Yep.'

'Well according to this, that's the road we wanted.'

We trudged back up the hill in silence and then took the correct road.

Our route book warned us about a hill after Underbarrow that would 'probably require dismounting'. Well, not for two finely tuned athletes like us. We cruised up without even breaking sweat.

Actually, Ben had said that there was 'no way The Falcon was going to make it up the hill,' which made it the most important challenge I had ever faced. Ben was then forced to respond by powering The Horse up, too. We collapsed in a heap at the top, sweaty and exhausted.

The next three miles were all downhill into the town of Bowness-on-Windermere, which sits, unsurprisingly, on the banks of Lake Windermere – England's largest lake.

After 15 miles cycling through the quaint country lanes, Windermere was a big shock to the system. It looked pretty – from a distance – but was fairly horrible. The pavements were crawling with coach parties visiting the overpriced shops, buying overpriced tat, and filling their faces with overpriced food. The roads were congested with through-traffic, tourists and coaches.

We found a spot of grass near to a tacky kiosk selling ice-creams and souvenirs. Ben spotted an outside tap by the kiosk and went to fill up our water bottles.

'UH, EXCUSE ME! You can't use that tap. It's for customers only,' shouted a voice through the kiosk's hatch.

'Oh, sorry. We're just filling up a couple of drinking bottles. Is that ok?'

'No. They're for customers only. Are you planning on buying anything?'

'Sorry, we don't have any money.'

'No tap then,' he said.

Soon after leaving Windermere we saw a sign warning us of something that we had been dreading since getting hold of our route book: Kirkstone Pass.

The route that our book detailed took us over Kirkstone Pass, which is the highest mountain pass in England and would be the *toughest climb of the tour*. The road gains 1,300 ft in six gruelling miles, and promised to be unlike anything we had ever attempted.

In reality, it wasn't too bad. By this, I mean that we didn't have to get off and walk at any stage. We did, however, swiftly remove our t-shirts after the first half-mile struggle. A well timed break after about four miles broke up the journey nicely, too. We sat against a stone wall at the side of the road and ate our lunch.

Using the stale bread that the lady had given us in Lancaster and the bags of crisps from Bob – the student - we built two epic crisp sandwiches each.

The final two miles passed without any incident, and on reaching Kirkstone Inn – which marks the top of the pass – we had to ask someone if we were actually at the top.

We stopped to take in the view, which was stunning in every direction. The road behind us snaked its way back down the valley towards Lake Windermere, and then beyond us in the direction of Scotland. The sun was out and the visibility was excellent. It is apparently common for End to Enders to reach Kirkstone Pass and not be able to see anything because of fog.

We could see a lake at the bottom of the valley in the direction we were heading and it taunted us with its shimmering, cool, refreshing quality. Hot, sweaty, dehydrated and on the top of a mountain, the scenery was suddenly of little interest. We were in desperate need of a swim.

The descent from Kirkstone Pass was undoubtedly the fastest I have ever been on a bike. It was possibly the fastest that man has ever travelled, in any form of transport.

If The Falcon had had wings, I swear she would have taken off. It was one of the scariest, but most exhilarating things I have ever done. Braking wasn't really an option for me, as The Falcon's brakes only had any slight effect when travelling at a ridiculously slow speed, or uphill. I just gave in and let The Falcon do what she was best at doing - not stopping.

There was surprisingly little traffic in either direction, which meant that we were able to take the 'racing line' through the many twisting bends. Cars would be unlikely to reach such speeds on such a winding downhill stretch, so it meant that we didn't have to contend with any cars trying to overtake us. I flew past Ben, who swerved and nearly had a heart attack when he saw me pass.

The road slowly levelled out at the bottom of the valley, and I steered The Falcon up a grass verge to come to a stop. It was at least ten seconds before Ben reached me.

'How the hell did you go so much faster than me?'

'I told you. The Falcon is an elite racing bike.'

'No, you're on a crappy child's bike. I didn't brake once down there yet you still flew past me.'

'Never underestimate The Falcon.'

'It's because of your weight advantage,' said Ben.

'What do you mean?'

'Well, you're fatter so you get more momentum down the hills.'

'Shut up. You're just slow because the massive knob on your head creates lots of wind resistance.'

'Well your man boobs flap around like aeroplane propellers giving you extra speed.'

Conversations between Ben and me were rarely more mature than this. We did once have a discussion about politics, but it was based around the unlikely scenario that we had to shag either John Prescott or Margaret Thatcher in order to save the human race. We both reluctantly agreed on Maggie.

We reached the village of Glenridding at about 3pm. We referred to it as 'Glen-rid-a-ding-ding' because we thought it was amusing. Looking back, it is less so now.

Glen-rid-a-ding-ding is a little village on the edge of Ullswater – the second largest lake in the Lake District. Many people consider Ullswater to be the most beautiful of the lakes, and Wordsworth described it as, *'the happiest combination of beauty and grandeur, which any of the lakes affords.'*

As well as the lure of Ullswater, Glen-rid-a-ding-ding (maybe it will get funnier if I repeat it) is also a popular base for hikers, as it sits at the bottom of one of the popular routes up Helvellyn – England's third highest peak, behind Scafell and Scafell Pike.

The village (Glen-rid-a-ding-ding, that is) was a pleasant mixture of traditional buildings and modern convenience, with an outdoor store, gift shop and a tourist information.

We parked up on a patch of grass just beyond the village, and stripped down to our boxer shorts. We then waded into the water up to our waists. It was ball-clenchingly cold. Within nanoseconds my testicles had retreated up inside of me and my Glen-rid-a-ding-ding had shrivelled to the size of a cigarette butt. I squealed like a girl.

'Looks nice in there?' said an elderly lady who was walking along the bank with her husband.

'It's... ah... ah... certainly... ah... ah... refreshing,' said Ben.

'You should join us,' I said.

'Maybe next time,' she laughed.

The Glenridding Mini-Market was an unbelievable shop. It was packed to the ceiling with everything that you could ever want to buy, and plenty of stuff that you would never want to buy.

'We get some odd-bods in this shop, but we've never had people doing what you're doing?' said the lady behind the counter, after we told her our story.

Her name was Avril and she looked like she was born to run a village shop. I don't mean that in a belittling way. She just looked like exactly the sort of person that you would want to buy your daily paper or provisions from; a warm and friendly smile, a calming relaxed manner and all the patience in the world to stand and listen to two scruffy young men beg for food from her. She was like a younger Mrs Goggins from *Postman Pat*.

'Would you like one of these pies? I'm unlikely to sell many more of these, as it's getting late in the day. We've got a large chicken pie here... this one's a steak pie... and that one is apple.'

'That's very generous of you,' said Ben. 'Which one shall we have, George?'

'Oh go on, take all three,' she said. 'I'm sure you'll find room for them.'

It was nearly 6pm by the time that we left Ullswater.

'Where are we going to stay tonight?' asked Ben.

'Not sure,' I said, taking a look at the route book. 'We've only done about 25 miles today so it would be good to try and do as much as we can in the time that's left.'

'But it'll be dark in an hour.'

'Looking at this, it seems that there's nothing between us and Carlisle, which is another 25 miles away.'

'Carlisle? But that's in Scotland isn't it.'

'No,' I said confidently, only because I had the book in front of me and was able to check. 'Not quite. I think it might have been part of Scotland once, maybe.'

'We'll never do another 25 miles today. Especially with these bastard hills.'

'According to the book, there's a short section of uphill coming up, and then it's downhill the entire way. Let's give it a go.'

'Alright, but I don't want to end up having to sleep in a bloody field tonight.'

The route left the Lake District and followed back roads through the villages of Greystoke, Little Blencow and Hutton-in-the-Forest, tracing parallel to the M6. The route book had not lied; it was downhill the entire way and it made us feel like

245

proper cyclists for the first time. Well, it would have done, had I not had to stop every few minutes to reattach The Falcon's chain.

It was dark by the time we reached Carlisle.

'Bloody hell. Why did the English fight for this place? The Scots can have it back if they want?' said Ben.

'Yeah, it does look like a bit of a dump, but maybe we've just come in on its worst side.'

Within the first five minutes of arriving in Carlisle, we had been told we were 'a couple of fookin bike poofs', were asked if we wanted to buy any acid, and then preached to by a born-again Christian. This was three separate incidents, by the way, not just one lunatic with his finger in many pies.

We did a few laps of the town centre on our bikes to try and get some inspiration of where to try for accommodation. Carlisle was by far the biggest town we had tried to stay in, and we didn't really know where to start.

At the top end of town we walked past an extremely posh looking hotel called the Crown and Mitre. It was so posh that it had a doorman. I have never stayed in a hotel with a doorman.

'Excuse me. Is it ok if we take our bikes into the lobby?' Ben asked the doorman. He stared back at Ben with a look that didn't say no, but didn't say yes.

'Or would you mind just keeping an eye on them for a couple of minutes if we left them outside?'

He continued the same stare and didn't say a word. We wheeled them up the steps and into the swanky foyer.

The receptionist looked up from her computer with the automated smile that she would greet all guests with, but this soon dropped and her eyebrows raised with a look that said, 'how did you get past security?' Ben gave her our spiel.

'No, we won't be able to help you, I'm afraid,' she said, before he had finished.

'Oh, ok. Would it be possible to speak to the manager at all, just to check?'

Her face didn't alter. 'No, I don't think so.'

'Why did she look at us like that?' asked Ben when we were outside.

'I guess because we look like a couple of tramps.'

'Yeah, but we could've been millionaires, for all she knew.'

'But we look like a couple of tramps, and we were asking for a free room.'

'True. But, even so.'

We tried another hotel – The County Hotel – and got a similar response, albeit this time with a smile. The receptionist was working alone and had no authority to offer a complimentary room without a manager's consent. Unlike at the Crown and Mitre, it was clear that if she could have helped, she would.

We then tried the Ibis on Botchergate, which seemed to be Carlisle's main commercial street. The receptionist was stunning; blonde, Swedish (probably) and had a name that neither of us could even attempt to pronounce. The more we looked at her name badge, the more it seemed that we were staring at her breasts. She thought the whole idea of our challenge was hysterical, and kept asking to hear more details about it.

'So you slept in a barn with a bull?' she asked in perfect English but with a hint of Scandinavian sexiness. 'You guys are hilaaaaarious.'

'Do you think you might be able to help us with anywhere to stay tonight? We don't even need a room. We could sleep in the cleaning cupboard,' I said.

'Hold on, I'll check for you.'

'The manager says the best he can do is £30 for the two of you,' she said. 'The normal price would be about £60 so this is a very good deal.'

'Thank you,' I said 'That does sound like a very good deal. Unfortunately, we don't have any money at all. We're not allowed to spend a single penny.'

'Hold on. I will try him one more time.'

A few minutes later, she returned.

'He said he could offer you both a room for £11. This is the staff rate, I think, with an extra discount added.'

Ben and I looked at each other with the same feeling of helplessness. We were being offered a room in a bright, clean, comfy, fresh hotel with hot showers, big beds, and no workmen drilling metres from our heads, for just £11.

We said farewell to the Swedish beauty, and she waved us off and wished us good luck.

It was 9.30pm and we were still standing in Carlisle town centre. It began to rain.

'Eleven sodding pounds. We were so close. We could be having a bath in our hotel room by now,' said Ben. 'I feel like I could cry. I love the Ibis.'

'I would rather be standing out here in the rain, than having a bath with you,' I said.

'I didn't mean together, you bellend. What's the plan now?'

'How about we go to a pub and just ask people if we can go and stay at theirs?'

'It doesn't look like we have many other options.'

Walkabout is a chain of Australian themed bars. Not just any old Australian themed bars, they are OFFICIALLY the coolest Australian themed bars this side of the planet. Well, that's according to their website anyway. I'm not sure that I've ever been to an Australian bar in Britain that was not a Walkabout, so the competition isn't huge.

There were picnic tables outside the front of the pub, and a few groups of people were sat under parasols in the rain watching Manchester United play a Champions League game on a screen through the doorway. We surveyed the groups of people and decided on our plan of attack. We headed towards a group of lads who looked like students.

We asked if any of them would be willing to put us up for the night, but nobody was forthcoming. We tried the same approach at another table of guys who were too absorbed in the football to even acknowledge that we were speaking to them.

'Yous can sleep at mah hoose,' said a Scottish voice from the other end of the table. We turned to see a man in his early seventies, with tightly cropped grey hair, a badly rolled cigarette hanging from his mouth and a woollen jumper that looked like it had been knitted by someone with severe colour-blindness. His eyes were wild and piercing. They were magnified by a pair of badly sellotaped glasses that made him look genuinely terrifying. I doubt he had ever lost a staring competition in his life.

'Really? Ok, great. Thanks. That's very kind of you,' I said, looking at Ben for some sign of acknowledgement.

'Thanks, that's really good of you. But we really don't want to put you out,' said Ben.

'Aye, it's nae bother. Yous both need somewhere to sleep. I have space. It's th' leest ah can dae. Nae bother,' he said, knocking back the shot of whisky that sat next to his half-finished pint of Guinness.

'But we might be a pair of serial killers,' joked Ben.

'That's awe rite. I'm a serial killer tay,' he said flashing us a glance that made Hannibal Lecter look like a teddy bear. He then burst out laughing and we laughed, too, although somewhat less convincingly.

'The name is Mick. Here, go get yerselfs a wee drink,' he said, handing over a £10 note.

'That's very generous of you, but we're ok,' I said.

'C'mon ya pussies. I insist. Get me another pint, too.'

'This is going to sound really stupid,' I said, 'but we're on this challenge to cycle the length of the country without spending any money.'

'Uh huh,' said the man. 'Aam askin' you ta spend mah money.'

'I know, I know, but part of the deal is that we're not allowed to use money at all – even other people's money.'

'Ah for fuck sake,' he said, grabbing the arm of a guy sat watching the football. 'Go and get these wee lads a fecking drink. And one for me and yous, too.' He fumbled in his pocket and handed the guy £20 instead.

The young student didn't know what to say. He was just being ordered to go and buy drinks by a drunk Scottish man. You could see him weighing it up in his head, and then it suddenly clicked that he was getting a free drink.

'Alright. What will it be then?' he said.

'Two pints of Guinness please,' I said.

'Ack, that's more like it,' said Mick. 'Yous gotta stop being such southern nancies.'

What followed was, without exception, the strangest night of my life.

We sat talking to Mick on the bench outside Walkabout for another hour. During that time, he sent the young lad at the end of the bench to buy another round. It transpired that Mick had been an alcoholic for many years. He had managed to stay 'dry' for five months up until the day we met him. That morning he had been to the doctor to receive the results of some tests. He was told that the cancer that he was being treated for had spread throughout his body. Mick then arrived at Walkabout just as it was opening, and had been there ever since. Ten hours of solid drinking had caused his words to slur slightly, but it hadn't hampered his energy or his memory.

'Aam the greatest living English-speaking poet in th' world today,' he declared.

'You're a poet?' I asked.

'Ah huh.'

'Cool,' and before I even had a chance to ask him, he launched into a recital. Much to the annoyance of the other drinkers.

'This one's called The Gargoyle,' he said.

The Gargoyle
Has wings…of stone
He's alone and feeling
All those things
No mortal creature knows
The clothes, of dreams
He shows
As though to seem to mean to see.
Belief – in fantasy – be fact
And acting out its part
The rain
Wears out his tears
With deadly animosity
Yet he succeeds to be
Totality
And passes, temporary
Man.

I was genuinely speechless. I don't know why, but I had

expected his poetry to be, well, shit. I didn't fully understand the poem the first time I heard it – I'm still not sure I do - but the way he recited it from memory with his prominent Scottish accent, intense stare and perfectly measured delivery was incredibly captivating.

Mick then took us to the pub across the road, and we took a seat by the window so that we could keep an eye on our bikes that we had pretend-locked to a lamp post just outside. The place was huge, but almost empty, apart from a group of about 15 blokes standing on an otherwise deserted dance floor. The music was so loud that Mick's Scottish accent became even more difficult to understand. He bought us both a shot of whisky and another pint, and also ordered us a burger and chips each, without us having time to protest.

The more he drank, the more he opened up about himself to us. He told us that he was gay, but had never disclosed this to anyone throughout his life, nor had any sort of relationship with anyone.

'When ah was yoong you could be pit in jail for being a buftie like me,' he said. 'Ye ken whit aam sayin? Aw mah life I've hud tae pretend aam somethin' aam nae.'

He talked a lot about 'God's will', too, and he gave us the impression that he was ashamed of his homosexuality, and felt that he had betrayed God.

'Ah dornt fancy either ay ye, by th' way,' he said, necking his whisky.

'Why not?' asked Ben, slightly offended. 'What's wrong with us?'

'Well you ah not my type, and his legs ah too hairy,' he said pointing to my exposed white thighs.

'I've killed people,' he then said a while later. 'I've killed lots of people.'

This was a conversation-stopper like no other.

'It was mah job,' he said after a long pause. 'Aam nae proud 'bout whit ah did.'

'What do you mean it was your job?' I asked hesitantly.

'Ah worked fur th' british government killin' terrorists. IRA mostly.'

'Surely that's an admirable job?' said Ben.

'Aye, you would think so, wooldnae ye? All mah life I've hud aw thes guilt inside me abit th' things I've dain an' th' things I've seen. I've never talked aboot this tae anyone before. Aam nae supposed tae. But after whit happened at th' doctor's this morn, ah cooldnae give a fuck anymore.'

He told us more about the places he had lived and the things he had done. At one point he started talking in Russian – a requirement for one of his missions, apparently. Ben and I were both totally gripped by his stories. We had met some interesting characters on our trip, but Mick was in a league of his own.

We were then faced with the moment of having to go back and sleep at his house. We suddenly longed for the easy, unthreatening nature of the other people that we had stayed with - Monica in Ludlow, or David and Annie in Nanstallon – rather than facing the uncertainty of a night with Mick.

He led the way back to his house which was a 15 minute walk from the pub. He was staggering all over the pavement and occasionally had to hold onto a wall or lamppost to regain his balance. Despite his age, and poor dress sense, he looked fairly fit and had a powerful athletic build.

'Are you sure this is a good idea?' whispered Ben.

'Yeah, we'll be fine,' I said, not entirely convinced.

'I'm absolutely shitting myself. We're going back to sleep on the floor at a trained killer's house, who is absolutely shitfaced. Are we insane?'

'When you put it that way, it does sound a bit stupid, but he seems like a genuinely nice bloke who just wants to help us out. What's the worst that can happen?'

'Errr, that we get bummed or killed, or both,' said Ben.

Mick lived in a small council flat on the edge of Carlisle. It had not been decorated since the 1960s. Either that or Mick was into retro-styling in a big way. A few meagre possessions dotted his front room; library books, a radio, an overflowing ashtray, and, somewhat surprisingly, a windowsill full of seedlings.

'If ye move those chairs outta th'way ye can sleep on the floor,' he said. He disappeared into the kitchen and emerged with a bottle of whisky and three glasses. 'Time for a wee dram before bed?'

This was more of a statement than a question, as despite our polite declines we were both given a huge neat whisky. Ben sipped at his like a connoisseur, and I downed mine in the hope that it would make me sleep better. Mick slumped into his armchair and seconds later he was asleep.

'Shit! What do we do now?' asked Ben.

'I don't know. We can't just go to sleep with him sat there can we?'

'No. But I'm not going to try and wake him and put him into bed. Are you?'

'No way.'

'I'm so glad I've got the sleeping bag. At least if he wakes up you'll be the easier one to attack,' said Ben.

'Stop boasting about your bloody sleeping bag. Besides, if he wakes up in the night and tries to rape or murder us at least I'll be able to make a quick getaway whereas you'll be hopping round the room like you're in a sack race.'

We both started laughing at the thought, but then stopped quickly when Mick started fidgeting. Mick asleep was far less terrifying than Mick awake.

Ben climbed into his sleeping bag and I covered my legs with my towel and we lay on the floor longing for the morning.

We had been quiet for about ten minutes when I decided to release a fart. Now, I'm a fairly prolific farter – I would even go as far as saying that I'm a master – but this was like nothing I had ever done before. It lasted for about ten seconds and the vibrations of it rumbled through the floorboards, echoing round the entire room. We looked over towards Mick who shuffled in his chair, sat forward, opened his eyes briefly, and then went back to sleep.

Ben almost wet himself with laughter and I had to put my fist in my mouth to stop myself shrieking. It was just what we needed to break the tension.

'Holy shit,' said Ben, 'we're sleeping next to a drunken killer and you go and let out something like that. I've never heard anything like that before.'

'It was definitely one of my best. I think it's a combination of the Guinness, the burger and the fear.'

It's fair to say it was not one of my best night's sleep.

I drifted in and out of consciousness, kept awake by the presence of Mick slumped in his chair a few feet away. He would swear loudly at himself at regular intervals throughout the night – seemingly in his sleep.

At some point in the early hours of the morning, Mick heaved himself up from the chair and staggered down the corridor to what we presumed was his bedroom. Ben then pushed the sitting room door closed behind him, so that we would at least get some sort of warning when he returned.

The temperature dropped considerably and the wind and rain battered the flimsy council flat windows. I put on my suit trousers but they did little to keep me warm. Ben lay smugly next to me in his sleeping bag.

255

Me and The Falcon, Kirkstone Pass

Ben before the ascent of Kirkstone Pass

Ben, halfway up Kirkstone Pass

The Falcon

The road up Kirkstone Pass, from Ullswater

Day 13
Welcome to Scotland
Carlisle to Dumfries - 39 miles

'Guid mornin', campers,' said Mick as he burst through the door. He stood in the doorway bouncing around on his toes shadow boxing. He was full of energy and enthusiasm, and was clearly not feeling any after effects from the previous day's drinking.

'Ah heard voices comin' frae in here an' it took me a wee while tae remember ah hud brooght ye home.'

'Yeah, it took us a while to remember where we were, too,' I said.

'What did ah tell ye mah name was?' he asked.

'Mick,' said Ben.

'Ach, noo. Ah say 'at tae fowk ah dunnae kinn. Mah real name is Ronnie.'

Ronnie offered us breakfast but then discovered he didn't have any food in the house. Instead he made us a coffee and topped them up with the remainder of the whisky. He then sat back in his arm chair and spent an hour retelling most of the stories about his life that he had told us the night before. Neither Ronnie nor his flat seemed quite so daunting in the daytime.

From his sitting room window, you could see into the back garden which was shared with a row of six other flats. Ronnie, it transpired, was the designated head gardener.

'Nobody else aroond here gi'es a jobby abit plants,' he said.

He had done a brilliant job. It wasn't going to win any awards at Chelsea, but you could tell he had put a lot of time and effort into the garden. It was fascinating to witness the two extreme sides to Ronnie's personality. Part of him was an angry, bitter, cynical, former killer. The other part was a generous, thoughtful, kind, nature-loving old man.

Shortly after completing the trip (damn it, I've spoilt the ending again), he sent me a lovely long letter saying how much he had enjoyed us both staying with him, and to thank me for some audio books that I had sent him. He enclosed a couple of poems – including a new one, which he said he wrote about me.

Out of your eyes
The love of life appears
Seeking liberty to feel
The actual, the real.
Your solitude absorbs
So gladly…
Knowing and yet unknowing me
I've no need to explain
The want of wanting
The haunting of you shall be me
And love completely
But teardrops on the windowpane
Of experience this is youth.
And I passing through your life
Hope to stain that glass… with truth.
And leave it with you.

When I tell people of our experience with Ronnie, I admit that his stories do sound far-fetched. Out of all the people in Carlisle, we happened to end up with a drunken hitman, who was in his final weeks of life. Most people laugh and say that it sounds like a load of bullshit. Ronnie's story, that is, not my version of events.

I don't consider myself a very gullible person. In fact, I tend to be very suspicious of people. Especially those that I don't know. But in Ronnie's case I never doubted anything he said. Looking back, this seems a little naïve.

I have been told on a couple of occasions since, that it is a classic sign of senility, that people will have delusions about a fabricated heroic past. In a way, I hope that Ronnie was just a delusional old man and that none of his shocking past life actually happened. I would be comforted, to some extent, if it turned out he had spent most of his years holed up in that council flat tending to plants and listening to the radio.

Minutes after leaving Ronnie's we were caught out by a torrential downpour. The raindrops battered the road surface like machinegun fire, and within seconds the gutters were full. The torrent of water elbowed its way down the high street looking for its escape. We did the same, and found refuge in the doorway of a shop. The window was well stocked with random household things, such as varnish and carriage clocks, but there was also a random selection of bike accessories.

'Surely there are some bike bits we could ask for while we are here?' said Ben.

'Like what?'

'I don't know, but your bike is rubbish. It must need some new bits.'

'It probably does, but I've got no idea which bits would make it less rubbish if we replaced them.'

Ben stared at The Falcon as though the answer would appear to him at any moment. 'Hold on, I've got an idea. Wait there,' he said, propping his bike up and disappearing into the shop.

I stood there wincing at the thought of him asking the bemused shopkeeper for a free derailleur, tyre, brake cable or inner tube, just for the sake of it. He emerged from the shop with a big grin on his face and two black bin bags in his hand.

'The latest in waterproof cycling gear,' he said.

'You are a genius.'

We tore a hole in the bottom of each bin liner for our head and a hole in each side for our arms. The bin bags were big enough to cover our rucksacks, too, and keep our few belongings sheltered from the rain.

As we set off again, it felt like we were on a movie set. Despite it being 9.30am, the streets were eerily deserted. The rain was so dramatic that the film director would have asked to tone it down because it was too unrealistic.

We had no idea where we were going. I had left the day's route in my rucksack, which was now inaccessible because of the bin liner. We cycled in the direction which our instinct told us was north. Two weeks on the road had given us an acute natural awareness of our location and direction.

Or so we thought.

'This is the road we came in on last night. We need to be going in the opposite direction,' I said.

'I thought it all looked a bit familiar,' said Ben, as we turned around and retraced out steps.

Less than a mile north of Carlisle on the A7 we passed a branch of Morrison's - the supermarket (other supermarkets are available). We both agreed that cycling in such horrendous conditions was particularly unpleasant, so decided to stop and try and get some breakfast.

We entered the supermarket followed by the glare of several exiting shoppers, who seemed a bit confused by our attire. The fashion of knee-length bin bags and skimpy shorts had apparently not taken off in Carlisle.

'Shall we try and get some bread and butter like we did in Ellesmere Port?' I suggested.

'I really fancy a fry-up. What do you say we try our luck at the café?'

We approached the lady at the till and tried our well rehearsed routine.

'Ye want a free breakfest? Ah cannae authorize 'at. Yoo'll hae tae gang an' spick tae th' stair manager. Gang ower th' the customer services desk.'

Everyone in Carlisle seemed to be Scottish. And not just a bit Scottish, but extremely Scottish. It was almost like they were pushed out of Scotland for being too Scottish.

'What the hell did she just say?' asked Ben as we walked away.

'I'm not sure but I think she told us to go and ask the store manager.'

We eventually located him at the Customer Services desk. He was Scottish.

'Sae ye want a free breakfest?' he said. 'Och aye, Ah hink we can sort 'at it fur ye. Whit will it be? Two full Englishes? Or shoods ah said Scottishes,' he said with a cackle.

'Two Scottish breakfasts would be amazing. Thanks so much.'

'Nae problem. gang an' tak' a seat an' i'll gie a body ay th' kimers tae sort ye it.'

'Ok,' we said, without the faintest clue as to what he had said.

Five minutes later, we were brought two large fry-ups and a pot of tea. If the Scots in Scotland were even half as nice as the Scots in Carlisle then we were in for a treat.

The rain had not relented by the time we braved it back outside, almost two hours after we entered. Our bikes, which we had unsubtly pretended to chain to the trolley depot, were still there. On this rare occasion, I secretly hoped that the bikes would have been stolen. That way, we could have abandoned the whole trip – due to circumstances beyond our control – and then headed home to our warm dry beds and home comforts. There would be no shame in admitting defeat, having made it so far, only for our trusty steeds, that we had worked so tirelessly to acquire, to be taken from us by a couple of pesky Carlislians.

Unfortunately, nobody had seized the opportunity, and the bikes remained where we had left them, ready for us to climb aboard with our damp, bin-liner-coated arses.

Reaching Scotland was certainly an anti-climax.

A bridge across the River Sark marks the border and we were greeted with a brown *'Scotland Welcomes You'* sign in the town (if you can call it that) of Gretna.

Gretna is of course famous for its registry offices. In Scotland, the 19th century law that allows 16 year olds to marry without parental consent is still taken advantage of. The first building you see after entering Scotland is one such registry office. The *'First House in Scotland Marriage Room'* or *'Last House in Scotland'* - depending on which direction you approach it - is a single storey white and black building, right next to the main road. I've definitely seen more romantic wedding venues, but it did have a certain charm.

It was noon and still raining heavily. There was no sign of any brides or grooms, but I got quite excited by the idea of a couple turning up for a spontaneous marriage, and urgently requiring two witnesses. Unfortunately, nobody did. The only way that a wedding by the side of a busy road, on a wet Thursday in Gretna could have been less romantic, would be if Ben and I had been the witnesses.

'Have you ever been to Scotland before?' asked Ben as we stood hugging the *'Scotland Welcomes You'* sign (this is a compulsory rite of passage for anyone that enters Scotland by bike or on foot).

'Yes. This is my second time,' I said.

'When was the other time?'

'About five minutes ago.'

'Eh?'

'I had to nip back into England a few minutes ago because my route instructions blew back over the border.'

'You're a moron. So you've never been to Scotland before today?'

'No.'

'Me neither.'

'Rubbish, isn't it?'

'Yes. It never stops raining.'

We posed for a photograph by the sign (again, compulsory), and then set off again. We followed a fairly quiet road that ran parallel to the busy A75, but the cycling was incredibly unpleasant. The rain had collected on the road so much that we were cycling through an inch deep puddle that stretched all the way from Gretna to Dumfries.

'Ben, do you remember that ear stud that Eric gave me back in Cornwall?' I said as I cycled alongside him to avoid being sprayed by his back wheel.

'Yeah, why?'

'I've lost it. It's been attached to my t-shirt all this time, and now it's gone. It must have got knocked off by the bin liner.'

'Oh well. It looked stupid anyway.'

'That's not the point. He gave it to us for good luck.'

'And?'

'Maybe our luck has run out.'

'Cheer up. You're becoming as miserable as me.'

On the way into Dumfries a car pulled out of a side road right in front of me. I applied the brakes, which were ineffective at the best of times. In water, and at high speed, they were completely useless. I was half off the bike by the time I hit the car. The Falcon's pedals and frame slammed into the back driver-side corner of the car, leaving a hefty scratch and a slight dent. Most of the skin was missing from my right knee, but other than that, The Falcon and I had come away quite lightly. The lady's car (I'm not being sexist – she was a female driver) definitely came off worse. She pulled to a stop and got out of her car to inspect the damage. Not to me, but to her car.

'What have you done, you idiot?' she shouted. By this point I had picked The Falcon up off the floor, and was cycling as fast as I could down the hill to catch up with Ben. Yes, technically I was leaving the scene of an accident, but there is no doubt that it was her fault. After all, she did pull out in front of me. But I also knew that my bike didn't have adequate brakes, and when it comes to driving they say that if somebody hits you from behind, it is always their fault. I assumed this probably applied to cyclists, too, but I didn't want to hang around to find out.

'What happened to you back there?' asked Ben as we pulled into a side road.

'I just had a bit of a run in with a car. I told you our luck had run out.'

'If your luck had run out then you would have come off a lot worse. Are you ok?'

'Yeah, I'm fine thanks,' I said. 'It was a bit scary. I think that's my first ever bike accident involving a car.'

'Really? I've had plenty of them. If you think Dumfries is bad, you should try cycling in London.'

'So what's the deal? Whose fault would it have been, and should I be responsible for getting her car sorted?'

'I've no idea. I've never hung around to find out either.'

We happened to have stopped right next to Robert Burns House, which is *'one of Dumfries's most notable tourist sights'*. Or so our route book claimed.

Robert Burns, or Rabbie Burns, or Scotland's favourite son, the Ploughman Poet, Robden of Solway Firth, Bard of Ayrshire or just plain old Bob, as I like to call him, is Scotland's most famous poet. I'm sure most of you know this already, but for those – like me – whose history is missing a few key events (such as everything that happened, ever) then I think it's sometimes helpful to give a bit of historical background. Where was I? That's right... Robert Burns is Scotland's most famous poet. He wrote poems, and he... errr... he did something with Liberalism or Socialism or both. And I think he probably invented Burns night, too. That's all I know, I'm afraid.

'Shall we go and have a look around Robert Burns House?' I asked Ben.

'We might as well, I suppose. At least it will be dry in there.'

'I was thinking more that it would be good to learn a bit more about Robert Burns and where he lived.'

'Yeah, of course. That too. But mostly because it will be dry in there.'

Robert Burns House is a small sandstone house just outside Dumfries city centre. It is where he wrote many of his most famous poems, such as that one about the thingy, and that other one about that place.

The man who worked there – the only other person in the building – was very nice and did his best to generate enthusiasm, but in truth, we were both much more interested in the electric heater that sat in the corner of the gift shop. We lurked beside it for a few minutes, pretending to read leaflets and look at postcards, until we had regained feeling in our lower legs and feet.

'Please, feel free to have a wander around the rest of the house. There are lots of interesting things to look at,' he said.

We did. There wasn't.

Don't get me wrong, I understand that Robert Burns was a remarkable man and that his work gives happiness and inspiration to many people, but that doesn't make the house that he grew up in any more interesting.

Robert Burns didn't live a particularly showbiz life. His house looked like any person's house from the 1700s. It had bedrooms, with beds in. A kitchen with a table in it, and a desk where he wrote. There were also windows that you could see through, and doors that both opened and closed.

I can see the appeal in looking around a house such as Graceland, with all its extravagance, or even Michael Jackson's Neverland, but Robert Burn's house just looked like a house. And a fairly unremarkable house at that.

I think my distain for unnecessary 'places of interest' stems from my visit to the Henry Ford Museum, just outside Detroit, Michigan. Henry Ford was… how can I put this politely?… a complete freak. He created, during his lifetime, a model village of significant buildings and things that had influenced his life. This sounds fair enough, but then you discover he had a favourite text book when he was at school, so he located the birthplace of the author of that particular book, and had her entire house shipped to his model village. That's not a normal thing to do. Still, at least Robert Burns House was dry and warm.

'If that was one of the best things to do in Dumfries, then I don't think there's much hope for this place,' said Ben, once we were outside. 'I would rather go to the Northampton Shoe Museum.'

A little further down the road we came across a shopping centre. There was nowhere suitable for us to leave our bikes, so we wheeled them into the shopping centre. Within seconds we were apprehended by a security guard.

'Ye cannae brin' those bikes in here,' he said.

'I know, sorry. It's just that we don't have any way of locking them up. We've just come in to get something to eat.'

'Whaur ur ye gonnae eat?' he asked.

'Wimpy!' I said, spotting a Wimpy close by.

'Awe rite. Weel jist prop yer bikes up by th' dyke thaur ootwith. an' dornt gang ridin' them aroond in haur.'

'Did you get that? What are we supposed to do?' I asked Ben.

'I'm not sure. I think he told us to leave our bikes by this wall and not to ride them inside.'

'Dammit! I've always wanted to ride my bike around a shopping centre. Why did you tell him we were going to Wimpy?'

'I just saw it here and thought he might let us bring our bikes in if we weren't going far. Also, I was genuinely excited about seeing a Wimpy. I thought Wimpy became extinct in the 1980s.'

'Me too. But how are we going to get free food here?' asked Ben.

'Same way we have for the last thirteen days, I guess.'

Pam, the manager, was a large, jovial lady in her late thirties. She had a huge mane of black hair and an even bigger smile. We tried to win her over by telling her about the appalling weather and how kind and generous all Scottish people that we had met had been.

'Are ye takin the pish? Ye want free burgers?' she said with a laugh.

'Errr, yeah, I guess so. I know it sounds cheeky, but we're decent blokes, I promise,' I said hopefully.

267

'Alrecht. Tak' a seat an' I'll brin' them ower tae ye,' she laughed.

Not only did she bring us a burger each, but fries, milkshakes and a couple of bags of crisps. She stood chatting to us for a while as we ate.

'Ae ye boys got any sort ay raincoat?' she asked.

'We've got a couple of bin-liners that we got in Carlisle this morning,' said Ben.

'Hang oan thaur. I'll gie ye some e'en bigger ones,' she said, and disappeared back behind the counter. Ben and I smirked at each other convinced that there was no way she could trump the bin-liners we already had. We were wrong.

'Hoo abit these bad jimmies?' she said, holding up the most ridiculously big bin bags we had ever seen.

'Oh my god. What do you use bags that big for?' I asked.

'I've got nae idea. They sent us them frae heed office, but they're far tay big e'en fur th' wheelie bins 'at we use. Ah hink they might be body bags.'

'Let's hope not,' said Ben. 'Thanks, Pam. These are amazing.'

We sat and drank our milkshakes as slowly as possible, to delay our return to the cold, wet world outside.

It was 3.30pm by the time I suggested that we leave.

'Do we really have to do more cycling today?' asked Ben.

'We've only done about 35 miles today. We were hoping to do at least 70.'

'But it's been pissing it down all day. It's no fun cycling when the weather's like this.'

'I know, but it would be good to do a few more miles today, because then that's less we have to do for the rest of the trip.'

'How many miles are you thinking?' asked Ben dejectedly.

'20-25?.'

268

'Oh bloody hell. You're such a masochist. Where will another 20 miles take us?'

I looked at the route book, and it was clear that there was very little in the way of civilisation until Kilmarnock, which was almost 70 miles away.

'I'm not sure. There looks like there are plenty of places we pass through,' I lied. 'How about we aim for the town of Moniaive, which is less than 20 miles away?'

'Give me that!' said Ben, snatching the book from me.

'There's bugger all on the route for bloody miles. We'll end up getting stranded in the middle of nowhere in this pissing weather,' said Ben, becoming increasingly frustrated with my stubbornness.

'Let's at least get to Moniaive. Tomorrow you'll be glad you did it.'

'I don't care about tomorrow. I care about today, and I don't think we should go any further. Look what it says here about Moniaive in the guide book: *'Moniaive has a marker post in the main street dating from 1638.'* That's all it says. What makes you think we'd even find somewhere to stay there?'

'I just think we're better off trying to get as many miles done today as possible.'

'But why? It's not like we're in a race, as you keep reminding me. We've done 35 miles today. Let's just consider the rest of the day a write-off.'

I knew Ben was right, but the idea of calling it a day at 3.30pm when we had planned on a big day's cycling just seemed wrong.

'How about another ten miles then as a compromise?' I suggested.

'How about NO? Seriously, what's the point? We can just do those extra ten miles tomorrow. If you want to do more cycling today then fine, but I'm staying in Dumfries tonight. You go on and stay in that stupid place with the stupid wooden post.'

I reluctantly agreed to call it a day and stay where we were for the night. Dumfries, that is, not Wimpy.

We sat in silence for another ten minutes before thanking Pam, retrieving our bikes, and venturing back outside into the rain.

'Are you going to sulk all day?' asked Ben.

'I'm not sulking,' I said sulking.

'Yes you are. Trust me, you'll thank me later.'

We found a bar further up the road and decided to ask inside whether there were any hostels or B&Bs around.

The building was very odd. It wasn't a pub, as such, but it wasn't a bar or a working men's club either. It was more like a community room that happened to have a bar in it. It was 4.15pm on a Thursday and there were at least a dozen men in there. The strange thing was that nobody was talking and every single one of them was sat facing a small TV screen in the corner that was showing *Deal or No Deal*.

The tension in the room was unbearable. At the time, I didn't really understand the program – I've since become hooked, too – and it was baffling to watch a group of men with such focus and concentration in their faces. Even the barman didn't take his eyes off the screen as we walked to the bar. We asked him about accommodation – in whispered voices, so as not to spoil the moment – but he still kept his attention on the television.

'There's a few hotels doon 'at way ye coods try,' he said, pointing his arm to his right, but not adjusting his gaze.

'Ok, thank you,' I said, and we slunk from the bar.

'DEAL, YOU IDIOT! DEAL! TAKE THE BLOODY MONEY!' one of them shouted at the TV on our way out.

We tried a B&B and then a hotel. The first was full, and the second was unable to help. We then stumbled upon the Aberdour Hotel.

'How can I help you, lads?' said the man at reception. We explained our situation and he gave us the look of a headmaster issuing a detention. 'Is this some sort of thing for charity, because I've been scammed before?'

'No, it's not. I mean, some people have sponsored us, but that's not what it's about,' I said.

'I've been scammed before by people saying they're doing something for charity and then they just take advantage.'

'We completely understand. Well, the point of this trip is that we're trying not to exploit people's generosity by using charity.'

'So you're not doing it for charity?'

'No. We're doing it as an experiment to see how kind and generous the people of Britain are,' said Ben.

'But you said that people have sponsored you?'

'Yes, some people have, but only because they insisted on it.'

'So you are doing it for charity then? Cos I've been stung before by people claiming they were doing something for charity.'

We were getting nowhere. He thought for a moment
'Wait there for a second, and I'll see what I can do.'

He returned a few minutes later with a key in his hand.

'I'm going to take a chance, because you seem like a couple of decent guys. Sorry to sound so suspicious, but I've been stung before by people claiming to be doing something for charity.'

'Of course, we completely understand,' I said, not really understanding. I was unsure whether he wanted us to be raising money for charity or not, but I knew that we had been honest with him, so left it at that.

271

The sight of two clean hotel beds was a welcome change to Ronnie's living room floor. We took off our soggy shoes, shorts and socks and hung them on the radiator. We then lay on our beds drifting in and out of sleep. After a few minutes there was a tentative knock on the door.

'Come in,' said Ben instinctively, forgetting that we were both lying on our beds, in matching pairs of Union Jack boxer shorts and nothing else. It was Colin – the manager. He did a double take and then looked very embarrassed.

'Sorry,' I said. 'We were just drying some of our clothes on the radiator. We don't really have any spares, which is why we're in our pants.'

'Right. Ok,' he said. 'I just wanted to let you know that I've had a word with the chef downstairs, and you can have whatever you like off the menu for dinner. I've also left £10 behind the bar so make sure you have a couple of beers each, too.'

Scotland was bloody brilliant.

Colin said goodbye, but then reappeared a few minutes later to give us a pair of tracksuit bottoms that he had salvaged from lost property.

'I think I better have these as you've got your suit trousers and a pair of shorts,' said Ben, staking his claim on the tracksuit bottoms immediately.

'Ok. But you did have a pair of tracksuit bottoms before. Remember? And you decided to just cut the legs off them.'

'Yeah, well I won't be cutting the legs off these babies,' he said as he pulled on a pair of dry, cosy tracksuit bottoms. I sat on the bed in my damp pants looking on enviously.

After dinner and a couple of beers we returned to our room. It was only 7.30pm and we had accommodation and were showered, fed and watered. Most nights we would still have been on the road at this time.

'What shall we do now?' I asked.

'I don't know. We could just have an early night?'

'Let's have a wander around Dumfries. This is our first night in Scotland after all.'

Dumfries didn't have a lot going for it during the day. There was even less happening at night. To be fair to Dumfries, it was a wet Thursday in September. I'm not quite sure what we expected.

We then spotted an old cinema down one of the back streets.

'Fancy the cinema?' suggested Ben.

'I can think of nothing better. Let's try.'

We checked the listings board outside. There was just the one screen and it was showing a film called *John Tucker Must Die*.

'I think I've heard of that,' said Ben. 'It's supposed to be shit.'

'Well it doesn't look like we've got much choice.'

The foyer was empty, and the girl behind the counter didn't look old enough to see a PG on her own, let alone work in a cinema. She was texting on her phone and finished writing her message before looking up to acknowledge us.

We gave her our sob story about how it was our first night in Scotland, and how we wanted to relax etc. She just shrugged her shoulders and said: 'Whatever. Doesn't make any difference to me. Just go on in.'

I can't remember a single thing about *John Tucker Must Die*. I've seen trailers of it on YouTube since, and nothing about it looks familiar. I didn't fall asleep, but I just completely zoned off and my mind shut down completely. It was two of the

273

most relaxing hours of my life.

That's not an endorsement for the film, by the way. It was just the first time in two weeks that I was able to just completely switch off and not have to talk to anyone, or ask anyone for anything, or worry about where we were going to eat or sleep.

There was also something soothing about being at the cinema. It was something that 'normal' people did. People with money. People who had fun. Not that we hadn't been having fun, but every moment of the day was occupied with some sort of physical exertion or mental and emotional test. *John Tucker Must Die* required none of this.

I could tell Ben felt the same way.

As we walked out of the cinema behind an elderly couple who had been the only other two people at the showing, Ben did a little skip along the road.

'That was just what I needed. I feel great now,' he said.

'Me too,' I said, and skipped alongside him, arm-in-arm, past the old couple back to our quaint little guest house.

Scotland sign, Gretna

Day 14
A place of our own
Dumfries to Neilston - 83 miles

'Make sure you have some breakfast before you go,' said the lady in the office, who we presumed to be Colin's wife. 'Colin has had to go out this morning, but he said to pass on his best wishes and to make sure you both had something to eat before heading off.'

It was a bright, sunny day and we both felt so much better than we had the day before.

'Good call getting us to stop when we did yesterday,' I said to Ben, during breakfast.

'I told you. I'm always right,' he said. 'Scotland doesn't look too bad in the sunshine does it?' He was right, for once. It didn't look too bad at all.

The road climbed gradually for twenty miles after Dumfries along the picturesque B729. We passed through the villages of Dunscore and Moniaive and in 20 miles we saw no more than a dozen cars. Moniaive, it turned out, had little more than the wooden post and it would have been a real struggle to find somewhere to stay.

We had been told that the Scottish highlands were beautiful, but the scenery north of Dumfries took us completely by surprise. It all looked a lot greener than anything we had passed through, and the rolling landscape was scattered with small copses of pine trees and the occasional ancient ruin. In any other country these would be made into tourist attractions. Scotland has so many of these, that most of them go unnoticed.

There was very little in the way of civilisation between

Dumfries and the town of Dalmellington where we stopped for lunch. Dalmellington was a peaceful, but sad looking town. Iron and coal were discovered in the nearby hills in the 1800s, and for over a hundred years it was a thriving mining town. Iron production ended in the 1920s and the coal mine closed in the 1980s, and now the town feels slightly neglected.

We called into a café on the main street. I say 'main street', but I think there was only the one street. We were particularly conscious of asking for free food in a place that was clearly struggling, so we insisted that we do some work in exchange for something to eat. The lady behind the counter insisted that we didn't need to do anything to help, and provided us with a sausage bap and a cup of tea.

As an example to illustrate just how quiet and peaceful Dalmellington was, I was nearly run over by a man in a wheelchair.

I was cycling down the main street, when he pulled out in front of me to cross the road without looking. I managed to swerve out of the way at the last moment but my foot caught the floor as I tried to regain balance and the pedal spun and smacked against my shin, shortly before grazing the back of my leg quite badly on the main cog. I turned around to see the man in the wheelchair continue to the other side of the road without even an acknowledgement.

I gave him the benefit of the doubt, assuming that he had some form of mental impairment, as well as physical, but then watched as he engaged in a loud conversation with a friend once he reached the other side.

We followed the busy (by Scotland's standards) A713 to Patna, which was another strange looking town. Patna is basically a big housing estate plonked right in the middle of some beautiful Scottish countryside. The town was built in

1802 to provide houses for the workers of the nearby coalfields.

Patna did attract tourists for a while when a nearby manor turned its grounds into a caravan park. This eventually closed in the late 1990s, and the caravan park became vandalised, eventually resulting in the manor house being burnt down and left as a ruin.

We called into Costcutter to try and get something else to eat. The girl behind the counter was in her teens, and she smiled when we told her our story, as though it was the most exciting thing that she had ever heard. She had lived in Patna all of her life, so the chances are it probably was.

'Aight, that's bloody wicked, guys,' she said. 'I'll get yers some food. I should probably check with ma manager first but a cannae be bothered and she'll never notice anyway. Yous wait there.' She picked up a shopping basket from the doorway and began scouring the shelves, aisle by aisle, looking for things to donate to us. She filled the basket with bread rolls, a packet of ham, a block of cheese, tomatoes, a tin of baked beans, some digestive biscuits, two steak pies, apples, pears and two drinks.

'Will this keep you going?' she asked, handing the basket over. We stood open-mouthed.

'Un-be-lieve-able,' said Ben. 'Thank you so much. Are you sure you're able to give us all of that?'

'Yeah, sod it. It's probably all past its best-before date anyways,' she said, knowing full well that it wasn't.

We always seemed to stumble upon generosity in the most unlikely of places. It was moments such as this that our faith in human kindness was given its biggest boost. Patna, as it turned out, was a damn fine place.

We ate the steak pies and an apple each, and stuffed the rest into our bags to have for dinner.

The road climbed after leaving Patna, and then descended for about eight glorious miles through lush farmland. We reached the town of Drongan and stopped for a quick break. I took a moment to check our progress in the route book. There was a little bit of information about Drongan. It said:

'*...another mining community whose fortunes suffered when the local pit closed in 1986. The town's youth reportedly have a strong local rivalry with neighbouring Coylton.*'

We didn't hang around very long. For the next twenty miles we didn't stop. Not because of the Drongan gangs, of course. That would have been silly. Simply because we were keen to cycle as many miles as we could to make up for our paltry distance of the previous day.

We passed through the town of Tarbolton, which has some association with Robert Burns, but decided not to stop to find out what. After our experience with Robert Burns in Dumfries, we knew we would not be missing out.

The weather was great, we had a surplus of food, the gradient of the road was in our favour, and Scotland was stunningly beautiful. But, there was still just one small problem: the Falcon could not manage more than a quarter of a mile without the chain falling off.

I had become a seasoned-pro at reattaching it, but it was still incredibly frustrating. I could sense Ben's anger increasing each time, and he would always mutter an 'oh for fuck's sake' or a 'here we go again' under his breath. If it happened when I was behind him, I would try to reattach it secretly and then catch him up without him noticing. I was successful on a couple of occasions, but most of the time he would glance back and see me fumbling with the bike. He would then make a point of stopping to let me catch up, just so he could mutter something like: 'I told you we should have replaced that piece of shit back in Bath.'

'Don't listen to him,' I said, stroking The Falcon's

handlebars.

'You're as messed up as your bike,' said Ben.

'Well, you're big... and... errr... big and stupid like your bike,' I said. It wasn't one of my best comebacks.

We arrived in the village of Kilmaurs just before 6pm. The Falcon's chain had fallen off yet again, and Ben was close to detaching it completely and wrapping it around my neck.

'Oh my god,' said Ben, 'I don't believe it.'

'I know, I know. I get the message,' I said as I tried to reattach it.

'No, I'm not talking about the bike. Look over there.'

Just across the road from us was a bike shop called Walkers Cycling.

'Would you believe it? It's a bloody bike shop. It's fate,' said Ben. 'We've got to go and see if they can do anything about that bike. I can't go on like this.'

'Ok,' I said, 'but it's 5.55pm. I reckon it'll be closed.'

It was open. We were greeted inside by a bearded man, who looked more like a friendly maths teacher than someone who should work in a bike shop. I explained what we were up to, and that we were having a few bike problems, and asked if they had any tips or advice on how we could prolong the life of The Falcon.

'No problem. I'll get one of my guys to come and take a look at it,' he said.

We were joined outside by two young mechanics who spent at least ten minutes oiling and tweaking the rear-derailleur and chain.

'We've stopped at a couple of bike shops along the way already and both of them told us that it was completely broken and that there was no hope,' I said.

'That's not in the spirit of your adventure,' said John, the bearded man, who owned and ran the shop with his wife

Susan.

'So you've really come all this way without spending any money at all?' asked Susan.

'Yes.'

'And you've managed to get somewhere to sleep every night, and plenty of food?'

'We've gone hungry a few times and we have had to slept in a few odd places, but we're doing ok.'

'We get a lot of End to Enders calling in because Kilmaurs seems to be on many of the popular routes,' said John. 'But I think in all the years I've been working here that you two are the craziest.'

'Definitely,' laughed one of the guys, who was still seeing to The Falcon. 'These tyres are pretty flat, too. You should probably put some more air in them if I were you.'

'We don't have a pump unfortunately,' I said.

'You're joking? You are cycling a thousand miles and you don't even have a pump. What about a puncture repair kit?' asked John.

'No,' I said, feeling like I was being told off.

'What happens if you get a puncture in the middle of nowhere?'

'We did get one. In Wales. We had to walk to the nearest house.'

'You guys are absolutely bonkers. Susan, go and grab these boys a pump, puncture repair kit and anything else that you think they might need. And what the hell were you doing in Wales, anyway?'

'I don't really know,' I said.

Susan returned a few minutes later with a pump, puncture repair kit, a 'Walkers Cycling' drinking bottle and holder, and a handful of energy bars.

'There you go,' said the man who had been attending to

281

The Falcon. 'You should be able to get a few more miles out of it now.'

'You mean The Falcon isn't broken?' I asked excitedly.

'No, The Falcon is far from broken. It just needed a bit of love and affection.'

I wanted to hug him but I managed to contain myself.

'Doesn't your back hurt riding something so small?' asked John.

'Yes. Quite a lot,' I said.

'He LOVES pain,' said Ben.

'Thank you all so much for your generosity and enthusiasm,' I said as we climbed back on our bikes.

'Not at all,' said John. 'We should be thanking you. You've made our day.'

All four of them stood on the tarmac in front of the shop and waved us off. If you are ever in East Ayrshire – or further afield – and have bike problems, then I would wholeheartedly recommend Walkers Cycling. Although, I think most people have to pay for their supplies and repairs.

Interestingly, John Dunlop – the inventor of the pneumatic bicycle tyre – was born just a couple of miles west of here. Actually, on re-reading that, it is not very interesting at all.

I would like to add that, after leaving Kilmaurs, The Falcon's chain never fell off again.

We were in such good spirits that we failed to notice that we had been cycling uphill for ten miles.

'Will this fuckin' hill ever end?' said Ben.

'I hope so,' I panted.

'Shall we look for somewhere to stay in the next town that we get to?'

'Yeah. There's a place called Neilston in another ten miles.'

'Ten miles? Are you kidding me?' asked Ben.

'Err, no. It doesn't look like there's anything else before

there anyway. We've done really well today. I reckon we'll have done over 90 miles.'

'WHAT? My god, you are such a slave driver. If I'd known we had done anything near that much, I would have stopped for the day ages ago.'

'I know. That's why I didn't tell you.'

The road continued to climb for several miles and then descended steeply for another three miles into the village of Neilston. Our first impressions of the town were not too favourable. It was 8pm and a girl in her early teens was being sick outside the Chinese takeaway on the main street.

Ben suggested that we try and spend the night in the church, but the church door was locked. We knocked but there was no response.

'That looks like the vicar,' I said, spotting a man walking down the road away from the church. We chased after him.

'Excuse me,' panted Ben. 'Are you the vicar for that church up the road?'

'Yes, I am. Is there a problem?' he asked suspiciously.

'No, no problem. We were…' Ben paused, trying to catch his breath, 'we were wondering whether there was any possibility of us sleeping in the church tonight.'

'Sleeping in the church? Whatever for?'

'We're cycling the length of the country without spending any money and we need somewhere to sleep tonight.'

'Sorry, I can't help you.'

'We don't need beds or anything like that. All we need is some form of shelter,' I pleaded.

'No. I can't help, I'm afraid.'

'Do you know anyone that might be able to help us?' asked Ben.

'No, I don't think so. Good night,' he said, and walked away.

A little bit further down the road we saw him walk into his house - a huge mansion.

'I never thought I would say this,' said Ben, 'but that vicar was a complete cock.'

'I know. Look at the size of his house. It must have at least five bedrooms.'

'They're probably all full of bound and gagged choir-boys.'

I would like to point out that this vicar may no longer work in Neilston. The current vicar is probably a very nice person, and I'm sure they would have welcomed us into their church with open arms.

Towards the bottom end of the village we spotted a pub called The Traveller's Rest. We hid our bikes around the back by the bins and went inside. It was a warm, cosy bar that would not have looked out of place on a snowy mountainside in Germany; lots of wood panelling, moodily lit, a lively atmosphere, and lots of people wearing lederhosen. I lied about the lederhosen.

There were about a dozen people in the bar, and most of them surrounded the pool table where a man wearing decorator's overalls was taking on some young challenger. The decorator swaggered around the table like Paul Newman, and proceeded to pot four reds in a row before following in the white off the black. The rest of the group howled with laughter and the young challenger raised his cue above his head in victory.

There was one lone man sitting at the bar, and we stood there for a few minutes until the barman appeared.

'Sorry lads. I don't think I can help you, I'm afraid,' said the landlord after we had asked him about the possibility of somewhere to sleep. 'We do have a few bedrooms available for rent, but I can't really give you one of those.'

'We wouldn't need one of your proper rooms. Would we

be allowed to sleep here in the bar?' asked Ben. 'We would be no trouble.'

'Sorry, no, I can't let you stay in the bar, I'm afraid. It would contravene our insurance policy.'

'Are you really going all that way without spending any money?' asked the man at the bar, who had been listening to our request.

'Yes. We've been on the road for two weeks.'

'Fair play to you,' he laughed. 'Let me buy you both a beer.'

Alec lived south of the border and was just up in Neilston overnight for business. He was quite vague about the type of business that he did, so we didn't pry. He asked us all sorts of questions about our trip, and then insisted on buying us another beer. It was 10pm by the time we remembered that we had nowhere to sleep.

The pool-playing decorator's name was Jim, and he was a joiner, rather than a decorator. Although, I'm not sure how someone who fits wood together can get so much paint on their clothes. Jim The Joiner – as his friends called him – was in his forties and extremely chatty. He was obviously 'the man' of the Traveller's Rest, and possibly the whole of Neilston. Within minutes of talking with him he had ordered the barman to get us both a beer on him.

'I wish ah coods help ye wi' somewhere tae stay,' he said mid pool shot, 'but our hoose jist isn't big enaw, aam afraid.'

'Sleep is overrated anyway,' said Ben. 'The beer is better.'

'Yoo've got a spare hoose, haven't ye, Les,' called Jim to one of the other men in the group.

'Very funny, Jim,' laughed Les. We didn't understand the joke, but laughed along anyway.

We spent the next hour drinking more free beer, playing pool and eating soup and bread that another of the men had ordered for us. We were sitting in a warm pub on comfy chairs, drinking free beer and eating broccoli and stilton soup with crunchy bread. We didn't have a care in the world. That was, until we remembered that the likelihood was that we would be spending the night on the streets.

'Oh well,' said Ben, 'our luck was due to run out sometime. At least we are full and drunk.'

'I still think we'll find somewhere to stay. We could walk down towards Paisley. It's only a few miles. It's much bigger and there's bound to be plenty of places to stay,' I suggested.

'There's no way I am going any further tonight. I'd rather sleep in the pub car park than walk any more. I'm knackered.'

Midway through our fifth pint - as we stood watching Jim The Joiner get beaten at pool yet again - Les approached us holding a bunch of keys. He was a fairly small man in his forties, with a friendly face and an English accent. He had lived in Neilston for several years and considered Scotland 'home'.

'I'm going to take a big risk here, lads,' said Les. 'These are the keys to my house. It's almost empty at the moment as I'm in the process of selling it, but you can both go and sleep there tonight, if you like.'

'Are you serious? So you really do have a spare house?' I said, unable to wipe the smirk from my face.

'Well, yes, I guess that technically I do. It still has all of my office equipment there and computer stuff, which is why I'm taking a bit of a gamble. I like you both, though, and I think you are genuine. Please don't let me down.'

He gave us directions to the house which was about a quarter of a mile back up through the village. We said our thanks to everyone, and then wheeled our bikes drunkenly to Les's.

We had slept in a canal boat, a posh hotel, and a self-contained flat, but we had just been given our very own

286

modern, three-bed semi-detached house in a quiet cul-de-sac for the night. We had raised the bar yet again.

Before going to bed, we made cheese, ham and tomato rolls from the supplies we were given in Patna. I lay on the carpet covered in a towel. Ben, predictably, was using *his* sleeping bag.

Ben and The Horse, near Dalmellington

Ben, somewhere in Scotlannd

Me, somewhere in Scotland

Walkers Cycling, Kilmaurs

North of Dumfries

Les, Neilston

Day 15
Another food festival
Neilston to Crianlarich - 42 miles

We awoke to the sound of something falling through the letterbox. We had only been in our new house for one night, and already people were sending us post. I staggered downstairs in my pants and discovered a scattering of five disposable razors and a gel bike seat lying on the doormat.

'Ben?' I shouted upstairs. 'Why has somebody posted razors and a gel seat through the door?'

'Huh? Oh, that will be that guy from last night. Dave, I think his name was – the bloke who bought us soup.'

'How do you know?'

'Cos he said we were looking scruffy and he was going to give us some razors so we could shave.'

'Oh. What about the gel seat?'

'That's for you. He went to have a look at our bikes by the bins last night, and then said he couldn't believe you'd been riding such an uncomfortable looking bike.'

We got our things together and managed to tidy up the mess that we had created in the kitchen just as Les arrived to check on his house. We thanked him for his immense generosity and asked him to pass on our thanks to all the others at The Traveller's Rest.

We were on the road at a respectable 9am. It was a cold but clear morning. The first three miles were downhill all the way, and we freewheeled into Paisley on the lookout for breakfast. Paisley is a town in itself, but it has gradually been swallowed up by nearby Glasgow.

At the time, we were both extremely disappointed with Paisley town centre. We cycled around for 15 minutes looking for any sign of life, but couldn't find a single shop or café that was open. It was as though it was the end of the world, but someone had forgotten to tell us.

Having since done some Googling, I have discovered that Paisley does in fact have a town centre with a nice looking pedestrianised shopping street. This somehow managed to elude us.

As we were leaving town we came across a café called Korner Kitchen. Inside, there was a queue of three workmen all waiting for their breakfast.

The café was run by two loud, smiling ladies. We watched as they flipped bacon, fried eggs and poured tea with a genuine love and enthusiasm for their job. By the time it came to our turn to be served, they had already clocked us and had raised their eyebrows at our clothes. We did differ slightly to their usual clientele of boiler-suit clad workmen.

'What can I get you two hunky lads?' said the younger of the two ladies.

We explained our challenge and asked if there was anything we could do in exchange for some free food.

'Oooooh, what do you reckon, Jan? Should we give these two strapping young lads any food?' she said to her colleague.

'Yeah, why not. If that one with the skimpy shorts shows us a bit more leg,' she laughed.

'That'll be you then, George,' said Ben. This was a new low. I was being made to flaunt my body in exchange for food. I felt used. I felt cheap. I liked it. I lifted up the side of my skimpy blue shorts, and exposed my flabby white thighs.

'Phwooooooaarr,' said both ladies in unison, before erupting into laughter.

'How about a sausage bap, a cup of tea and a custard donut each?' she said.

By the time we had finished our breakfast it was 10.45am,

and our early start had vanished. We followed the A726 out of Paisley and crossed the Erskine Bridge. For bridge enthusiasts out there, the Erskine Bridge is a 524m, cable-stayed, box girder bridge, built in 1971 and designed by William Brown. It connects West Dunbartonshire with Renfrewshire. For those less interested, the Erskine Bridge is a big bridge that crosses a river.

We stopped halfway across the bridge to admire the stunning views of the River Clyde. Public telephones and adverts for The Samaritans were installed at regular intervals along the bridge's railings, and our mood took a sombre turn when we realised that we were standing at one of Scotland's most notorious suicide spots.

We had a decision to make when we reached the other end of the bridge. We could either follow the busy A82 to Loch Lomond, or take the longer route which followed a cycle path and minor roads described by the route book as: *'badly surfaced'* and passing *'behind urban areas not recommended for solo cyclists.'*

'We definitely take the A82,' said Ben adamantly.

'Why? We're not solo cyclists,' I said.

'Yeah, but it sounds dodgy. Anyway, the A82 will be much quicker.'

'It won't be dodgy. I bet we're much more likely to be injured on the main road than on a cycle path.'

'If I'm going to get injured I would rather be hit by a car than stabbed or shot.'

'You really are a weirdo,' I said. 'Let's take the scenic route. I'll protect you.'

'Fine, well I'm not going to protect you and if you get stabbed then it's your own fault.'

The Clyde and Loch Lomond Cycleway, as it is officially called, is a cycle route that extends 20 miles from the centre of ҙow to the shores of Loch Lomond. It was absolutely brilliant to cycle along. Although we had followed relatively quiet roads throughout the trip, we still had to be alert to the prospect of other cars. The cycleway was all ours and it was extremely liberating. I even pulled a wheelie.

There were a few sections that deviated through slightly rundown housing estates, but there was never any threat of danger. Ben did have a slight confrontation with a fly that flew into his mouth, but they managed to resolve that between themselves.

We arrived in the village of Balloch at about 2pm, during yet another food festival. The Loch Lomond Food & Drink Festival took place in the car park of the Loch Lomond Aquarium.

Most of the stalls offered free tastings, which should have suited us perfectly. It was actually more hassle that it was worth, however, as we had to listen to a tedious sales pitch about the benefit of Scottish olives over Greek olives, and nod away enthusiastically for ten minutes in exchange for a single Scottish olive. We then had to endure the same for a morsel of Scottish cheese, and again for a Scottish chipolata. It was not the best return for 30 minutes effort.

We decided to resort to our tried and tested honest approach. We still had a bit of cheese and some tomatoes from the previous day, so only needed a little more for lunch.

Ben managed to get a small loaf of bread, and I was given some sun-dried tomato focaccia.

'My god, you are such a middle class blagger. Foccacia? What the fuck?' said Ben.

'Look at you with your peasant bread,' I said. 'I'm embarrassed to even know you.'

Cycling along the shores of Loch Lomond had promised to

be one of the highlights of our journey; 25 miles without a single hill, the sparkling lake on one side and the ragged mountains on the other. The route book made us salivate at the prospect:

'The A82 north from Balloch is a beautiful road.'

It isn't. In theory it should be, but it's actually a fairly horrendous road. The A82 serves as the main route linking the lowlands and the western highlands, which means that almost every person travelling between Glasgow and the north passes along this road.

We hugged the verge closely, as a constant stream of coaches, cars, caravans and motorbikes growled along the narrow road. As for the view, that probably would have been nice if we had been able to see it. During the occasional lull in traffic the view was obscured by a thick barrier of trees that grew along the shore.

The most frustrating problem, however, was the actual road surface. It wasn't a problem with potholes, as such. For some reason – possibly deliberate – the entire surface is textured like a cheese grater. It was absolutely exhausting to cycle along. We should have been able to cover the distance in no time, as there was no gradient, but it felt like a real effort just to keep going.

In summary, the A82 should be a beautiful road. All it needs is complete resurfacing, to be closed of all other traffic, and to have some serious deforestation.

We eventually reached the hamlet of Ardlui at the northern end of Loch Lomond. It was 7pm and we were ready to call it a night. Ardlui has a hotel and a campsite but we had no luck finding accommodation at either.

'There's a few places in Crianlarich - that's the next village – that you could try,' said the man at the campsite.

'Ok, thanks. How far is that?' I asked.

'Ooooh, it's only another 3-4 miles.'

'Crianlarich, baby!' said Ben.

Crianlarich was closer to ten miles further up the road, and every inch of it was uphill. Both of my hands were raw from rubbing on the handlebars and my back felt as though I had been snapped in half. It was one of the most painful day's cycling of the trip, and it was made worse by the belief that it was supposed to be our easiest.

I know that it's a cliché, but cycling – and all other physical activities, for that matter – is completely reliant on being in the correct mental zone. In order for your body to achieve its full potential, you need to be able to focus all of your mental energy into distancing yourself from any pain, discomfort, and the realisation of the challenge that you are facing. I'm not speaking from experience here, by the way; I'm quoting from a book that I read. I have never reached this mental zone and every form of physical exercise I have ever done has caused severe amounts of pain and discomfort.

It was almost dark by the time we reached Crianlarich. We followed signposts to the Crianlarich Youth Hostel, which we felt confident would be able to help us out. Our hopes were dashed by a smiling, bearded man, who told us, politely, that there were no rooms available at all, and that no we couldn't sleep on the floor, or sleep in his office, and no he didn't have a tent that we could borrow. Instead, we got into a long conversation with him about CAMRA (the campaign for real ale), but I'm not sure why, or what the relevance to our trip was. But if you are ever in the area and want to talk to someone about beer, then the guy at the Crianlarich Youth Hostel is your man.

'We're buggered,' said Ben, once we were outside. 'If a

Youth Hostel won't let us stay, then what chance have we got of finding somewhere?'

'Don't worry. We say this every night. That bloke at the campsite said there were loads of options here. We'll find somewhere.'

'Yeah, but that bloke also said it was just a couple of miles up the road. And he forgot to mention that it was halfway up a bloody mountain.'

We pushed our bikes back into the village and called into Londis to ask for some food. The man behind the counter said he was unable to help, but suggested that we try the Ben More Lodge for somewhere to stay, which was just on the road out of the village.

Whilst we were outside, the man from Londis came out. He came out of the shop, I mean. He didn't announce to us that he was gay. That would have been very random.

'Here you go. I found these for you. Two tuna pasta bake ready meals, and two spag bol ready meals. They are all past their best-before date, but I'm sure they'll be fine,' he said.

'Fantastic. You are a star. Thank you,' I said.

They were microwave meals. All we needed was a microwave.

The Ben More Lodge is a single-storey long white building, surrounded by a few wooden chalets. The place had a lovely cosy feel to it, with a roaring log fire. One of the white walls of the bar area had been completely covered in graffiti. Not an act of mindless vandalism, but hundreds of tiny little messages written in pen from visitors to the Ben More Lodge. Most were from fellow cyclists or hikers who had passed through on their journeys. Phrases such as *'Pain is just weakness leaving the body,' 'Scotland Rules,'* and *'Ease the chaffing,'* were scrawled all over the wall and it was fascinating to think of all of the different groups of people who had undertaken challenges of their own and shared similar moments of pleasure reading the tales of others.

We decided to add our own message. After spending several minutes trying to think of something witty or motivating to write, we settled for *'LEJOG – with no money. George & Ben.'* Truly inspirational.

The manager walked over to us after ten minutes. His name was Graham and he was in his early thirties, stocky with spiky black hair.

'I understand you are looking for free accommodation tonight as part of some challenge,' he said, in a barely noticeable Scottish accent.

'Yes, that's right,' said Ben.

'Well that's not something I can authorise myself. I would need to check with the owner. Is that ok with you both?'

'Yes, of course. Thank you.'

'She's not working today so I will have to give her a call at home, but she may not be back for another hour or so. I'll bring you over a free beer in the meantime.'

'An hour?' whispered Ben, when the manager had left, 'We can't wait for an hour.'

'Why not? We've got nothing else to do, and he's bringing us a beer. What could be better?'

'What happens if he speaks to the manager and she says no. It'll be gone 10pm by then and we'll be in the middle of the Scottish mountains with nowhere to stay.'

'I hadn't thought of it like that. I guess we'll worry about that if it happens. Let's hope she says yes.'

It was an incredibly long and anxious hour. Forget A-level results day. Forget your country being 1-0 down in the World Cup Final with five minutes of injury-time added. Forget waiting to see if Jack Bauer will save the world yet again. This was real tension.

Just before 10pm, Graham strode over to us. His face was completely emotionless.

'I've just spoken to the owner,' he said, 'and she said that I can't let you have one of our rooms or lodges, I'm afraid.'

'Oh, ok...' I said.

'BUT,' he interrupted, 'she said you are welcome to have one of the bunks in the staff bunkhouse. Is that ok with you?'

Ben and I looked at each other and then laughed.

'No. Actually, that's not good enough, Graham. We want your best lodge or nothing at all. Of course that's ok, you're an absolute legend,' said Ben, standing up and giving him a huge hug.

I did the same, and we had an awkward group hug for a few seconds. Graham's face remained completely emotionless. I imagine he would have probably looked the same if he won the lottery or when he was having sex. Not that I have imagined him having sex. That would be weird.

'When you said 'bunkhouse', I thought you were going to show us to some rat-infested shed. This is amazing,' I said.

'Well, it's not The Ritz, but hopefully it's adequate for you both,' said Graham.

The bunkroom had six beds and an en-suite bathroom. We were the only tenants so had the pick of any of the beds.

'It's more than adequate, Graham,' said Ben. 'I think I'm the happiest man in the world right now. I thought we were going to be sleeping in a cold Scottish field tonight.'

'Good, well I'm glad we could help. Is there anything else I can help you with?'

'Actually, there is something,' I said. 'We were given these microwave meals from Londis up the road. We don't have a microwave, obviously. Is there any chance that you could heat these up for us, or let us use a microwave, please?'

'That's no problem. I'll go and sort that out for you. Come

back over to the bar area in ten minutes or so.'

'We did it again, Georgie Boy. Look at this place, it's awesome. Bagsie having this bed,' said Ben, diving onto one of the bottom bunks.

We both had a quick shower - not at the same time – and put on the least skanky of our t-shirts before returning to the bar.

'I thought you could save those meals for another day,' said Graham. He was carrying a tray with two big bowls of soup, two plates of chips and two buttered baguettes.

'Dammit, I was really looking forward to my out-of-date Londis microwave meal,' I said sarcastically.

'Graham, you truly are my hero. I might have to give you another hug,' said Ben.

'No. That really won't be necessary. I'll bring you over another couple of beers. Oh, by the way, you can have breakfast in the morning. Just tell the person who is on duty that you cleared it with me.'

Korner Kitchen, Paisley

Ben, Loch Lomond Food & Drink Festival, Balloch

Day 16
The highlands
Crianlarich to Fort William - 42 miles

'Where are those razors that Dave gave us?' asked Ben.
'In the bottom of my bag, I think. Why?'
'I'm going to shave. It's time.'

Whilst Ben was shaving, I went to check on our bikes which we had hidden around the back of the lodge. The Falcon's back tyre was very flat. I had noticed it the day before but it was much worse. Thanks to our new pump and puncture repair kit this was of little concern at all. I borrowed a washing up bowl full of water from the restaurant kitchen and then set to work on The Falcon.

Ben emerged from the bunkroom a few minutes later looking like a 12 year old boy. The beard had actually made him look more mature, albeit in a dirty, trampy way, and now he was back to his pre-pubescent self.

'How do I look, eh?' he asked.
'Youthful,' I said.
'You should give it a go.'
'No. I can't really be bothered to be honest. Wasn't it painful shaving that much beard off?'
'Yes. I went through four of those razors. What's going on with the washing up bowl and puncture kit?'
'I was just checking The Falcon's tyre for a hole.'
'Why?'
'Because it was flat.'
'Did you repair it?'
'No, because there wasn't a hole.'
'So you've got a bike whose tyres go down without punctures?'

'Yes.'

'My god, that bike is such a pile of crap.'

We ate porridge and a fry-up for breakfast and set off shortly before 10am.

The A82 climbed for a bit after leaving Crianlarich before descending to Bridge of Orchy; a hamlet consisting of a hotel, a railway station, and a couple of houses. Oh, and a bridge, of course.

The route book mentioned that the Bridge of Orchy Hotel served a 'great banoffee pie', which we fantasised about as we cycled past. Incidentally, a very good friend of mine claims that his Grandma invented banoffee pie. I don't believe him.

Just after Bridge of Orchy we passed Loch Tulla - a mirror-like lake surrounded by windburned heather and a scattering of ancient pine trees. It was beginning to look like the Scottish highlands that I had envisaged.

The weather was still dry, but the sky ahead of us was black and we knew that rain was inevitable. The road climbed steeply through a switchback that seemed to go on for miles. We were now in true *Braveheart* country. With the exception of the road, there was no sign of civilisation in any direction.

Unfortunately, bank holidays and roads make a lethal combination. The traffic was relentless, and an uninterrupted torrent of motorbikes treated the road like Brands Hatch. Not only did it make cycling unpleasant, and potentially dangerous, but the noise was insufferable. It was like having a mosquito trapped inside your eardrum. It was not how we imagined the remote Scottish highlands would be.

Just before the summit, we reached a lay-by where we stopped for a break. There was an ice-cream van and a souvenir stall selling bits of tartan crap. Crap souvenirs, I mean. Not tartan faeces. Although I'm sure there's probably a the market for that.

There was also a bagpipe player who looked to be packing away because of the impending rain. We stopped next to him and pulled on our state-of-the-art waterproof cycling gear - the trusty bin liners. He offered to play us a tune, despite us telling him that we didn't have any money to offer. His name was Sandy and he drove from Glasgow every day to play his bagpipes in that particular spot.

'Hae ye nae got proper waterproofs?' he asked, when he saw what we were wearing.

'No, unfortunately not. Just bin liners,' said Ben.

'Yoo'd better ride canny in those. Two people ur killed everyday on these roods. Yoo'll be gonnae home in a feckin' body bag.'

As we left the lay-by the weather closed in completely. An impenetrable blanket of fog had fallen onto the mountainside, cocooning us in its damp, cold flesh. Our route book described this part of the road as follows...

'On a fine summer's day this is a beautiful ride... But when it's misty, wet and windy the crags close in, and a headwind can make this section tough going.'

This was definitely an understatement. The bagpipe player's words were haunting me.

'Two people ur killed everyday on these roods. Yoo'll be gonnae home in a feckin' body bag,' I said out loud, in my bad Scottish accent. It sounded more Jamaican.

'I know. What the hell did he have to say that for? Thanks, Sandy, for scaring the shit out of us,' said Ben.

'He probably had a point, though. Look at us! We couldn't be more dangerously dressed if we tried. Maybe we should push our bikes for a bit, just until the fog clears.'

'That sounds good to me. I hate sharing a road with these stupid coaches and motorbikes anyway.'

There was very little room to safely walk on the edge of the road, so we wheeled our bikes along the verge which was extremely boggy and uneven.

After about half an hour we could make out what appeared to be a set of traffic-lights through the mist. The steep mountain road was being repaired and was down to one lane. The traffic was filtered as a result, and oncoming traffic was forced to wait at the lights. A workman stepped out from his cabin when he saw us approaching.

'Are you heading down to Glencoe?' he asked. Ben looked to me, as he never had any idea where we were going.

'Yes, we are,' I said.

'I can't let you go down like that, I'm afraid. The visibility is too bad and it would be dangerous.'

'OK, no problem. We'll just push our bikes down then if that's ok?'

'No, I'm sorry. I can't let you do that either. The road is too narrow and cars wouldn't be able to see you, even if you were walking.'

'What can we do then?'

'If you hang around for ten minutes, I'll give you a lift down the mountain in the van.'

'Brilliant. Thanks mate,' said Ben excitedly.

'Sorry to be awkward,' I said, 'But we're cycling from Land's End to John O'Groats and, I know this sounds petty, but if we got a lift with you then I would feel like we've cheated as we haven't technically cycled the whole way.'

'Oh, George, stop being such a stickler. It's only a couple of miles, and we don't really have any choice,' said Ben.

'No, no, he's right,' said the workman. 'I can see that it would feel like cheating to get a lift. Here's what I'll do. I'll radio down to the guys at the bottom, and in a minute we'll stop the traffic in both directions while you cycle down. Let me just go and get you a couple of high-vis vests too, just in case. You look ridiculous like that. Just hand them to the guys at the bottom when you get there.'

'THIS IS AMAZING!' I shouted, as we descended down the mountain with the road to ourselves.

'Yeah, but it would have been even more amazing in the back of a warm van,' said Ben.

'Would you not have felt bad doing that?'

'No. Not in the slightest. Although, it is pretty cool them closing an entire mountain for us.'

'If only they could close the next 200 miles of road for us, too.'

It only took a few minutes to reach the bottom, but already the traffic was backed up at the lights as far as we could see. We handed in our vests to the man in the cabin and cycled off, followed by the glare of many frustrated motorists.

During our descent, I remembered that The Falcon's brakes were completely inoperative in the wet. The last time we had cycled in wet weather was in Dumfries and I had ended up sliding into the back of a car. I had somehow forgotten this fact, and carried on as if they would fix themselves.

On those treacherous roads, my inability to stop could have resulted in me taking a detour over one of the many precipices. The wind, mist and rain were relentless, and it was a challenge just to keep the bikes on the road. That, and the added threat of the menacing traffic, made cycling on this stretch of road particularly dangerous.

'This is stupid,' said Ben, 'let's just walk again.'

'Fine by me,' I said, dismounting in a split second. It was 4pm and I had become slightly concerned that we wouldn't make it to any civilisation before dark.

'How far is it until the nearest town or village?' asked Ben.

'A few more miles… probably,' I responded vaguely.

Every inch of our bodies was sodden, and for the first time on the trip, we started to feel the cold. Even when the weather had been cold before, we had maintained a good body temperature whilst cycling. Walking had allowed our circulation and heart-rates to slow down and our bodies were suffering at the hands of the weather. I immediately regretted being so disparaging towards the three pairs of gloves mentioned in our guide book's sample kit list. Just one pair of gloves would have made a big difference.

We walked for several miles with no sense of our surroundings whatsoever. The fog was so thick that we couldn't even see the other side of the road, let alone what lay ahead of us. Then, emerging from the fog, a sign appeared.

Glencoe Visitor Centre

It was like an oasis in the desert. Only without the sand, certainly without the sun, and with lots more rain.

'Please be open, please be open, please be open,' we repeated, as we walked up the long drive to the visitor centre. There wasn't anything in particular that we thought the visitor centre could do for us to ease our situation, but the idea of being indoors and warm was all that we desired.

It was open.

'They've got a café!' said Ben. 'I wonder if they'll heat our microwave meals up for us.' It was nearly 5pm and we hadn't eaten since breakfast.

The kitchen was being manned by a man named Paul, a smiley, bearded gentleman with huge glasses. He was wearing a badge that said 'Visitor Centre Manager', so he seemed like the right person to ask. We told him our story, and he smiled and nodded away enthusiastically.

'Yes, that's not a problem to heat up your meals,' he said. 'You both look like you could do with a hot chocolate, too.'

It really was the best hot chocolate I have ever tasted; thick, overly sweet hot chocolate, topped with cream, marshmallows and a flake. I think you probably need to spend hours walking in the wind and rain, dressed only in a pair of shorts and a bin bag to fully appreciate it, but it's definitely worth sampling, if you are ever in the area.

The Londis microwaveable spaghetti Bolognese wasn't too bad either. Again, I think our enjoyment of this was partly due to the circumstances.

'I don't think I've ever felt as miserable as I did half an hour ago,' said Ben after a while.

'Yes, it was pretty grim,' I said. 'At least we're dry now and it's not far to go today.'

'That's the problem, though. Today isn't the end of the bike ride. We've still got hundreds of miles to go until John O'Groats and I just want it to be over.'

'Are you not enjoying it at all?'

'No. It's horrendous. I keep thinking how I could be at home sitting on the sofa, drinking tea whenever I like, going to the cinema, going to the pub. The only thing getting me through this is knowing that each day means we're another day closer to finishing.'

'Just imagine the sense of achievement we'll feel when we've finished.'

'I used to think that, but now I don't see the point. I mean is it really worth all the effort?'

'I'm having great fun. Of course I'm looking forward to finishing, too, but I'm really enjoying each day. Today has been horrible, admittedly, but most of it has been good. Besides, we've been to the cinema and pub, and drank plenty of tea since we've been on the road.'

Ben gave a huge sigh. He had shown moments of frustration before, but this was the first true sign of dejection. I hoped that it was nothing that a place to sleep and a change of weather couldn't fix.

We stayed in the café for as long as we could, but Paul eventually encouraged us to leave as he was closing up. We spent a few minutes trying to dry our clothes under the hand-dryers in the toilet, and then braved it back outside.

It was still raining outside, but the fog was clearing and the sun was fighting to break through the clouds. Ben looked thoroughly depressed as he pulled the already wet bin liner over his head and climbed aboard The Horse. Out of context, that last sentence would sound very strange.

'Cheer up, mate. It's downhill all the way to Glencoe,' I said.

'Yeah right. I've heard that one before.'

'It is, I promise you. It's only a couple of miles.'

'Is that where we're going to stay tonight?'

'It's up to you. We can try and find somewhere there, or it's another 15 miles along the banks of a loch to Fort William, which is much bigger. It'll be flat all the way.'

'We'll see. I'll let you know when we get to Glencoe.'

Ben pedalled like a man possessed, and we reached Glencoe in no time.

'What do you want to do, Ben? This is Glencoe. We can stop here if you like.'

'No. Let's keep going. The further we go, the closer we get to finishing.' This was a first. Things were clearly worse than I thought.

The A82 crosses Loch Leven just after the village of Ballachulish and then follows the edge of Loch Linnhe all the way to Fort William. The road was still incredibly busy, but the cycling was easy and the views were striking.

Fort William is the largest town in the Highlands with

10,000 inhabitants (I assume they have rounded that figure to the nearest thousand). The city of Inverness is the only larger settlement.

Fort William describes itself as *'the Outdoor Capital of the UK,'* due to the huge number of tourists who use the town as a base for climbing, hiking and mountain biking in the surrounding mountains. Despite its relative grandeur in Highland terms, the town centre is relatively modest and the main street had a distinct lack of high-street chains, which made for a welcome change.

We asked an old lady who was standing in a shop doorway if she knew of anywhere cheap to stay.

'Ye coods try th' Bank Street Lodge. It's halfway up towards Glen Nevis.'

'HALFWAY UP BEN NEVIS?' I shouted, after mishearing her.

'Ack noooo. Up towards *Glen* Nevis. It's nae far.'

The Bank Street Lodge sits on a steep side-road, not far from the centre of Fort William. The reception was staffed by a no-nonsense lady in her sixties.

'Sae ye want somewhaur tae sleep an' yoo'll dae some jobs in return?' she said, as though it was a request she had heard many times before. 'Yoo'll hae tae hang oan fur a minute while ah phone th' owner.'

'I've got some wee jimmies haur who want tae bide at th' lodge tonecht fur free... Ye explain it tae 'er,' she said, thrusting the phone towards me.

'Errrr... hello... yes... errr... my friend and I are looking for somewhere to stay tonight, for free, as part of a challenge that we're doing. We're happy to do any odd jobs that you need doing; cleaning, washing, decorating... ' I said.

'And this is a charity bike ride, is it?' asked the well-spoken lady on the other end of the phone.

'Well no, not exactly. We travelling from Land's End to John O'Groats without spending any money and we're trying to prove how nice the people of Britain are.'

She gave a half-hearted laugh.

'And you have made it all the way to Fort William from Land's End without spending any money?'

'Yes.'

'Well, I wouldn't want to ruin it for you now. I'm sure we can sort something out for you. Pass me back to Tootie and I'll have a chat with her.'

'Uh huh... ok... ay... ok... ha ha... uh huh,' said Tootie, as she continued the conversation with the owner.

We watched on, trying to work out what they were talking about.

'Ok,' said Tootie, after hanging up the phone, 'Ah can lit ye sleep in a bunk in one of th' dormitory rooms. In return, she would like ye tae clean out uir dryin' room which is under th' buildin', an' clear up aw th' fag butts frae in th' front ay th' hostel. Diz 'at soond awe rite?'

'Sounds like a great deal. Thank you,' I said.

Tootie showed us to a nice room with two sets of bunk beds. It was unoccupied, and she said it was unlikely that she would need to put anyone else in with us.

We collected a bucket, dustpan, mop, cloths, bin bags and a couple of brushes, and Tootie showed us to the drying room, which was located in an underground car park area. It was used by customers and staff to hang wet hiking gear and to store ski equipment.

We spent about an hour removing the mats, sweeping it out, bagging up rubbish and giving it a general tidy. It then took another 20 minutes to pick up hundreds of cigarette butts that lined the road outside the hostel entrance. I have a feeling that a high-proportion of these were Tootie's.

During the cleaning we got talking to a chef who worked in a posh restaurant just down the road from the hostel. He was fascinated to hear all about our adventure and was keen to help us out.

'I can't offer to feed you tonight, I'm afraid, because we're so busy, but I'll make you up a packed lunch in the morning if you fancy it.' We hadn't even asked him for anything, and already the following day's lunch was taken care of.

'What shall we do about food tonight?' asked Ben when we were back in our room.

'We've still got those Londis tuna pasta bakes.'

'Ughh, I don't think I can face one of those. I fancy fish and chips.'

'You make me laugh. We've got two perfectly decent microwave meals, yet you still want to go out and try and blag fish and chips.'

'Yeah, what's wrong with that?'

'Nothing. I would like fish and chips, too. Let's go.'

Twenty minutes later we were back at the hostel with two portions of haddock and chips. We had got lucky at a takeaway on the main street. The manager wasn't in, and the girl behind the counter handed over two fish suppers without any hesitation.

We ate in the communal lounge area where the only other people were three young Chinese students who were all immersed in guidebooks about Scotland.

After we had finished dinner, Ben decided - for no known reason - to make a scrabble set out of a couple of bits of paper, which he tore into lots of individual letters. Ben had always seen himself as an expert scrabble player due to the amount of time he spent playing the game on set during his acting jobs. This is not a result of him having a particularly wide vocabulary, but simply because he had memorised all of the possible two letter words.

He was infuriating to play against. At one point he simply added the letter 'X' to score 50 points with the word 'Xi' in two directions. I had to sit through an hour of his smug face as he piled on the points with a series of two letter words that he had no idea to the meaning of. Xi is the 14th letter of the Greek alphabet, in case you were wondering.

Ben then got talking to the Chinese students. They were in Scotland as part of a two month tour of Europe. The conversation soon became an in-depth discussion about the advantages and disadvantages of communism in modern China. I didn't have the knowledge or mental willingness to take part, so slunk off to bed and left them to it.

Ben modeling state-of-the-art waterproof clothing

Paul, Glencoe Visitor Centre

Sandy, the bagpipe player

Benmore Lodge, Crianlarich

Fixing The Falcon, Crianlarich

Day 17
The hunt for Nessie
Fort William to Beauly - 63 miles

After the brutality of the previous day's cycling I slept for nine hours straight. Ben's sleep was somewhat shorter after his lengthy late-night communism tutorial with the Chinese students.

Breakfast, on the other hand, was not one of my most memorable; a Londis tuna pasta bake cooked in the hostel's microwave. They were already two days past their use-by date, but we didn't have the heart to throw them out, or the desire to take them both with us. On our way out, Tootie - who seemed to be on a 24-hour shift - gave us the packed lunches that the chef had promised us.

The A82 was much friendlier once the fog had cleared. The bank-holidaymakers were all still asleep, and so the road was almost deserted.

A few miles north of Fort William we passed a sign for the Nevis Range, which is one of Scotland's main ski areas. Seeing as we were passing, we decided to call in and take a look. We regretted this decision instantly, once we realised that it was actually a mile-long uphill graft away from the main road.

I had always been very sceptical about Scottish ski resorts. I imagined them being little hills with a couple of rickety drag-lifts transporting people the 15 metres to the top of the slope. At the Nevis Range I was shocked to see several chairlifts, and an actual gondola. Not the *just one Cornetto'* type that you find in Venice, but a proper cable-car that stretched up the mountain as far as we could see.

In the winter, it carries hundreds of skiers and snowboarders, and in the summer it transports hikers and

313

ıtain-bikers to the top.

ᴸet's see if we can get a free trip up the mountain. It might be fun to check out the view,' I suggested.

'What would be the point in that?' asked Ben.

'I don't know. I just thought it would be nice to try and do these things while we're here. It's unlikely we'll be passing through here again anytime soon.'

'But what's the point in going up a stupid mountain in a stupid cable-car?'

'I bet the views are brilliant from up there. You'd get to see all the mountains and lochs.'

'We've seen nothing but bloody mountains and stupid lochs for the last few days. I think I've seen enough of them, to be honest. Also, look at the sky. It's going to chuck it down soon and we'll have wasted loads of time pissing about up a stupid mountain.'

'I thought part of the point of this trip was to do fun things along the way, too?'

'Yeah, FUN being the operative word. There's nothing FUN about going up a big hill for no reason.'

'Why are you in such a bad mood today?'

'I'm not. I would rather just get cycling. I want to get to John O'Groats.'

I wasn't that bothered about going up the mountain either, to be honest, but I was enjoying riling Ben, so decided to continue. The ticket office was closed, and a sign with the opening hours showed that we had ten minutes to wait, which made Ben even more furious.

Once it had opened we explained to the lady in the ticket office that we were hoping for a free gondola trip in order to fully appreciate Scotland, and other such bollocks.

We were asked to wait and two very attractive ladies soon approached us and introduced themselves as Katrina and Sarah from the marketing department.

314

'We'd love to be able to allow you up the gondola for free, but looking at the state of your bikes I don't think it would be a good idea to cycle back down the mountain,' said Katrina.

'Oh sorry, you misunderstood,' I choked. 'These bikes aren't even good enough to go along roads, let alone a mountain. We just wanted to go up the gondola, have a quick look at the view and then come back down IN the gondola.'

'Ok. That's a relief. Absolutely, it's well worth doing. The scenery at the top is amazing. Especially on a clear day like this,' said Katrina.

'We've got a couple of these Ski Scotland t-shirts for you, too,' added Sarah.

'I bloody LOVE Scotland,' said Ben as we boarded the gondola. It's amazing the difference that a free t-shirt and a couple of good looking girls can make.

'Shit, this thing is fast,' said Ben sarcastically, as the gondola set off up the mountain. 'It's like being on Nemesis at Alton Towers.'

'It's a cable-car, not a rollercoaster, you idiot.'

'Wow! Look at the views! They are like sooooo amazing. Look there's some grass. And there's a hill. This is the best day of my life.'

'Stop being a dick. We're not at the top yet.'

'Actually, I admit that this is pretty cool. I've never been up a cable car before. It's much better than I was expecting,' he said, almost sincerely.

We were the first people up the gondola after it opened, which meant that we had a completely unspoilt view. A patchwork green carpet stretched as far as we could see. That was a metaphor for what the forests and fields looked like from above, by the way, not some Scottish sewing experiment.

315

The landscape was interrupted only by the many lochs, and the town of Fort William down to our left.

'Happy you came up here?' I asked.

'It's alright, I suppose. Anything beats cycling.'

We wanted to stay and soak up the views for longer, but we had places to go, and people to meet. Also, it is bloody cold and windy on the top of a mountain in a pair of silky shorts and a t-shirt.

We retraced the road back to the A82 and then followed it uphill to Spean Bridge, where we stopped briefly at the Commando Memorial; a bronze statue to commemorate the elite commando unit who trained in the area during the Second World War. We then descended to the shores of Loch Lochy – surely the most excellently named loch in Scotland.

Like Loch Ness, Loch Lochy also has its own mythical creature living beneath its surface. Her name is Lizzie. There have been many reported sightings over the years, but Lizzie has always been overshadowed by the legend of her big sister Nessie just up the road.

We stopped for a rest at the Bridge of Oich, and I was disappointed to discover that the area wasn't a hangout for hooded youths, as the name implied. In fact it was a beautiful cantilevered suspension bridge, built in 1854 and designed by James Dredge, don't you know?

It was 1pm, so we unpacked our lunch. The schoolboy memories came flooding back as we tore open the carrier bag to see what the chef had given us.

'Yeahhhh,' said Ben. 'Good 'ol chef. This is a proper packed lunch. Ham and cheese sandwiches, a yoghurt, an apple, fun-size Mars Bar, Dairylea Triangle and a carton of fruit juice. Perfect.'

We borrowed a tin opener from a nearby café and then supplemented our lunch with the cold baked beans that we had been given in Patna.

We stopped at a pub near Fort Augustus to fill our water bottles, and Ben went to dispose of our lunch wrappings in a nearby wheelie bin.

'There's a whole bunch of bananas and an unused loaf of bread in that bin,' said Ben when he returned.

'Really? Do they look ok?'

'Yeah, they look perfectly fine. Shall I go and take them?'

'Definitely. Perhaps you should ask in that shop, just in case, as the window looks out onto the bins. It might be a bit weird if they saw you scrounging through their dustbin.' Ben skipped back across the road and entered the shop. He emerged a few minutes later with four yoghurts.

'Those ladies were well lovely,' he shouted from across the road. 'They said we could have these yoghurts as they go off today.' He reached into the bin to retrieve the bread and bananas, and skipped back across the road.

The bananas were slightly bruised but otherwise fine, and the bread had only just reached its best before date. We ate a banana and yoghurt sandwich there and then (try one, before you judge me) and kept the rest for later.

Loch Ness had promised to be another highlight of our trip. Unfortunately, it didn't quite live up to our expectations.

The A82 (yes, still that same bloody road), sits fairly high up the hillside and not along the shores of the loch as we had expected. The views are also fairly restricted because of a barrier of vegetation, wall, fence or field. It was slightly underwhelming

Just then, we saw a disturbance of the surface and out rose a giant serpent like creature. Its huge body rippled out of the water behind it, as it glided effortlessly through the loch. It must have been about 30 feet long, and I'm fairly certain it smiled just before it submerged again into the deeps.

I may have made that last paragraph up. Such is the fame and legend of the Loch Ness Monster, though, that every visit to Loch Ness is likely to be a disappointment. Even for the most sceptical unbeliever, there must still be that small element of excitement on seeing the Loch for the first time, that maybe, just maybe, a mysterious creature might poke its head out of the murky water right in front of your eyes. Then the realisation hits you that there is no monster, and it's just a lake. And a fairly unremarkable lake at that.

The one exception along its shores is the magnificent Urquhart Castle. The splendid ruins sit on a rocky outcrop by Loch Ness. Despite its ruinous state, it remains an impressive sight and the castle has had a fascinating history. It is not known exactly when it was built, but records show a castle on the site from 1230, with a fort previously occupying the spot from as early as the 6th century.

The castle became an important stronghold in many battles and has changed hands several times, as the Scots battled for independence. It is now owned by Historic Scotland, and the only things that are fought over these days are the postcards in the gift shop.

We had a stroll around the site and another look for Nessie, from one of the viewing areas, before rejoining our beloved friend the A82, which we had been following for over 130 miserable miles.

The pretty village of Drumnadrochit - which I still don't know how to pronounce - sits two-thirds of the way along the loch, at the point where we finally left the A82 and headed north.

Drumnadrochit is the most popular tourist centre for Loch Ness and boasts a couple of rival Loch Ness museums. One of them – Loch Ness 2000 – has a giant fibreglass Nessie in the car park. We had to stop. With a name like Loch Ness 2000 it promised to be a museum of the future.

The gift shop was manned by a silver-haired lady, but was otherwise empty. Absolutely everything for sale was Nessie shaped, had 'Nessie' written all over it or was tartan. Some were all three. The lady didn't really understand the concept of our bike ride, but agreed to let us have a look around the exhibition free of charge.

It really was one of the strangest museums I have ever been to. And this is coming from someone who has visited The Pencil Museum in Keswick. Although seemingly a permanent exhibition, all of the 'Entrance', 'Exit' and 'Toilet' signs were written on bits of paper, in pen, and sellotaped to the doors as though they had been made the day before. Perhaps this is how the museums of the future will look.

The exhibition itself consisted of an eclectic mix of framed photos of OFFICIAL sightings, documentation that PROVED Nessie's existence and a half hour video featuring EXPERTS confirming that Nessie did UNDOUBTEDLY exist. Various scientists also gave scientific PROOF that the monster was genuine. I was more of a believer in the Loch Ness Monster before I visited the museum, than I was afterwards.

We ate another banana sandwich as we perched on the wall in the car park. It was 6.30pm and we debated calling it a night, but we (I) decided to try and reach the slightly larger town of Beauly before dark.

We left Drumnadrochit on the A831 before turning off onto the A833. The next three miles were some of the toughest of the entire trip. The road climbed very steeply and The Falcon's lack of low gears caused problems. Even in its lowest gear it required a huge amount of force to complete one rotation of the pedals. I was determined not to be beaten by

319

the hill, so persevered. Ben, on the other hand, with his endless number of gears, decided to dismount as soon as he caught sight of the hill.

'Bollocks to this. I can't be bothered to cycle up,' he said.

'You loser,' I panted. 'I... will... not... be... beaten... by... a... hill.' I made it all the way to the top without stopping, but Ben had beaten me by several minutes and he had walked the entire way.

'You're such a stubborn idiot,' he said. 'Well done. What have you proved by doing that? You were slower than me and you'll be ten times more knackered.'

'It's a... it's a... good... sense... of... achievement,' I said, collapsing onto the verge to try and ease the pain in my thighs.

'Do you have a sense of achievement?'

'None whatsoever. Just pain.'

We were rewarded with an easy nine mile descent, past fields of inquisitive Highland cattle, down into Beauly. On the outskirts of town we called into Lovat Bridge Camping and Caravan site, but the lady who ran the place – despite being very pleasant – was unable to help us out.

It was almost dark by the time we reached Beauly, and we received two rejections from B&Bs on the main street in quick succession.

The impressive looking Lovat Arms Hotel dominates the main street, and we knew we were pushing our luck when we entered. After a long chat with the friendly manager, he informed us that they had no rooms available, but if we were able to find somewhere else in town to stay, we could come back for a free meal that night. This was almost a better reward than somewhere to sleep.

We chatted to a coach driver who was parked up outside the front of the hotel. He was staying in Beauly overnight as part of a coach tour and was checking on the bus before dinner with his group of oldies.

'Any chance we could sleep on the coach tonight?' Ben suggested. 'We wouldn't dirty the seats or anything. We'd just sleep in the aisle.'

'Are you serious?' he asked. 'You're that desperate you would sleep on the bus?'

'Completely.'

He thought for a moment.

'Well, I suppose you could. I can't see a problem with that. I've just got to pop into the hotel to get the keys. Back in a minute.'

'Nice one,' I said to Ben. 'You've blagged us a bus.'

'It'll be like we're the Famous Five or something. Only there's just the two of us, and we don't have a dog.'

'Errr, yeah, and I don't think the Famous Five ever slept on a bus, either. Otherwise it's just like that.'

'I'm really sorry, guys,' said the coach driver when he returned. 'I've had a think about it and I'm not going to be able to let you sleep on the coach, I'm afraid.'

'Oh, ok,' I said dejectedly. 'Can I ask why you changed your mind?'

'It's for insurance reasons, I'm afraid. I remembered that I'm not covered for people staying on the bus overnight. If it was to catch fire or something I would be held responsible.'

'We promise not to start any fires,' said Ben.

'It's still a no, I'm afraid. I'm really sorry that I can't help you out.'

We tried at another B&B just off the main street, but were politely refused. Further down the main street we reached the Caledonian Hotel; a slightly shabby looking hotel/pub. The lights were off, but the stairwell was lit and we could hear the noise of a television from upstairs. Assuming that the

321

reception was upstairs, we made our way up and opened the door. A dog began barking frantically and a lady, who was sat on the sofa in the dark, shouted at it to be quiet.

'Excuse me, we're really sorry to disturb you,' I said hesitantly.

'Och jesus christ ye scared th' life out ay me. Ah didne hear ye come in. Ah wondered whit Rufus was barkin' at.'

Ben and I both had a sudden rush of panic that we had walked into someone's living room. The lady was sitting on a big sofa in the dark, watching TV with a dog on her lap. It's not the usual set up for a hotel reception.

'I'm really sorry,' I said, 'we didn't mean to scare you. Is this the reception for the hotel?'

'Och aye, ye could say 'at. Are ye lookin' fur a room?'

'Yes, well sort of.'

'IAIN!' she yelled. 'Will ye come out here please. We've got customers.'

Iain emerged from another bar at the back of the room drying a pint glass with a tea towel. He was a giant of a man; at least six foot tall, with a pub landlord's body. He was in his sixties, had a white moustache and patches of curly white hair on the sides of his head.

'What can I do for you two gentlemen?' he asked, in a voice far more gentle than his appearance suggested. He smiled as we explained our challenge.

'I'm sure we can sort you out with a room. We're not too busy tonight. In fact, you're the only people here. I'll get Cathy to show you to a room.'

The room was absolutely fascinating. It would have looked very posh 'back in the day' - perhaps the early 1970s. Everything from the floral print wallpaper to the bed covers, the carpet to the radio/alarm clock looked like it was unchanged in many decades. I loved it. It felt like we were staying in a museum.

After a quick shower and change into our new Sunday Best – the Ski Scotland t-shirts – we walked back up to the Lovat Arms Hotel. The manager seemed a little surprised to see us back, but was happy to honour his word and found us a seat in the restaurant – tucked away in the corner hidden from the eyes of the respectable paying guests.

It was an amazing meal; steak pie with delicious chunks of beef, thick gravy, a light puff pastry lid and chunky chips. But the highlight for me was the vegetables. Carrots and peas have never tasted so good. Not that they were particularly special carrots and peas; just that vegetables of any sort had been almost absent from our diets since we started.

If a nutritionist had analysed what we ate during the bike ride, I think they probably would have concluded that we should not be alive, let alone fit enough to cycle. I read somewhere that beige food is bad for you. Almost everything we ate was a shade of beige; bread, pasta bakes, chips, pasties and bananas. Anyway, all I'm saying is that peas and carrots taste unbelievable if you only eat beige food for 17 days beforehand. Give it a try.

The Caledonian Hotel was buzzin' when we returned. By that I mean, that there was another person in the bar. She seemed to be a regular as she was sat on a bar stool and deep in conversation with Cathy and Iain.

'Thanks again for letting us stay,' I said as we passed the bar on our way to our room.

'Aren't you going to stay and join us for a drink?' asked Iain.

'But we…'

'Ah don't worry about that, I'll get you both a beer,' he said.

Two hours, four pints and two 'nightcaps' later, we were still at the bar. The lady – Susan, I think her name was, as my memory of that night is slightly hazy – was a permanent tenant of the campsite we had called at earlier. Since her marriage ended, she rented a mobile home at the site, worked in a factory during the day and drank in the Caledonian in the evening. They were all great company, and Ben and I were made to feel very welcome.

I looked up the Caledonian Hotel on the internet after our trip, and was staggered to read the reviews. Out of 18 reviews, 12 of them rated it 'terrible'. Here is one such review:

'This hotel is without question the worst hotel in the world. It smells of stale beer and cigarettes as soon as you walk in the door. The staff are rude and equally as smelly. Avoid this hell hole at all costs. You would honestly be better sleeping in your car!'

The Caledonian was, without a doubt, one of the friendliest and most unique hotels I have ever stayed in. If you want a modern, featureless hotel, then the Caledonian is certainly not for you. If, however, you fancy a slightly different experience, where usual hotel policies don't apply, then I would wholeheartedly recommend it.

Katrina, Nevis Range

At the top of the gondola, Nevis Range

Nevis Range gondola

Loch Ness 2000, Drumnadrochit

A82, near Loch Ness

Urquhart Castle

Day 18
Whisky tastings and llama farms
Beauly to Berriedale - 79 miles

The closer we got to John O'Groats, the greater the sense of enthusiasm we woke with each morning. For the majority of the journey, our first thoughts on waking would be of mild fear and anticipation of the day that lay ahead. These thoughts turned more towards excitement, as we felt the finish line getting closer.

Iain gave us a delicious bowl of porridge for breakfast and we acquired an out-of-date quiche from one of the nearby shops before setting off.

Just after leaving Beauly the route turned right and we climbed the road up to a ridge. The sky was black as far as the horizon, and we could see the haze of torrential rain in the distance ahead of us. The weather gods were on our side, because for the next 20 miles a massive tailwind propelled us, and the clouds, so that we fortunately never crossed paths.

We joined the A9 and crossed Cromarty Firth via the Cromarty bridge – built in 1982, bridge fact fans – and then diverted onto minor roads through the villages of Evanton and Alness. We passed alongside beautiful evergreen forests with the road still fresh from a battering by the rain.

After Alness, the road followed the coast along Cromarty Firth for several miles. The terrain was perfectly flat, and the wind so strong that even when we stopped pedalling it had the force to propel us along. We continued as far as the village of Milton where we turned inland again. Here we had an option to either follow the A9 to Tain, or take the 'shorter route,' as I described it to Ben.

'Definitely the shorter route. That's a no-brainer,' he said, taking the bait. I had neglected to mention to him that the shorter router was significantly hillier.

'This is hell,' he said, as we panted up a road through thick woodland. 'I bet the A-road was dead flat.'

'No. It's just as hilly as this,' I lied, 'but with much more traffic.'

We then had a nice long downhill into the town of Tain. We didn't stop, as we had a more appealing destination in mind a couple of miles further on; the Glenmorangie whisky distillery.

I have never been a fan of whisky. In fact, I would even go as far as saying that I hate the stuff. It always seemed to be the drink of choice towards the end of a long drinking session in my late teens. Ever since, the slightest taste takes me back to the feeling of wanting to spew my guts out. Still, when in Scotland…

Glenmorangie has been the best selling single-malt in Scotland since 1983. About 10 million bottles are produced each year. Not all of these are drunk in Scotland, however. A couple of bottles are sent elsewhere.

The distillery itself is a beautiful old building sitting just off the A9 on the banks of the Dornoch Firth. We hid our bikes in a bush in the car park, and walked down to the distillery. The lady in the gift shop explained that they ran hourly tours of the distillery and the cellars, followed by a tasting session. On this occasion she was happy to waive the admission fee, on the basis that we seemed like 'a couple of decent guys'.

'The next tour doesn't start for another 30 minutes, so maybe you would like to join in with the tasting session for the tour that has just finished,' she suggested.

We sat in a room with about ten other people – mostly Americans – and tried a series of different whiskies that were described with terms such as earthy, oaky, grassy and cerealy.

'What does the aftertaste of this one remind you of?' said the lady.

'Vomit,' I said under my breath.

'Caramel,' said Ben.

'Exactly,' she said. 'It has definite caramel undertones, and hints of woodchip and oak.'

'You brown nose,' I said to Ben. 'Do you really like this stuff?'

'Yeah, I love it. Don't you?'

'No. It's rank.'

'Some people like to have a drop of water with theirs,' she then said, passing around a jug of water.

'Do you have any Coke?' I asked, only half jokingly. The room erupted in laughter, and I went along with it as though I was a comic genius, rather than a whisky heathen. 'Ha ha, whisky and Coke,' I laughed. 'As if!'

To be fair to Glenmorangie, their whisky was definitely the least offensive that I had ever tasted. I would not go as far as saying that I enjoyed it, but it didn't make me gag and I managed to finish each of the three shots.

'Do we really have to go on the tour?' whispered Ben. 'I bet it will be really boring. I only wanted to do the tasting.'

'Yeah, it would be rude if we left now. We might as well do the tour. It might be fun.'

We met the other tour group – again, mostly Americans – at the designated spot with their guide Sandra.

The tour was actually fascinating and well worth doing. We were guided through all of the different stages of whisky production, which, although seemingly complex, still use the same basic processes that have been used for hundreds of years.

The distillery looked like something out of a sci-fi film, with giant cauldrons (I think that's the technical name) of fermenting 'stuff'. The odours that emanated around the room were completely overpowering, but not unpleasant.

At one point, Sandra opened the hatch on top of one of the cauldrons and we were told to put our head inside and take a proper sniff. Ben went first and put his entire head in and inhaled deeply. He gave a loud cough into the cauldron and emerged gasping for air with his eyes streaming.

'Oh my god. I wasn't expecting that,' he spluttered.

'It certainly clears your sinuses, doesn't it?' said Sandra. 'Who's next? There's no need to put your head in as far as Ben did.'

I was next up, and, after copying Ben, my eyes were streaming and I was coughing and spluttering too. It was how I imagine snorting a line of wasabi would feel. The rest of the group decided against having a go.

This particular batch of Glenmorangie single malt is best avoided. It contains traces of our spit.

The highlight of the tour was a visit to the cellars, in which thousands of barrels are stacked up until they are ready to be bottled. Every single element of the process is considered an influencing factor on the product, such as the natural spring water that is used from the nearby spring, to the type and age of the wooden barrels, to the sea air and the temperature. I felt guilty that I had entertained the thought of ruining all of this with a splash of Coke.

'Ok, now you can all come and take part in a tasting of some of our whiskies,' said Sandra at the end of the tour.

'Thanks, but we already did one before this tour,' I whispered to her.

'Lucky you. You might as well come and do another one.'

We duly obliged. It would have been rude not to. Besides, we had both become fascinated by studying the different people in the group. They were a very strange bunch. One particular bloke took notes on a little notepad the entire way round, and then asked Sandra very specific questions at the end, referring back in his notebook to how Glenmorangie was different to the other distilleries he had been to. His wife could not have looked more depressed the entire time.

We got talking to Bruce and Anne - a couple from Vermont, USA. They too were whisky enthusiasts, but not as hardcore as the freaky notepad guy.

'I've been to Vermont,' I said, to try and impress them.

'Really? Where did you go?' said Bruce.

'Errr, the Ben & Jerry's factory,' I said.

'Yeah, Ben and Jerry's is about the only thing that brings people to Vermont.'

We sat through another tasting session, and talked with Bruce and Anne about their vacation. They were spending three weeks in Scotland, hiking, eating and drinking.

'This is our address,' said Anne, 'if you are ever in Vermont again, make sure you stop by.'

Sandra, the guide, then presented Ben and me with a rare bottle of Truffle Oak Reserve single malt whisky - one of only 800 bottles produced.

'What's this for?' asked Ben. 'We don't deserve this'

'Yes you do. It's our gesture of goodwill. You can either enjoy it during your trip, or save it to celebrate with afterwards.'

'That's so kind of you. We better not have any more today otherwise we'll never make it to John O'Groats,' I said.

My rucksack was completely full, and there was no room in Ben's bag as it still contained the complete picnic set he had carried since Cornwall. After a bit of effort, we managed to strap the valuable boxed bottle of whisky to the back of The Horse, and we wobbled off with heavier bikes and lighter heads.

I'm not sure if it was the whisky or the weather, but the next few miles were incredibly tough going. We crossed the Dornoch Bridge which straddles the Dornoch Firth, and the wind had turned dramatically and was now blowing against us, as well as across from the left. This meant that not only did we have to fight against it just to move ourselves forward, but we also had to lean into it to avoid being blown under the wheels of the many passing articulated lorries.

We pushed our bikes for a large section of the bridge because we didn't want our trip to come to an abrupt end so close to the finish, and also because it was as quick to walk as cycle.

I'm sure Dornoch Firth would be very beautiful on a nice day, but the wind had turned it into a wild, intimidating body of water and we were glad to reach the other side. If the name 'Dornoch' sounds familiar to you, it is probably because it is the location of Skibo Castle where Madonna and Guy Ritchie married in 2000.

We continued uphill for a while before descending to a causeway across Loch Fleet, which forms part of a 19,000 acre wildlife conservation area that is a popular spot for birdwatchers.

The village of Golspie (population 1650) was a heaving metropolis compared to most of the places we had passed through that day. Places such as Evelix, Poles and Culmaily looked significant on the map, but often boasted one house, and sometimes not even that. Golspie even had a shop.

The whisky had clouded our minds and we had forgotten

about food. It was nearly 5pm and we hadn't eaten anything since our porridge at the Caledonian.

The young cashier of the shop – a pretty Scottish-born Asian girl – gave us a bunch of bananas, which would have seen us through the rest of the day if it had come to it. In that remote part of Scotland, we didn't know when we would eat again.

It was too early for us to stop for the day in Golspie, as we would have been left with over 70 miles to complete on the final day. Just beyond the village we passed the spectacular looking Dunrobin Castle. I say 'spectacular' because I have just seen pictures of it on the internet. I don't remember being able to see much of it from the road, though. Our route book said that it is *'well worth a stop'*, but I didn't read this until we were several miles beyond.

The wind had died down and the rain clouds were out of sight, which left us with some pleasant cycling for the rest of the day. Fuelled by the bananas we made good progress, cycling another 20 miles through the town of Brora and on to the village of Helmsdale.

It was 6.30pm by the time we reached Helmsdale, and we had to decide whether to call it a day or push onto the next village of Berriedale, another ten miles further on.

'I think we should try and get to Berriedale today. It'll be 10 miles that we don't have to do tomorrow,' I said.

'I knew you were going to say that,' said Ben. 'But what happens if we can't find anywhere in Berry Vale?'

'Berriedale.'

'Whatever. What happens if we can't find anywhere there? Shouldn't we look for somewhere here first? This place looks fairly big. There are B&Bs, a pub. I think we could find somewhere easily.'

'We probably would, but I'm sure we'll find somewhere in

Berriedale, too. It looks as big as this place on the map.'

'Ten miles, you say?'

'Yeah. The other thing is there is a massive hill for the next 4 ½ miles, which would mean that if we stayed here we would have to do that first thing tomorrow.'

'But if we do it now, it means that we have to do it NOW! Either way it's crap.'

'But if we get it over and done with now, then we'll have just 43 miles left tomorrow, and it will all be fairly flat and easy.'

'Fine! If it shuts you up, let's get it over and done with. But if we end up homeless tonight then I'm going to fucking kill you.'

The hill was every bit as gruelling as our route book suggested, and Ben moaned every bit as much as I thought he would. We left the coast behind as we crawled slowly up into the hills. By 'crawled' I mean that we cycled slowly. Things had not got that bad.

The descent into the village of Berriedale was one of the steepest we experienced on the entire trip. Those doing the route from north to south would have this to tackle on their first day.

Just before we reached the village, I managed to come to a stop using my feet in the gravel of a lay-by. Ben screeched to a halt behind me.

'What did you stop for?' he asked.

'Did you see the gates to that house back there?'

'No. What was special about them?'

'I'm not sure. I couldn't see the actual house, but it looked quite important.'

'So what?' asked Ben.

'Well, it's our last night. Maybe we should try to stay somewhere really special?'

'I like your thinking.'

The sign on the gateway to Langwell House was modest enough - there was nothing to indicate that it was a hotel or guest house - but there was something about the driveway that stretched out of sight into the woods that gave a hint that it was more than just an average semi, and it made us want to find out more.

We pushed our bikes down the wooded driveway. I'm not sure why, but it felt more polite to walk, rather than cycle down someone's drive. We turned a corner expecting to see the house in front of us, but instead the drive continued. The road then emerged from the woods and was suddenly clinging to the side of a deep valley, with a river flowing peacefully at the bottom.

'What the hell is this place?' asked Ben.

'It's like we've ended up in Narnia or something.'

'Is it just me, or is it all a little bit creepy?'

'I'm glad you said that. I'm shitting myself.'

There was no evidence of human habitation anywhere. One minute we had been on the outskirts of a village, and the next we had ventured into another world. We got on our bikes. Not because we were scared, you understand, but because we had been walking for ten minutes and still not reached the house.

The drive continued for what felt like several miles and we eventually saw the house; a fairly humble building, considering its location. It was a beautiful white farmhouse sat in a prime spot on the hillside, with views stretching across the wooded valley and out to sea.

We began to walk up towards the house when we heard the roar of an engine, and a quad bike came shrieking down the track towards us. A man dressed in army camouflage trousers, a wax jacket and a flat cap climbed off and then reached for his shotgun from the back of the quad.

A huge Alsatian ran salivating and barking down from the house and stood beside him.

'Can ah help ye?' he said with an angry glare. Being confronted in the middle of nowhere by a man with a gun, and a dog with an apparent lust for blood, was not the most welcoming of greetings I had ever had.

'I'm really sorry to bother you,' I said. 'We've travelled the length of Great Britain without spending a single penny. Everything we own has been acquired along the way including all of our food and accommodation. Tonight is our last night, and we saw this place and thought it would be fitting to end our journey somewhere really special.'

The man's face remained as stern as before, and he still held on tight to the shotgun.

'Yes,' continued Ben. 'Would there be any chance at all of us sleeping here tonight? We're happy to do some work in return.'

He paused.

'Nae. That willnae be possible.'

'Oh, ok,' said Ben. 'Are you the owner?'

'Nae, aam th' gamekeeper.'

'Would it be possible to speak to the owner?'

'Nae. That willnae be possible.'

'We're kind of a bit stranded,' added Ben. 'It's almost dark and we're in the middle of nowhere and we've got nowhere to stay.'

'Ah cannae help ye,' said the man.

'Would it not be possible to have a quick chat with the owner? Maybe they have an outhouse we could sleep in?' I said, beginning to sound a bit desperate.

'Nae. i'm gonnae hae tae ask ye tae leave now.' With that, we got back on our bikes and followed the long driveway back to Berriedale. The gamekeeper appeared behind us on his quad for the last section, and shadowed us to make sure that we left the property.

Berriedale was nowhere near as big as I had promised Ben. In fact, the term 'village' would be very generous. It was 8.30pm and completely dark. We knocked on the door of the house with lights on. Despite a car being parked outside and the flickering of a TV visible through the curtains there was no answer.

'Should we knock again?' asked Ben.

'I don't think so. It's a bit late and they obviously don't want to answer.'

'Let's try the next house then.'

'I think we should keep going.'

'What?'

'I don't like knocking on people's doors late in the evening like this. It feels wrong.'

'Yes, it's not bloody ideal, but we don't really have much choice, do we? If you had stopped being so stubborn and looked for somewhere in that last place then we wouldn't have this problem.'

'Well hindsight is a wonderful thing isn't it?'

'So is foresight, and it was pretty obvious this was going to happen.'

'Alright, I'm sorry. You're right. But at least we've got that big hill out of the way, and it's not much further to John O'Groats.'

'Yes, but that doesn't resolve the small problem of not having anywhere to stay tonight.'

'Ok, well let's keep going and see what happens.'

Cycling was not an option. We had no form of lighting whatsoever, and only a single Tony-the-tiger reflector on The Falcon's front wheel to keep us safe. The busy, unlit A9 meant that even walking was dangerous. We walked along the edge of the road and moved onto the verge each time a car passed.

'What happens if we don't find anywhere?' asked Ben as we lumbered around a steep uphill switchback on the way out of Berriedale.

'Then we keep walking. It's the last night. It doesn't really matter if we don't get any sleep. It just means that by the time it gets light we'll be even closer to John O'Groats.'

'And you'd be happy to walk all night?'

'Yes, if it came to it,' I lied, desperately hoping to find somewhere to sleep.

After a couple of miles, we reached a bungalow which was set away from the main road. There was a sign outside that said:

Kingspark Llama Farm
Bed and Breakfast

But then below that, another sign, with two words that made our hearts sink:

No Vacancy

'I'm going to ask anyway,' said Ben. 'At least they'll be able to tell us what there is ahead of us and how far away.'

The door was opened by a smiling, grey-haired man, with a grey moustache and a flat cap.

'Good evening. How can I help you?' he said, in a thick West Country accent, which was a little surprising considering that we were less than 50 miles from the top of Scotland.

'Hello. We're really sorry to disturb you this late, but we're kind of stranded and we are looking for somewhere to stay tonight,' said Ben.

'We saw that you have no vacancies, but wondered if you have any shelter at all or if you knew of anywhere nearby that might be able to help?' I added.

'Well we're actually closed at the moment for refurbishment. That's why the sign says *No Vacancy*. How come you are stranded out here?'

His name was Brian, and we told him how we came to be stranded on his doorstep. He nodded along enthusiastically, and laughed at various points including our visit to Langwell House just down the road.

'They are a strange bunch down at Langwell House. I'll tell you what, you two wait there and I'll go and have a word with my wife Mary. I won't be a minute.'

'Mary says that it would be too difficult to sort you out with a bed tonight, but you are welcome to sleep in the polytunnel,' said Brian when he returned. 'There's lots of hay in there and I don't think it will be too cold tonight.'

'That sounds amazing. Thank you. We're sorry again for disturbing you.'

'Not at all. Come in and have a quick cup of tea before I show you to your lodgings.'

We were led through to the sitting room and Mary arrived a few minutes later with a tray of tea.

'I've decided I can't have you sleeping in the polytunnel when we have all these empty rooms,' she said, sounding very flustered.

'We're more than happy to sleep out there,' said Ben.

'We'll I'm not. It wouldn't be right. I'm sorry, I'm just a bit stressed by all the renovations, and I've been a bit under the weather recently.'

'Yes, of course. We completely understand. We feel really bad just turning up like this.'

'I'll go and make up a bed for you both,' she said and

disappeared out of the door, before we had a chance to protest further. We hated the idea of being a burden to people, and had tried to avoid it at every stage of the trip. It was late, they had a sign saying 'no vacancy', yet they were giving us a room because they felt a sense of guilt and it didn't seem right.

'Brian, we would honestly be much happier to sleep in your polytunnel. We feel really bad just turning up like this and we hate being a burden on people,' I said.

'No, no, it's fine. Mary doesn't mind,' said Brian nonchalantly.

'I know, but it's clearly not a good time. This trip is all about adventure and to be honest a polytunnel would be more exciting for our last night.'

Brian thought for a moment.

'Yep, I suppose I can appreciate that. I spent some time in the paratroopers and I can see what you're saying.'

'We would honestly be so much happier if we didn't take up one of your rooms,' said Ben.

Brian went to speak to Mary and after a lot of protesting, Mary finally accepted.

Brian led us out the polytunnel, which – in case you are wondering – is basically a greenhouse made with cling film instead of glass.

'There are a few holes in the roof, but it's not going to rain tonight,' said Brian. 'You'll be fine. You can make a bed with the hay, and I've probably got a spare blanket somewhere that I can give you. What about dinner? Have you eaten at all?'

'No, but could we ask you one more favour?' said Ben.

'Of course.'

'We got this quiche,' said Ben, retrieving the out-of-date quiche that we'd acquired from the shop in Beauly. 'Could we possibly zap it in your microwave?'

'No problem at all. I'll go and sort that out for you.'

He returned a few minutes later with two plates of quiche,

and a welcomed accompaniment of baked beans.

There was something very poetic about lying on the hay, beneath the polythene roof. This was how we had spent our first night, on the hay next to the bull in Harry Mann's barn. During the 18 days in-between we had slept in a posh hotel, a canal boat, a student house, a pub, a tent in a car park, a hitman's sitting room, an elderly lady's spare bedroom, a hostel, a bunk house, a farm house, our own self-contained flat, our own house, and now we were back on the hay. We had gone full circle.

Out of all of the different types of accommodation, our two nights on the hay were undoubtedly our most comfortable. Next time you hear the nativity story, don't feel sorry for Mary and Joseph; they had it very lucky indeed.

Iain, Caledonian Inn, Beauly

Cathy, Caledonian Inn, Beauly

Golspie Beach

Day 19
The finish line
Berriedale to John O'Groats - 43 miles

Brian had been wrong about the rain. It pissed it down all night, and the roof leaked like a sieve. But it wasn't cold, and the sound of rain on a polytunnel is very hypnotic and we both slept like babies; waking up crying every hour with wet pants.

Barring any major problems, it was to be our last day's cycling. Less than 50 miles lay between us and John O'Groats.

'Mary is making you a fry-up,' said Brian when we went to say goodbye, 'and you're not getting out of this one.'

'Oh alright then. If you insist. It smells amazing,' said Ben.

We chatted to Brian and Mary over breakfast, and asked them how two Bristolians had ended up in North-East Scotland running a B&B and a llama farm.

'It just sort of happened,' said Brian casually. 'We liked the area here in Caithness and decided to move here a few years ago. We got the llamas because we heard they adapt well to the climate, and the rest is history.'

'Can we have a look at your llamas before we go?' I asked.

'Of course. You're going to help me feed them after this.'

We finished our breakfast then followed Brian into the field behind his house. We passed a set of aviaries housing several large parrots.

'Those just sort of happened, too,' said Brian.

We fed the five friendly and scruffy-looking llamas - or 'natural looking' as Brian preferred to describe them – and had a wander around the rest of the farm.

We then followed Brian over a fence and a few hundred metres across another field. We reached a snooker-table sized

342

concrete platform, on which sat a round metal turret like you would find on a tank.

'This came as a bit of a surprise to me after we bought the place. I didn't even know it existed,' he said as he unscrewed the large metal lid of the turret.

'What is it?' I asked.

'It's an old war bunker. Come and take a look.'

We climbed down the ladder into the darkness and Brian lit a lantern. The room was the size of a small single bedroom with benches lining each wall and shelves for supplies. There were many items scattered about from 'back in the day' such as tins, pots, cans and a half-finished bottle of whisky stashed on one of the shelves; although this was possibly Brian's. Why the wilderness of Caithness was ever considered at risk during the war, I am not sure.

'This is a fantastic place, Brian,' said Ben.

'Yes, isn't it just? I often come down here for a few hours to escape from the wife,' he said with a wink.

We returned to the house to collect our things and say goodbye to Mary. They had both been incredibly generous despite us turning up on their doorstep late at night during a particularly difficult time. Our last night was not the extravagant manor house that we had hoped for, but it was certainly one of our most enjoyable and memorable.

The route between Berriedale and John O'Groats was fairly uneventful. Brian had given us a list of places that we MUST see while we were in the area: Dunbeath Castle, Laidhay Croft Museum, Hill O' Many Stanes, and an excavated Iron Age village. Despite our best intentions, once we were on the road we only had eyes for the finish line.

'Wasn't that the turn off for Hill O' Many Stanes?' I called to Ben half-heartedly.

'Oh bollocks to that,' replied Ben. 'We're nearly at John O'Groats. And anyway, the English for that translates as 'hill of lots of stones'. I've seen plenty of those before, thank you very much.'

We stopped briefly in Wick to fill our water bottles at a petrol station - with water, not petrol – and then set off on the final 15 miles to John O'Groats. During these last few miles we passed many End to Enders heading in the opposite direction, all fresh-legged with happy smiles and no idea of what lay ahead of them. We gave each group a good-luck wave and exchanged brief cheers of support as we passed. It is only on these approach roads into John O'Groats and Land's End that you are likely to bump into other End to Enders. The complex network of British roads is such that there is no particular favoured route, as cyclists, runners and walkers navigate their way from one end of Britain to the other.

We reached the outskirts of John O'Groats just after 1pm, having covered the 43 miles from Berriedale in three hours. We paused for a moment and looked down the road towards the harbour.

'This is it, Ben,' I said. 'Just a few hundred metres to go.'

'Thank fuck for that,' said Ben.

'Do we cross the finish line holding hands or what?'

'Hell no! Let's just cycle across it like we have for the last thousand miles.'

As we freewheeled down the hill towards the famous sign, I felt a sudden swell of emotion that caught me completely by surprise. I had never doubted that we would complete the trip, but I was suddenly hit with the realisation of what we had achieved.

We had cycled between the two most distant points in Great Britain in 18.5 days. This was an achievement in itself, but we had started our journey at the foot of England in a pair of underpants, and nothing else. There we were, less than three weeks later, at the top of Scotland, fully clothed, with bikes, having found somewhere to stay every night and food for nearly all of our meals. I felt immensely proud.

The actual finish line lies, randomly, in the hotel's car park, and we crossed it valiantly watched by a welcome party of none.

'You're not crying are you?' said Ben accusingly, as we came to a stop.

'No. As if! It must just be the wind,' I said, and I looked up to see his eyes welling up, too. I gave him a big hug.

'You big gaylord,' he said.

We had been given an 'official' End to End card from Jemma at Land's End that we had to get stamped in the John O'Groats hotel to prove that we had made it. Although, I'm not quite sure who we needed to prove this to.

The hotel bar was empty apart from the barman, who was leaning on the bar whilst watching a TV across the room.

'Hello. Is this where we get the Land's End to John O'Groats certificate thing stamped?' I asked.

'Can do,' he said, not taking his eyes off the TV.

'Great, thanks,' I said, sliding the piece of paper along the bar to him. 'We've just cycled the whole way from Land's End without spending any money and we had to blag all of our clothes and food and accommodation and we stayed in a stable with a bull and with a hitman and in a posh hotel and in a polytunnel and in a canal boat and we had to work for lots of our meals and we didn't even have a bike pump and then this one time we got a puncture and then we had to...'

'There you go,' he interrupted, stamping the card and passing it back to me, still without averting his gaze from the

345

TV.

To us, we were the most courageous human beings to have ever stepped foot into the John O'Groats Hotel. To the barman, we were just the latest in the long line of people completing the trip, often, like us, with their own 'wacky' take on it. He had seen it all before, and he didn't give a shit. He just wanted his shift to finish so that he could go home. I loved him for this, and it was almost preferable to a cheesy greeting from an over-enthusiastic welcome party. It certainly brought us right back down to earth.

My body was drained of all life, but my mind was alive and racing at thoughts of what we had achieved and of the things that we had experienced.

I had fallen deeply in love with Great Britain. I secretly always had been, but I was no longer afraid to admit it. As a nation, we don't give ourselves enough credit. We are, according to public perception, a country full of ASBOs, underage drinkers, bitter, arrogant moaners and pregnant teenagers. Yes, we have our problems, but it truly is a wonderful place to live. Britain is far from broken; it just needs a bit of love and affection.

At every stage of our journey we were overwhelmed by the generosity and kindness of the people that we met. Complete strangers went out of their way to offer us food, accommodation, clothes, bikes, directions, beer or conversation. Britain is a melting pot of cultures, races and personalities, and this eclectic mix of characters should be embraced and celebrated.

And it's not just the people; Great Britain is stunningly beautiful, too. We expected Cornwall to be pretty, and we knew the Scottish Highlands would be spectacular, but it was the bits in-between that surprised us. There was not an inch of the 1000 miles that didn't have an appeal. Even Runcorn had a certain charm. Nowadays, with cheap flights and the channel tunnel, it is so easy to disappear to some faraway land, rather than explore all of the beauty right on your doorstep.

This journey was never about money. I don't want to preach to you about consumerism or society's obsession with money – I'm sure you have got your own opinions on that. Travelling without money was simply a way to put us at the mercy of those around us, and allow us the opportunity to meet people, see places, and have experiences that we would not otherwise have had.

It did, however, teach us about the endless opportunities that are open to us, even without money. It doesn't cost anything to get out and explore your local town. It doesn't cost anything to cycle or walk through the beautiful British countryside. It doesn't cost anything to stop and talk to people. It doesn't cost anything to swim in the sea or a lake, or to visit many of Britain's most impressive sights. It doesn't cost anything to ask for help. It doesn't cost anything to make new friends, and it doesn't cost anything to smile and have fun. It took this experience to help me realise that Great Britain is undoubtedly a Free Country.

It is amazing what adventures you can have when you step outside your front door. Get out there. Take a look for yourself. You won't be disappointed, I promise.

It is claimed that cycling can lead to impotence. This thought had been niggling away in my mind throughout the three weeks that I spent sat on The Falcon, with a saddle made from the hardest, most ball-destroying material known to man. However, exactly nine months after getting home, my wife gave birth to our baby daughter, and, with that, a whole new adventure began.

Brian and Mary, Kingspark Llama Farm, Berriedale

Ben feeding the llamas

A parrot, Kingspark Llama Farm

A llama, Kingspark Llama Farm

The final stretch to John O'Groats

Almost there

If you would like to see more of the photos from the trip, hear about future projects, or simply want to say 'hi' then please keep in touch via the links below.

facebook.com/GeorgeMahood

twitter.com/georgemahood

george@georgemahood.com

I have a website too, but there is really not much to see there. But if you sign up to the newsletter you will be one of the first to hear about any new releases

http://www.georgemahood.com/newsletter/

If you enjoyed reading Free Country, I would be extremely grateful if you could leave a quick review on Amazon. As a self-published author, your reviews and recommendations to friends are essential for me to help spread the word about the book.

Thank you so much for reading. You are OFFICIALLY a very nice person.

My second book *Every Day Is a Holiday* is out now!

I also published a new book at the end of 2015 –

Operation Ironman: One Man's Four Month Journey from Hospital Bed to Ironman Triathlon

You don't need to have any interest in triathlons or sport to enjoy it. It contains plenty of the nonsense that is in my other books.

Here's what others have said about it:

"…it won't fail to entertain, enthral and motivate…"

"…hilarious and heart-warming…"

"…I laughed, I cried, and am proud of a man I have never met…"

Operation Ironman is available on Kindle and in paperback on Amazon.

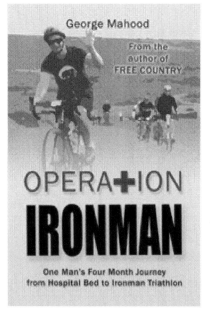

Printed in Great Britain
by Amazon